A Divine Accident

A Divine Accident

A Memoir of Life, Love and Learning

CAROL SORKIN HUNTER

What lies behind you and
What lies in front of you,
Pales in comparison to
What lies inside of you."

- Ralph Waldo Emerson-

To my beloved Prince Ian for all reasons, thru all seasons.

.

Preface

LIFE HAPPENS. IT happens while we're busy making plans for the day, the week, the month, our future. It spits in our eye and creates stumbling blocks, one after the other. We climb over them with every good intention and with hope for a better day and greater rewards for our efforts. Everyone has problems. Everyone deals with failure of one kind or the other. Everyone makes mistakes. At first, we take them in our stride, despite the struggle. Then the failures seem to mount along with our self-esteem. Maybe we're not as smart or talented as we thought we were. Maybe we're not as attractive as our peers. Maybe no one cares if we're struggling against unbeatable odds.

We grow weary and miss the pats on the head that encouraged us as toddlers learning to walk. We're on our own now. We'll have to live with the consequences of our choices.

A Divine Accident relates my personal journey from a Hollywood childhood that may seem like a fairytale of privileges and accesses, but which left me unprepared for an adulthood of person decision-making. I had been treated like a princess by people living their own hopes and dreams, but children grow up and adults aren't cute and cuddly. I was expected to make my own way. Make a name for myself. Find lasting love. Create my own family.

Adulthood brought unexpected loneliness and challenges that sent me spiraling into food addiction and one poor choice after the other as I attempted to fill the hole in my soul by filling my stomach.

My confidence plummeted. Hopelessness grew. Poverty threatened my very existence. From this low point in my life, I heard the words that triggered my journey toward self-worth, the fulfillment of my talents and by Divine Accident, my soul mate, who has contributed immeasurably to my contentment and confidence.

Like Benjamin Button, I learned that we can always start all over again to become whatever or whomever we want to be. It begins with making the choice to do so.

Table of Contents

Preface · ix
Acknowledgements · xiii

1 · 1
2 · 13
3 · 23
4 · 31
5 · 45
6 · 60
7 · 82
8 · 99
9 · 112
10 · 125
11 · 140
12 · 156
13 · 173
14 · 180
15 · 184
16 · 188
17 · 203
18 · 217
19 · 233

20 ·249
21 ·269

Addendum ·288
About the Author ·297

Acknowledgements

W ITH GRATITUDE TO my beautiful family: Ian, Lisa, Jenny, Taylor, Carson and Hayden, for gifting me with encouragement, joy and love. To the best sister in the world, Sandra, and the rest of the chorus of my treasured two and four-legged God-Family.

To Nancy Johanson, who put lyrics to my music, so generous with her time and expertise. Thanks to Lee Swidler for fixing all the computing glitches; special kudos to Leila Meacham and Wendy Thomson, who paved the road with stardust.

With gratitude to my Teachers and Masters, who prayed with me during my darkest depths of despair, and to Dr. Joseph Murphy, who eventually made me believe I was a "Child of God."

1

1943: Los Angeles

I HEARD THE telephone ringing in the foyer just off our living room, and from my peripheral vision, I saw Daddy's head turn in that direction. My properly-curved fingers froze on the piano keys, but I remained stiff-backed in the correct playing position.

"It's for you, Barney."

My mother's voice was like music to my ears.

"Keep playing, Carol. And turn on that metronome. Your timing was off."

The second my father left the living room, I reached for one of the chocolates from the two-pound box of Whitman's Samplers that always sat atop the piano next to a box of Los Angeles' famous See's chocolates and popped it into my mouth, rolling my tongue pleasingly around the strawberry cream. It was my favorite, but I wasn't picky when it came to chocolate. The fancy chocolates were available at all times for guests, especially for my father's band members when they came to the house to rehearse a new number. They called him Maestro, and he found that to his liking. Barney Sorkin was becoming a "somebody" in the city of stars and film producers, and he wanted his home and his two daughters to live up to the favorable image his name evoked whenever mentioned.

"Maestro means a rare talent, Carol. An expert. A whiz. That's what you can be, if you keep working on your scales. You need nimble fingers to play the piano well. You have to know those keys so well you can play in the dark or with your eyes closed like I do my saxophone. You have to feel it down deep and hear the notes in your head."

"I' m trying, Daddy. It's hard. I'm only eight."

"That's no excuse. Everything in life is hard. Where would we be if we quit trying every time the going gets tough? Someday, when you're older, you'll learn about Knute Rockne, the most famous coach of any football team ever. Unfortunately, the man died in a plane crash a couple years ago, may God rest his soul. They just made a movie about him. He told his team that 'when the going gets tough, the tough get going.' That means they had to work even harder if they wanted to win games and come up national champions. That's me, Carol. A champion saxophonist. I work hard. So does everyone in the Sorkin family. We're tough. We make our own way in life. No handouts. And be grateful you can have piano lessons. Little Jewish girls in Russia, Poland and Germany have nothing anymore. No pianos. No toys. Nothing. Absolutely nothing."

I knew my grandparents came from some place called Russia, but I didn't know where it was or exactly what he meant by those 'other' places. I remembered hearing the words on the radio and in school, along with the word Japan. On days when the alarm system would come on, scaring all of my classmates and me, the teacher would hustle us into the corridor to sit close to the wall with our hands over our ducked heads. She said it was only a practice session for an air raid. We had to "be prepared" just in case there was cause for a real one. She didn't elaborate, but some of the other students talked about it. Especially the boys. They said the Japanese might send more planes and drop more bombs on us like they did at Pearl Harbor in a place called Hawaii. California was real close to Hawaii. I couldn't picture in my mind what that meant. I only knew nobody wanted such a thing to happen. For several seconds after my father's narrative, I thought about other Jewish girls my age and wondered why they didn't have any toys. They were lucky not to have a piano. I peeked up at Daddy from the sides of my eyes and saw him scowl. He never complimented me, no matter how well I played. At first it bothered me, but for a long time now, when he wasn't around to see me, I rewarded myself with one of the special chocolates.

The chocolate eating had become a ritual I looked forward to whenever my father made me prove I was taking my piano lessons seriously and not wasting his money or my teacher's time. His lack of hugs upon achievement at any level prompted my need for something sweet. Soon, it became a necessity. Anything would do—cookies, a slice of angel food cake slathered with 7-minute frosting, a donut dusted with powdered sugar, a scoop of ice cream, or even a few Tootsie Rolls. They all soothed my easily deflated spirit. My daddy didn't think I was good enough. I wanted to be, because I loved him with all my heart, but that heart just wasn't into music. Didn't he know? Couldn't he tell?

Although my father rarely lost his temper, he expected obedience, just like my mother expected politeness and good manners. When he asked me to play something for him, I'd get those flutters in my stomach that one of my aunties called butterflies. The mere thought of butterflies in my stomach was so disturbing that when I felt them there it was doubly hard for me to sit still. I'd slide onto the piano bench; turn the pages of the music book to the piece requested by father, and wait for the lecture, all the while willing the butterflies to stop flapping their wings.

"You're blessed with musical talent, Carol. You get it from me, you know, and from your grandfather. He was musically inclined and so are both of your uncles. You've got great piano hands. Look at your fingers. They're long and can stretch to reach the octaves. Even your teacher agrees with me. You'll be a famous concert pianist someday. If I say it, you can take that to the bank. Picture this, Carol. Your mother and I will come to Carnegie Hall to hear you play with the symphony orchestra, and all your mother's New York relatives will be there beside us. The marquee will have your name in big letters. Miss Carol Sorkin, daughter of Maestro Barney Sorkin. Spectacular. That's what it'll be. Spectacular! But it won't happen unless you practice, practice, practice. No daydreaming, Carol. Now show me what you can do."

My fingers moved lightly over the keys, but I don't think I breathed throughout the entire musical piece. I had been taking lessons since I was six, and on this occasion, I was barely past my eighth birthday. The thought of secretly eating a fancy chocolate was my only incentive for doing well. I'd much rather be in my room drawing a picture. I wanted to be an artist. Not a pianist, which was my father's dream. Not a dancer, which had been my mother's dream, until she sent me to tap dancing class and decided, after only two lessons, I wasn't going to become the next Shirley Temple. I had used up all the tubes of paint in the set someone gave me for my seventh birthday and wanted more colors and bigger brushes. I had a box full of paper dolls and the dozens of outfits I'd created for them, and I had colored every page in every color book ever given to me. I drew so many pictures, my Crayola color crayons were quickly stripped of their paper protection and worn down to one-inch stubs.

After rehearsing with his band all day or playing his saxophone as part of a larger band providing the musical background for a Hollywood film, my father would often return home in the late afternoon for early dinner. After showering and donning a dark suit or tuxedo, in order to perform at a night club, in the home of a wealthy Hollywood star or producer, or at a charity function, he'd sit at the piano and have me stand across the room.

"Okay, Carol, listen carefully," he'd say. "I'm going to play a few notes, one at a time. You know the drill. Tell me what notes I'm playing. It's important to train your inner ear, if you're going to be a great musician."

I was terrified I'd give the wrong answer. He never shouted when I said C instead of D, but he raised his voice and the look on his face and in his deeply penetrating umber eyes upset me. Although my bottom lip often trembled, I wouldn't cry or whine a protest. Part of being a "proper" young lady meant I should never talk back to my father. Not ever.

"When I was your age, I'd get up at about four o'clock every morning to deliver newspapers, Carol," he said on one of these occasions. "I had so many customers on my route, my carrying bag dragged on the ground until it was light enough to hoist onto my shoulder. I walked every inch of the way, because I didn't own a bike. Can you even imagine yourself doing that? Walking for blocks all by yourself in the middle of the night? Rain or shine, snow or sleet, it didn't matter. My customers wanted a newspaper to read with their breakfast. Whenever you think practicing your piano lesson is hard or boring, picture your daddy when he was your age. Now, what note am I playing?" He played sharps, flats and both major and minor chords. "What's this?"

"That's . . . uh . . . I think it's A flat."

"No, no, you're not listening! I give up." He rose from the piano bench and threw my lesson book at me.

Startled, I glanced at where it lay at my feet and didn't look up. I couldn't face him. I waited until I heard the front door shut before I let a couple tears trickle down my cheeks. Daddy had never done that before. I bent down to pick up the lesson book and walked with dragging feet back to the piano and placed it carefully on the bench. Then glancing around the room to ensure no one was watching me, I lifted the lid of the Whitman's box and chose the rich dark chocolate cherry cordial. After replacing the lid, I bit through the chocolate shell, sucked out the white cream to get a good look at the cherry, and then popped it all into my mouth. The cherry was like a kiss.

One day I was watching my mother cook in the kitchen. She chopped an onion, several carrots, two long stalks of celery and scooped them into a pot of chicken broth on the stove. She was preparing another pot of soup. We'd been having soup almost every week for what seemed like forever. Sometimes there'd be chicken in it and other times noodles or big, fluffy matzo dumplings. "Why do we have soup so much, Mommy?"

"Because it's our patriotic duty to be thrifty. These vegetables come from our Victory garden in the backyard. Your grandfather takes good care of it for us."

I watched and waited. Finally, I gathered up enough courage to speak my deeper thoughts in a mumbling voice. "Why doesn't Daddy ever tell me how good I played my piano piece, Mommy? He only tells me what I do wrong."

"How *well* you played, Carol, not good. Daddy has a lot on his mind these days. We all do. You're too young to understand, but the whole world has been at war since you were a little girl and we lived in New York. Millions of Americans are either serving with one of our armed forces and are away from their families, or they're at work in factories making things our government needs. Your daddy hasn't been sent to war, because they said he wasn't tall enough, but he feels obligated to offer his services in other ways. He loves our country. That's why he's away so much."

"Sometimes, I'm scared of Daddy. He used to hug me and throw me in the air and catch me. I remember when we'd go to the park. Now, he never does anything fun. He just wants me to practice on the piano. Other kids get to go outside after school and ride their bikes." I folded my arms on the counter and dropped my head on them. "Daddy threw my practice book at me last week. He was really mad," I mumbled, eager to get the secret off my chest.

My mother turned down the gas burner of the range to simmer and reached for the soup pot cover. When I didn't budge, she went to the refrigerator and brought out the bottle of milk, shaking it so the cream that always rose to the top would be evenly dispersed. "How about some milk and a couple cookies? Will that make you feel better?"

I nodded.

"You have to forgive your daddy, Carol. He had a lot on his mind. Daddy does plenty of fun things with you. You're choosing not to remember them. He takes you to the movie studio with him, doesn't he? Only a very few little girls get to experience how a movie is filmed. Think of all the movie stars you've met."

"Those people all want to hug me, Mommy. They ask too many questions and I don't know what to say. I want to hide behind Daddy, but he always pushes me towards them. I miss our old house in New York. Why do things have to change?"

"That's life, Carol. Things have changed for everyone. You're too young to understand how our country suffered during the long Depression, before Americans got involved in the war and our people could go back to work in the factories. We drove all the way across the country to Los Angeles, because your daddy heard he could get steady work playing his saxophone in bands at the movie studios. You've met the men who play in Daddy's band. Their children don't see them very often either. They work all day at the studios and then entertain at parties or charity events at night to bring a little cheer to weary souls. Hollywood producers and many actors are making movies that bring smiles and laughter into the lives of those whose daddies or sons are far away at war. You like the Shirley Temple movies, don't you? And Lassie?"

I sipped my milk and nibbled on the oatmeal cookie. "I guess so. Why aren't *those* people at war—those actors and producers?"

"Some are too young; some too old, some have health reasons. You can serve your country in many ways, Carol. When your daddy isn't at the studios, he offers his services to Lockheed Aircraft, over in Santa Monica. He's a wonderful draftsman who makes detailed technical designs and drawings for them. He also works with the Red Cross and entertains servicemen who come home wounded. You've been there with me. We take cookies and pack up gift boxes. This is a conversation for adults, dear. You can't really understand the seriousness behind my words."

"You always say I'm too young to understand."

My mother was right, though. I didn't understand much of what she was telling me, but I liked listening to her talk to me. I finished eating both cookies and reached for a third.

"No more, Carol. Two is enough. Sugar is rationed and you mustn't be greedy. Thousands of children never get a single cookie these days. We're lucky to live in the United States. I don't know what the future holds for us as a family or for you and your little sister when you grow up, but in your prayers, never forget to thank God for sending your grandparents this country where they are safe. Where we're all safe."

My mother stirred the soup, tasted it, added more salt and pepper, and then placed the ladle on a dish nearby to catch the drippings. Finally, she turned to look directly at me. "Your daddy might not praise you as much as you'd like, Carol, but I've heard him tell other people how talented you are. He's proud of you. And he took time to find you the best piano teacher in town, didn't he?"

"Mr. Raderman?"

"Yes, and Mr. Raderman doesn't usually take little girls. He did it as a favor. Someday, when you're all grown up, you'll be glad you can talk about music with your father. It's his special gift, and he hopes he's passing it onto you."

I loved my piano teacher, Max Raderman. Mother often said he was a movie-star handsome man, but I thought of him as being patient. He was the exact opposite of my father, and I dreamed about him being my parent. He never yelled or made me feel hopelessly stupid when I made a mistake. He did insist, however, that I use the metronome. In that way, he was just like my father. "You're a lucky girl, Carol," he'd say. "That concert grand piano you practice on is a Steinway—the best piano made in America. The greatest pianists in the world use Steinways. They're made to last and they have an exceptional tone. That piano will be around long after your parents and even you and your own grandchildren are playing with the angels in heaven." I learned much later that Max Raderman's brother was the concert master at MGM studios.

Today, the family Steinway grand sits proudly in my music room, and I still enjoy playing the pieces I learned for recitals so many years ago, including Rachmaninoff's Concerto No. 2, Chopin's Grande valse brillante in E-flat major, Op.18, and Clair de Lune by Debussy.

My father had instructed Mr. Raderman to teach me only classical music, so part of my strict training involved practicing pages and pages of Beringer scales. I would come home from school, have a snack, wash my hands and head for the piano to play until suppertime. First, I practiced scale and chord passages and finger studies with progressive movement, always conscious of my hand placement and using the proper fingers marked by numbers on the sheets of music. I could barely reach the pedals, but I still had to know when to push and let up my foot on a pedal, and when to strike the keys harder. The instant I made a mistake, I'd have to begin the piece over again until it was perfect.

I'd lay in my bed at night and think about my father as a boy. I pictured him getting up way before the birds in the morning to deliver newspapers and then come home for breakfast and a long day at school. I'd think of him practicing on the saxophone provided by his father. It wasn't until long into my adulthood that I fully realized how remarkable it was for him to learn this difficult instrument without the benefit of lessons from a professional, and then about how he used his acquired skill to support our family and make a good living, even during the war years. He had earned the nickname Maestro. I believe he placed greater demands on me to become an accomplished pianist, because he was providing me with what he had lacked at my age. He honestly believed that a fine teacher and time to practice, without the pressure of having to contribute to the support of our family, should and would produce great results. He didn't have time or the inclination to analyze the possibility of my developing any other talent.

He forgot that his drafting talent may well have been passed on to me. The ability to see the size and shape and depth of an object and to reproduce it in a recognizable form required as much skill as learning to play a musical instrument. Both a musician and an artist must practice persistently to reach the level required for a professional—a professional who is paid for an exhibition of her talent.

My father worked from dawn to long after dusk, not unlike others during the war years. After the Japanese bombed Pearl Harbor, the uncertainty and fear that always lay bare in their minds resulted in an urgency to take advantage of each day' s blessings. Not a day went by when my parents and other family members didn't worry that the bombings would be repeated. Looking back, I more fully understand the forced and too boisterous laughter of the attendees at every party, the indulgences when the lives of others were at risk, the "eat, drink and be merry" attitude, "because tomorrow we may die."

Fear that war produces abruptly changes daily routines and expectations. It alters priorities and creates a dread of answering the doorbell for fear a telegram courier will be there or an officer with news of the wounding or death of a loved one. Two of my uncles and cousins were in the armed forces. After my grandmother died, Grandfather Mitnick moved in with us. I would sometimes sit beside him as he listened to news reports several times a day on our console radio. He wanted answers to the questions that plagued him all his waking hours. Where were his sons and grandson and would they come home safely? Although the words of his favorite radio broadcasters—Gabriel Heatter, Walter Winchell and Edward R. Morrow—didn't make sense to me at my young age, I knew intuitively that these men were among his educators.

"Why do you have to listen to all that talk about war?" I asked him once. "Why don't you read the newspaper instead?"

"*Спокоцно*! Not now, Carol. When the news is on, you must be quiet."

When I asked my mother why he read the newspaper upside down and signed his name with an X, she said, "Your grandfather never learned how to read or write English, Carol. Before he immigrated to America, he was considered the one with the most authority in his village. Like a judge. Whenever a problem came up, he was the spokesman. He's very smart. He knows a little about everything, but he still thinks and reads and writes in Russian."

Stress. It wreaks havoc on individuals and families, and the unrelenting stress that war brings adds to the misery. It especially affects the children, because they are too often brushed aside. Whenever I complained that no one was any fun anymore, my mother became stern. "No more of that, Carol! You are living in the lap of luxury compared to other children your age. Now, no more questions. Can't you see how busy I am? Go find your sister and play with your dolls. You're the oldest. Set a good example. Better yet, practice your piano lesson. Surprise your father with a perfect performance today. Busy hands don't have time to get in trouble."

Busy. That defined the lives of most Sorkin adults in our house. They were too busy to go to synagogue on Saturdays, too. Saturdays were the busiest days of the week. My father was booked weeks in advance for private parties or charity events and often held a rehearsal with his band members earlier in the day. My mother had to either attend the party or hostess one at our house. Either way, the preparations took up hours. My younger sister and I would play in short spurts, wander around the house, and end up in the kitchen to eat anything available to relieve our boredom.

The desire for treats to soothe my troubled soul first came about with the captivating aromas that seeped from our kitchen into other rooms in the house. There were no frozen foods or boxed mixes. Cakes, pies, cookies or bars were made "from scratch." Mother loved to bake and I loved to sample whatever she produced. Whenever I smelled something fresh from the oven, I reacted like a Greek mariner being lured by the sweet singing of the sea nymphs into certain destruction on the rocks surrounding their island. The older I became, the less resistance I had to anything sweet or sugary.

When our guests were due to arrive for a special dinner party or buffet, my sister and I were usually banned to our rooms upstairs. "Stay out of the way and don't become a bother, Carol. This is an adult party tonight."

When I thought it was safe, I would sneak halfway down the stairway and perch behind the balusters to see what the ladies were wearing and listen to the music. If my father and his band weren't playing, musical guests would gather around the piano and sing. At times, when I was caught and shooed back upstairs, I'd take out my drawing supplies and recreate the women guests in their fancy dresses.

One evening, I was back on the stairway trying to be quiet while having a little fun. Rather than crouching to peer through the balusters, I decided to sit and dangle my legs over the edge of the stairway tread. I got my right leg successfully through the narrow space by slipping my foot through first. Not thinking, I pushed my left knee into the space and it got caught. I couldn't pull it out or push it forward. I was trapped. And scared. I did what any youngster would do in such a situation. I yelled. Help came running. Lots of it. I was scolded and banished to my room.

It is said by many writers of wisdom that our lives are defined by moments, ones that create never-to-be-forgotten memories. These moments, however small or insignificant and over our lifetime, have an effect on us, sometimes insightful, sometimes unpleasant or damaging.

During our childhood and adolescence, every moment experienced and every word spoken to us seems profound. We're easily hurt, easily influenced or swayed one direction or the other. We're eager to please and acquiesce. We make snap judgments. We harbor resentments. We misconstrue, distort and stretch the truth. Those around us do the same, even our parents and others we love and trust. And so we mature and make choices based upon these prejudices.

It often takes years to let go of things we didn't fully understand at the time the moments were occurring. In the meantime, we make a series of wrong choices and head down the wrong road for the wrong reasons, becoming what we vowed never to become. If we're lucky, another moment happens that illuminates us. We make a wiser choice, and then another. We are finally able to change course and redefine ourselves.

That's what I did, but it took far too long to understand that I alone was responsible for the outcomes of each wrong decision and why I had made them. Every moment, every opportunity presented me with an option, and I had a choice to make. Not my mother. Not my father. No member of the Sorkin family. The decision was mine.

The longer I continued to make snap decisions, unconstructive, harmful, selfish or image-damaging decisions that seemed like solutions for filling my love-starved soul, the more miserable I would be. Who did I want to become? The accomplished concert pianist in my father's dreams? No. Besides, I had killed the possibility for that achievement when I resolutely determined, at age twelve, to stand up to the maestro and declare, "I want to play the harp."

The harp wasn't the piano, but it was "piano-like."

My father frowned and narrowed his eyes, thinking. "I'll get you the harp, if you take piano lessons for one more year and you haven't changed your mind."

I changed my mind. No harp, but no piano either. I put my foot down. My piano lessons came to an end. Who would I be now, if not a concert pianist? "You decide," my parents said. "We've done our best."

2

I DIDN'T KNOW what I would be as an adult, but I had acquired a better understanding of my heritage during my preteen years and how that might influence my future. I was a Russian-American and a Jew. It wasn't until after the war that the atrocities committed against Jews was fully known in what history now calls the Holocaust, but there were plenty of rumors, and even as young girl I listened to those in my household talk about it.

My maternal grandparents were no strangers to the fear that comes from war and prejudices. They left their homeland during the Russian Revolution. Both were from the village of Minsk, Belarus, not terribly far from Kiev, Ukraine. My grandfather, Benjamin Mitnickski, married Dora Kupson at a fairly young age. In the few photographs they carried with them, I can see why he was enamored by her pretty face, smile and long, heavy braids. When I first saw one particular photograph, I laughed at the ankle-high, laced boots she wore, but now they're back in style.

My grandfather looked like a dapper young man, with a rusty-red mustache and blondish hair; his appearance spoke volumes for his deep sense of adventure, but not for his willingness to work hard to become a productive and contributing American. As with so many immigrants from this period of American history, it was only because of the unspeakable hardship in their homeland that they were able to leave their other family members and make such a long journey on nothing but a dream of a better life.

Over the years, I've gathered bits and pieces of my ancestral DNA through information gleaned from my grandparents' records and conversations with my mother. My grandparents, who had two young daughters to think about (my aunts Celia and Ida), made plans for Grandma Dora and the girls to remain behind in Minsk for a later journey to London, before sailing for America. This would allow my grandfather time to find work and provide a home for them somewhere in this new country. He said his heartfelt goodbyes and left in the back of a wagon with his three brothers and a sister and traveled for days to Bologne, France; they sailed from there on the S/S Maasdam Rotterdam, June 16th, 1899. It was a long arduous boat trip across the Atlantic Ocean arriving in New York, two weeks later, June 30th, 1899. He and his sister, Esther, settled in Providence, Rhode Island. The three brothers (Chane, Cibel and Leib) went on to South America, where many other emigrating Russians were settling.

Benjamin Mitnickski was eager to blend into the melting pot of nationalities that made up a rapidly growing America. Immigrants from many nations arrived in ships at the Ellis Island port every week. It wasn't unusual for those with difficult surnames of any nationality to shorten them for easier spelling and pronunciation. Grandpa changed his to Mitnick. Later, it was changed to Morton by my uncles, Jack (Jacob) and Moe (Morris), who wanted to pass themselves off as heirs of the Morton Salt Company.

According to my mother, Grandma Dora stayed in London with some man whose name and exact relationship to her remains unknown. She arrived in Providence a year after Grandpa. I have wondered many times if my sweet little grandmother, who looked like the caricature of Mrs. Santa Claus, might have had an indiscreet adventure with this "stranger" while biding her time in London. It is more likely he was only another Russian who enjoyed speaking with someone in his native tongue, until he, too, could venture forth on his emigrant voyage.

Benjamin and Dora raised six children—four daughters (Celia, Ida, Martha and Selma, my mother) and two sons (Jacob and Morris, who became Jack and Moe). Grandpa did a little of this and a little of that in Providence, competing for business in a city that had been growing nonstop because of the railroad network, turnpikes and the port. At the time my grandparents arrived, history figures show that more than sixty percent of the 175,597 residents were foreign born. They came because of the need for both skilled and unskilled labor; Providence was an industrial city that included cotton and worsted wool mills, machine tool fabrication, rubber products, and jewelry and silver manufacturing.

The Benjamin Mitnick Family

Immigrants were willing to work hard, and Grandpa Mitnick was no exception. But his labor was not producing the wealth he had envisioned would come when living in America, the land of the free. It was still a dream.

Still a dream, until the 1920's Prohibition, when bootlegging brought him all the money he'd ever imagined having. There's no way to write this delicately. Bootleggers were smugglers and distributors of illegal alcohol. When the Eighteenth Amendment to the Constitution went into effect in January of 1920, most of the public was opposed to it, especially those from major port cities like New York and Providence, where many of the immigrants were of German, Irish, Jewish, or Catholic backgrounds. Daily beer drinking was a part of their culture. History shows that the Protestants—especially the women who were often victims of domestic violence and economic deprivation because of their alcoholic or perpetually drunken husbands—had pushed for a prohibition of alcohol. They were joined in their efforts by many business or factory owners who wanted sober workers on the job to produce quality products.

The Amendment, called the National Prohibition Act, and also known as the Volstead Act, called for the restriction of the "production, sale, transportation, importation, and exportation of alcoholic beverages," but not the drinking of them. Laws rarely impede those who can see how to work around them. This one was no exception. Thousands horded alcohol or established ties with those who could buy it from foreign sources, especially from Canadian bootleggers, and smuggle it into the States. Of course, those with the most connections were mobsters. Grandpa Mitnick had his eyes and ears open and made his connections. For the sake of the family, of course.

My grandfather was not the only one capitalizing on the illegal distribution of alcohol. Several books and many other sources have documented that Joseph Kennedy, the father of U.S. President John F. Kennedy, made his fortune in the same manner.

Drinking of spirits of any kind and quality, from beer to the finest scotch, whiskey, rum or wine, continued to be big business. When we think of this period of history, we often envision it through the early movies that depicted the secret clubs called speakeasies, where drinks were served to those who knew the secret code to gain entrance. Reports say that at least 30,000 such establishments existed in NYC, and drinks that once cost patrons a nickel could be sold for 50 cents. The speakeasy owners grew adept at disguising the quality and taste of their bootlegged liquor, usually of a cheaper quality, by adding fruit juices or ginger ale or tonic; and thus, the "mixed drink" was born.

At a young age, by today's standards, my uncles frequented these speakeasies. Mother told me about her "spoiled brothers," who, even in their teens, had new cars and many girlfriends. Grandpa would buy Uncle Moe and Uncle Jack another car whenever they crashed one and filled their palms with as much cash as they needed. While the girls in the family were home tending to all the cleaning and laundry, bed linen changing, grocery shopping and cooking, the boys were cruising the town. This pattern was set way before I came along. Connections counted and secrecy worked. My uncles took their "work" seriously and understood how Grandpa was supporting the family and what it took to "keep a woman happy." It wasn't discussed in mixed company.

Perhaps that's why the Morton Brothers, as they became known, never really worked after the Twenties decade. They had money in abundance and thrived on the power and influence it could buy. Money and the discussion of how to make more of it was their reason for living. It's no wonder, then, that they moved to Los Angeles, where Hollywood glamour and show business captured their attention and added substantially to their business and personal interests.

After my family moved to Los Angeles, it wasn't unusual for me to see either uncle with a beautiful starlet on his arm, especially Uncle Moe. He would stop by our house long enough for a quick introduction and then be on his way. I usually tagged after him, my eyes taking in everything. I couldn't always follow the conversation. Once, when we were alone, I asked him, "What did you do when you were a kid my age, Uncle Moe?"

"I worked in a local movie theatre as a candy butcher."

"What's a candy butcher?" I asked, wrinkling my nose while gazing up at him, picturing the men in white aprons who worked behind a meat counter. "I don't get it."

"Do you know what a concessionaire is? No, of course you don't. Why would you? All you need to know is that when I was a boy I'd stroll up and down the aisles of a movie theater selling candy before the movie started and during the intermission." He reached into his jacket pocket and pulled out a candy bar. "Don't I always give you candy? I learned that little girls liked it way back when I was a candy butcher. And you don't even have to pay me for it, Carol. Just say thanks."

"Thank you, Uncle Moe." I never turned down anything made with chocolate.

"I wasn't the only kid who hawked stuff for a living back in Providence, Carol. Ever heard of Thomas Edison? No? I guess he died just before you were born. Well, he's famous. You'll learn about him in school. He was an inventor of lots of stuff, but I just remember the light bulb. When he was a kid, he sold candy and newspapers to people who road on the railway trains back and forth to work. Don't forget that. Your Uncle Moe isn't a famous inventor, but I'm pretty famous out here in Hollywood."

"But why were you called a candy butcher?"

"So many questions." Uncle Moe tousled my head of curls. "I don't have a good answer. Maybe it was because meat butchers would lay the chops and ribs and cutlets they carved out of the cow or pig onto trays in the meat counter. We candy butchers would carry the assortment of mints and fudge and bars on the trays we carried. See the similarity?"

I nodded, no longer interested in anything but the taste of chocolate in my mouth.

I loved Uncle Moe. He often slept in the same room as my sister and I on a rollaway bed, because he didn't keep an apartment of his own. I especially enjoyed the Smith Brothers licorice cough drops he kept on the night stand that I would occasionally sample when he wasn't around. I worried that he would catch me in the act or ask why some were missing from the box and decided he was a little scary, even when he was smiling and joking. Yet, when I was hospitalized to have my tonsils removed, he was waiting on the porch steps the day I came home with a huge teddy bear in his arms.

Several times, I watched him cut newspapers into neat stacks of dollar-sized rectangles and then wrap a few real bills around a wad of them, holding them in place with a rubber band before stuffing them into his pants and suit jacket pockets. Little did I know then that Uncle Moe would become one of the "major gambling figures in syndicated crimes." (Gus Russo, Supermob, Bloomsbury, USA, c2006, pp.337-343.)

My mother, Selma—or the more formalized Americanized form, Sarah—was the baby of the family. She had five older siblings who quickly tagged her with the nickname Babe, a name that stuck for the rest of her life.

I must admit that I called my mother Placenta throughout my adulthood, and believe it or not, she would always answer, even from across a room. She was quite a character and is the only woman I've ever known who donned a shower cap and a bathing suit to defrost the freezer in the years before the automatic defrosting mechanism was invented.

Her oldest sister, my Auntie Celia, was married to a good man, according to my mother, but he died shortly after I was born. Sam Rice and his family owned jewelry stores in Providence, Rhode Island. Unfortunately, Auntie Celia and Sam had no children, so she doted on my sister and me all our lives. A sweet and gentle soul, she was the epitome of kindheartedness and always spoke to me in a soft voice. She moved to California about the same time my family did and spent the rest of her life performing electrolysis for the Hollywood crowd. Years later, when she suffered from an inoperable brain tumor, she asked me for sleeping pills to end her life, but I had enough guilt in my life at the time and knew I couldn't live with such an additional burden. Euthanasia was and still is illegal.

Auntie Celia's nephew, Bob Rice, was one of the original investors in the Dunes Hotel in Las Vegas, and that became my family's "Vegas" connection. Bob's son—my cousin Jeffery Grant Rice, as he liked to be called—wrote the first "Night Stalker" television show, which starred Darrin McGavin, and became a successful screenwriter.

Mother was close to all three of her sisters. Aunties Ida and Martha, as well as Auntie Celia, mothered me whenever they visited. Sometimes it seemed as though I had four mothers instructing me about manners, my posture, and what was important or not important for women to have a satisfying life.

Auntie Ida was a Sophie Tucker lookalike. Her curly auburn hair and voluptuous diminutive body made her irresistible to me. Although she had a "sailor's" mouth, which didn't please my mother when she was around us children, she had the loving heart of a Mother Theresa. Her home was open to anyone who needed a hug or a meal. It took considerable eavesdropping on my part, but I eventually came to know that she never wore underpants, a shocking discovery I have never forgotten.

Auntie Ida had never learned to drive. But her lack of driving skills, which meant she was forced to stay at home on days when she'd rather be somewhere else, enhanced her ability to listen. She encouraged every visitor to spew their endless tales of woe and common gossip, and this uncommon trait eventually resulted in her becoming their confidant. When she didn't have a visitor, she watched the popular television soap opera "The Guiding Light.

Ida was always on a diet and talking about her growing waistline, even while she was indulging in daily teatime treats. My sister Sandra and I decided to play a naughty trick on her. "We helped Mother make homemade fudge yesterday," I declared, handing her a small square chunk on a napkin. Watching with widened eyes, Sandra vigorously nodded.

"Oh, my goodness, homemade fudge, girls? I adore chocolate, so I'm officially off my diet as of right this minute!" Ida used two fingers to carefully transfer the entire piece to her mouth. Bless her heart, she kept chewing and chewing on it, and our eyes threatened to pop out of their sockets. Finally, we had to confess. "Spit it out, Auntie Ida! It's chocolate-covered rubber! We played a trick on you! We're so, so sorry. Please don't tell Mommy."

Auntie Ida's husband, Samuel Diskin, could pass for Woody Allen's father. A rather short and well turned-out man, he was rarely without a cigar in his mouth. Ida, Sam, and their two sons, Jerome and Francis, designed home furnishings and ran a successful furniture store in Los Angeles called Diskin Art. Their daughter, Gloria, eventually became the designated driver for her mother.

As long as I knew her, Auntie Ida shopped, visited friends, indulged in several lunches, teas parties, and outings at the theater each week without ever getting behind a wheel. She'd ask anyone she knew with a driver's license for a ride to an event; most were more than willing to accommodate her request, as she'd generously treat them in some way for their services.

Uncle Sam was an impeccable dresser and Auntie Ida put on whatever fit her that day. While she struggled with weight throughout her entire life, Uncle Sam never gained or lost an ounce. Any night of the year, his dinner consisted of a T-bone or sirloin steak and a baked potato with all the trimmings. It certainly didn't affect his cholesterol, because he lived a long, fun-filled life, well into his nineties. He also had a passion for the ponies, as did several others in both the Mitnick and Sorkin families, and that kept his mind sharp.

Auntie Martha and my mother looked more like sisters than they did with their other two sisters, which had always raised questions in my mind after I learned about the birds and bees. In those days, Auntie Martha was gorgeous as a young woman, and counted Eddie Duchin, the famous pianist and band leader, as one of her suitors. Her heart, however, was captured by the wonderful and quite handsome Sol Hiller.

One of the most memorable and frightening sights to me as a young girl was seeing Grandpa Mitnick's teeth soaking in a glass of water. It made such an impression on me that, in the later years when he lived with us, I would make excuses about having to go to his room to deliver his laundry or fresh towels. I never asked him why he had "fake" teeth, but when I asked my dentist about it, he adamantly declared it was from eating too much "sugar." Unfortunately, that message never kept me from using anything sweet and sugary as a panacea for unhappiness, disillusionment, disappointment or loneliness and, eventually, more than my teeth would suffer the consequences.

Grandpa Mitnick enjoyed drinking strong hot tea, and it didn't take being in the room with him to know when he was indulging in his daily habit. I could hear the clanking of his spoon against the side of the cup even from the piano bench in the living room when I paused between songs during practice sessions. Years later, when my husband Ian and I visited St. Petersburg, I noticed other Russians doing the same thing. What once seemed annoying to me, I now find endearing and a happy memory.

As children, we're so quick to judge. We live on our emotions and form many inaccurate perceptions of people and events based upon our limited knowledge and experiences. We're fanciful and have the ability to stretch the truth if reality is too hard to understand or too difficult to accept. Although we know the difference between the truth and lies, we're all too willing to fabricate a reply that will please the ones we love . . . or who we want to love us. We grow up wanting to provide the 'right' answers.

I wonder now, in the waning days of my life, how much truth was spoken among my Mitnick family members during the Twenties decade of bootlegging that brought enough wealth to see them through the Depression of the Thirties and the war years of the forties.

3

THE PATERNAL SIDE of my family was very proper, and was a gentler version of my maternal relatives. My grandfather, Abraham Sorkin, married Esther Inoff in their hometown of Divinsk, Vitebsk, Russia. Esther was young, petite, and had facial features that resembled those of the beautiful china dolls only the wealthiest young girls of my grandmother's era were given as toys. Abraham was considered a "good catch." He was an exceptionally talented and artistic young man who worked hard in a local jewelry and watch shop, but he yearned to emigrate to England. After talking Esther into participating in his vision for their future, they packed their few belongings and left Vitebsk with their two very young children (Myron and Leih), saying goodbye to their family and friends. Their first destination was the Cape of Good Hope in South Africa, where they lived for a year with Abraham's sister Lizzie. When the time was right, they sailed to London, settling in Whitehall. It was there that my father was born, in 1903, and his brother Harry seven years later.

London, at the turn of the century, was the capital city of an empire that spanned the globe; historians still consider the British Empire the largest in history. Included under its rule were New Zealand, Canada, at least a third of Africa (including South Africa), India, Australia, Hong Kong, Switzerland, Pakistan, Ireland and many others. Needless to say, Britain was considered the center of power and London became the Mecca for many immigrants.

When I learned about the British Empire in school, I questioned my father about his years of being an Englishman. What I found interesting was that London, even in 1900, had many of the modern conveniences we enjoy today. When I watched films of this period of history, I didn't think of electric lights, gas heating, or a telephone network that allowed transatlantic calls to the United States. My father assured me he hadn't studied his lessons by candlelight or gas lantern.

Whitehall was actually a wide street in London lined by imposing government buildings and, at one time, the Royal Palace of Whitehall, which was destroyed by fire in 1698. I learned, on one of my visits to the city, that King Charles I was beheaded in the banquet room, which is still open for tours.

The Sorkin Family

Right before my grandparents immigrated to London, the city had celebrated Queen Victoria's Diamond Jubilee (1897). Visitors came from many foreign countries for the event and, evidently, a few commented on the daily fog and unimpressive town houses and "medieval street plan." In the next ten to fifteen years, while my father was living through his childhood and adolescent years, he said the city seemed to transform itself. A building was being constructed somewhere at all times, and the architecture incorporated those of many European styles, even Greek.

"Although your grandfather had a small cigar store in Whitehall, his love for anything having to do with artistic efforts interested him, Carol. He said the nonstop effort to create a more 'imperial metropolis' kept people employed, and that's what mattered to labor men like brick layers, especially to the immigrants who were grateful for the opportunity to support their families."

One of the first things I noticed about my grandfather, whenever he visited us in the United States, was the metal brace on one leg. But my memory now is mostly of a meticulous gentleman in both his fine manners and appearance. When his letters arrived from London, the handwriting on the envelope always caught and held my attention. As a budding artist, I was impressed by his beautiful penmanship, which was executed with the skill, style, and flourish of a calligrapher. In that respect, I was gifted with his talent in later life.

My grandmother, Esther, had her hands full with the four children, especially with the three boys. Fortunately, they all demonstrated musical talent at an early age, and a great deal of their free time was spent practicing on their chosen instruments. Uncle Myron played both the piano and the saxophone; my father and Uncle Harry also took up playing the saxophone, because the instrument was already in the house and they wanted to be like their big brother. Auntie Lee, as was typical of most middle-class daughters, helped her mother with the cooking, baking and housework, especially after my grandmother became a midwife to help earn extra money for the needs of her growing brood.

Russian Jews, at that time of history, were fairly diminutive in height, as were most Europeans. Several studies have traced the growth in height of people between 1900 and the present; they show that the norm was five-feet-five before WWI. Height numbers changed during later decades due to advances in medicine and improved economic circumstances and diets, but no member of my father's family grew beyond the norm. Their height, however, did not deter them from accomplishing their goals. In that respect, they were ten-feet tall.

Music was their passion, especially for my father. He couldn't listen to enough of it. After school, he would rush home and confiscate Myron's saxophone. Then, sitting on the steps of their modest home, he'd practice the scales and anything he "heard" in his head or on the radio. He took no formal lessons, and no one ever gave him special instructions. He was truly gifted and had the coveted "ear" for music. Increasingly consumed by what he could do with the saxophone, he took up various other woodwind instruments, including the flute, the clarinet and the piccolo. In his musical career, he played one or the other of these instruments—alto, soprano or bass—depending upon the song and the effect that best portrayed a desired sound.

At the age of only seventeen, Daddy was hired to play with the famous London Savoy Hotel's orchestra, in its popular ballroom. Night after night, he dressed up in his tuxedo and bowtie and rushed to board one of the railway trains in the three-level underground system established about the time he was born and known to everyone as the "tube." With his saxophone under his arm, he strode into the Savoy feeling like the royalty who frequented the hotel. Like many of his decade, he had not graduated from high school. It was unthinkable to him, later in his long career and to me now, that someone with such little formal education and no formal music lessons played for the rich and famous. Dignitaries visiting the Savoy included the Duke of Windsor, whose favorite song was, Mr. Sandman, U.S. President Harry Truman, and Jordan's Prince Hussein. In one of my guest bedrooms, I still display a framed photograph of the late King Hussein with his first wife, Princess Sharifa Dina, who is the mother of his oldest child, Princess Alia. There, in the photograph, is my father playing his saxophone for them.

Although I knew, from other members of the family, that Daddy traveled in the circles of the well-heeled and well-connected because of his job, it wasn't until full adulthood that I could truly marvel at the experiences that colored his life. Even as a "wanna be" artist who didn't take her craft seriously, even while taking art lessons in Europe, I wasn't aware of the Savoy's impressive history that contributed so richly to Daddy's musical artistry. For instance, after the Savoy opened for the first time in 1889— the same year my grandparents immigrated to London—the famous artist Claude Monet set up an art studio in his Savoy suite and created over seventy paintings of views he could see from its windows, especially those featuring the Thames. I recently read that after its major, multimillion dollar restoration ended in 2010, the hotel initiated an 'artist-in-residence' plan, allowing some of today's best artists to stay at the hotel while creating new works that would go on display.

My father's first trip to the United States was in 1927, when he was twenty-four. He sailed on the ship known as the Berengaria, whose passageway was from Southampton, England, to the Port of New York. After checking out many of the nightclubs, listening to countless bands and determining whether or not he had a chance to "make it" in this equally bustling city of immigrants, he returned to London and continued to play at the Savoy.

In preparation for writing this memoir, I discovered there were still recordings or "zonophones" of my father playing with a group known as The Rhythmic Eight, a section of the Bert Ferman Dance Orchestra that played nightly at the Savoy. Produced in Middlesex, England in 1928, the mostly jazz album called "My Pet" featured him playing the alto sax. The jazz style represented what they called the "red hot, naughty, risqué jazz" of the 1920's. (http://grammercy.com/app/albums/view/166/The-Naughty-1920s-Red-Hot--Risque-Songs-Of-The-Jazz-Age-Volume-1)

Daddy played on other albums featuring Bert Ferman's band, which included "Let's all Sing the Lard Song," "Ain't That a Grand and Glorious Feeling," and "Let's All Go to Mary's House"; they can be viewed and heard on YouTube videos. There is also a 1927 album called "Sax Appeal," where Daddy played his instrument with Bert Ferman as part of the Devonshire Restaurant Dance Band. (http://musicuc.com/barney-sorkin) The photograph below is of The Rhythmic Eight. Barney Sorkin is seated on the far right.

Happily, the remodeled Savoy maintained the look and feel of the original foyer, where The Savoy Orpheans 1928 played such numbers as "Five-Foot-Two, Eyes of Blue" (1926) and "The Girlfriend" (1927). Today, I get misty-eyed whenever I envision Daddy playing his beloved saxophone in the same venue where Noel Coward, Rudy Vallee and Caruso used to perform.

Left to right: Sylvester Ahola (1st trumpet), Harry Robbins (drums), Irving Brodsky (piano, arranger), Andy Richardson (2nd trumpet), Ben Oakley (trombone), Reggie Batten (violin, leader), Barney Sorkin (saxes), Dave Thomas (banjo), Claude Hughes (saxes), Jim Bellamy (brass bass), Jerry Hoey (saxes), Jack Cressy (saxes).

A year later, Daddy was ready for a new musical adventure and sailed back to New York City. This time, he was more persistent in his search and landed a job with Emil Coleman's orchestra at the Waldorf Astoria Hotel. It was 1931, and he was just twenty-eight years old.

While playing at a wedding reception in New York, Daddy's eyes found those of my mother across the room. It was love at first sight for both of them. "With that porcelain china skin and flaming red hair, she looked exactly like the photographs of Ava Gardner," Daddy would say, his eyes sparkling. "What could I do? And that figure. It wouldn't quit. Can you believe it? I've loved your mother since she was seventeen years old."

When I listened to Daddy exclaim over my mother's natural beauty, I would sigh to myself. Why hadn't I inherited her genes, instead of his? Even in her housedresses, she demonstrated a flair for fashion, color and design. Even with her nearsightedness, she could whip together a stunning outfit fashioned from bed sheets. And she didn't have to wear an abundance of makeup to cover flaws. Even into her mid-nineties, Mother looked years younger than her age. She could have been a movie star herself. And yes, after Daddy's story of their first meeting had been repeated without change well into my teen years, I did look for a photograph of Ava Gardner to make comparisons with Mother in their wedding picture. It's true that beauty is in the eyes of the beholder, but I did see some resemblance.

Mother's story is all the more remarkable to me when I consider that she had contracted bacterial meningitis at age eighteen. At that time, there were no available antibiotics. Penicillin wasn't widely used until the mid-1940s. My grandparents were told their daughter wouldn't survive the night. Well, she obviously did, but the young girl in the bed next to my mother's died of the same disease, and this event had a profound effect on Mother. Because her life had been spared, she developed a sense of compassion not only for the sick and dying, but for the living. She taught my siblings and me to have an attitude of gratefulness and generosity and to always be kind to others.

Several years before Mother's stroke-induced inability to speak, she shared a dream she had experienced while in the hospital, fighting for her life at this young age. She said, "People were trying to pull me over a wall, but I wouldn't go, Carol. They kept tugging at me, and then I saw a brilliant light emanating from a tunnel. I wanted to investigate, but something held me back." She told me about this incident only once, but from what I've read and heard, it seems consistent with those of many others who had a near-death experience. I have to believe it wasn't her time to leave her earthly life.

Because of the depth of his love for Mother, my father took care of her and all her expenses while she recuperated in the hospital and, later, at home. They married shortly after her recovery. I remember asking Daddy, when he was recounting this story to me for the umpteenth time, "Did you and Mommy have a song you liked more than all the others you've played?"

"Now that is an easy question to answer, Carol," he said. "It is 'When the World Was Young.' It was a popular 1950's French song, with music by Philippe-Gérard and lyrics by Angèle Vannie. It was recorded by the incomparable Edith Piaf, often called the Little Sparrow, because she is as tiny as most girls are in grade school. She is only four-feet-eight-inches tall, but has a voice that can bring a man to tears. And she's done just that every time your mother and I have heard her sing our song." He'd lift his eyes to the ceiling and hum the melody. "Ah, the apple trees, sunlit memories. Where the hammock swung, on our backs we'd lie, looking at the sky, till the stars were strung."

4

I APPEARED ON the scene in March of 1934: Carol Elaine Sorkin. My parents named me Carol because Daddy loved the music of Christmas carols, and Elaine, because my mother loved the long poem "Lancelot and Elaine" ("Elaine the fair, Elaine the loveable, Elaine the lily maid of Astolat.") Apparently, she had great expectations, but my DNA was like "Boardwalk Empire" and "Downton Abbey".

In my early years in New York City, we first lived in the area called Forest Hills on Long Island. A white-uniformed nanny with "clunky" white, lace-up shoes was hired to take care of me. Julia dressed, washed and fed me. Among my first memories of her were those of her curling my wet hair around her fingers to form ringlets. I was about three, going on four. To this day, I haven't forgotten that Julia smelled like Ivory soap, whose slogan impressed both her and Mommy. It was "99.44% Pure," and the preferred castile soap of mothers everywhere, at least according to the convincing ads in women's magazines. What I loved about Ivory was that no matter how many times I pressed it under the surface of my bath water, it would bob to the surface, a game I played time and again until Julia would snatch it from the water before it had diminished in size. "It floats!" was added to the Ivory soap ads, and I repeated it with each dunking.

Although I'm sure Julia read to me from the many children's books on my bedroom shelves, a remembered favorite was The Real Mother Goose, with the Blanche Fisher Wright's cover artwork; it was published by Rand McNally in 1916 and remains a favorite of new parents and their children to this day.

Julia would have me recite the verses over and over again, and I had quite a repertoire, from "Humpty Dumpty" to "Polly Put the Kettle On" and "Old King Cole." Retaining this repertoire of much-loved verses came in handy later, both as a mother and a grandmother.

Mother took me to tap-dancing class and, after only two lessons, realized I didn't process the bodily grace or enthusiasm of my classmates. I was disappointed that I had to take off and retire my tap shoes, because the clicking sound when I merely walked across the kitchen floor was "dancing" to me. I didn't even attempt to put on dancing shoes again for eighteen years, when my interest in flamenco dancing spurred me into visiting a Hollywood dance studio once owned by Rita Hayworth's uncle.

One of my father's dancing friends was a great flamenco dancer from Spain, and I was privileged to meet her. Carmen Amaya was a lovely and impressive lady who gifted me with one of her recordings and two sets of her own castanets. They were tricky to play, but I worked hours on them until I could produce the right rhythm to songs I heard on the radio. Although I was twenty at the time, I found I wanted to learn how to dance while using them. The notion of whirling about a room while foot stomping and handclapping appealed to me, although I had no aspirations to work as hard as Carmen Amaya had to become world renown. I was told that one of the four flamenco elements was called Jaleo, which meant "hell raising." With my hormones in full development and plentiful supply, that vernacular amplified my determination. To this day, I play those castanets when listening to music and have often joined with a band at parties.

During a trip to Russia, my husband Ian and I visited Pushkin, about fifteen miles south of St. Petersburg. A six-piece band was entertaining while we enjoyed dinner. One of the members was using an idiophone instrument called a treshchotka, composed of a series of identically-sized wooden paddles. It sounded like the clapping of hands. I learned much later that Russians sometimes call people that (I'm sure they mean women!) who are too chatty. After some encouragement and a quick lesson, I played them during the next band performance. Again, as I had been the castanets, I was gifted with these treshchotka. They remain stored in a cabinet with the castanets and ready to use at a moment's notice. My family members also enjoy dancing and, quite impulsively, we will rise to our feet whenever we hear music with a strong beat. The castanets and treshchotka are put into play by both of my daughters and, now, my grandees dance with abandon until we're all laughing and they're exhausted.

With Daddy's continued success, we were soon able to move into a larger New York apartment with an elevator. I would play in Central Park, which was occupied by more pigeons than people. Today, I'm living in an area of Michigan where I can enjoy the beautiful Canadian geese that visit our back yard to feast on the tart red apples that drop from the trees. Although both "fowl" can become a nuisance when their increasing numbers aren't controlled, the geese offer more to my aesthetic sensibilities.

I thoroughly enjoyed the annual visits of my Mitnick grandparents. On one particular visit, their presence was providential. We lived near a pond that froze during the winter months, enabling me to pretend I was ice skating. One day, my best friend Lynne and I were outside playing, and the pond looked particularly inviting. We decided it would be great fun to walk all the way across the pond and back again. We joined hands and proceeded to amble slowly across the ice, giggling and sliding with our boots on the slick surface. We were near the middle of the pond when the ice snapped underfoot, then cracked with the sharp sound of gun fire and finally broke with our weight. In a flash, we both slipped into the frigid water. Scrambling to grasp hold of the edge of the ice above us, our efforts resulted in nothing but the breaking off of the ice into handheld fragments. We were too young and too frightened to scream for help. We just kept flapping our arms like they were flippers on zoo seals.

My grandfather Mitnick had been outdoors for a walk, heard our giggles and laughter, and watched as we glided on the ice. Then the heart-stopping accident occurred right before his eyes. He shouted for help and headed gingerly across the ice to rescue us. He told me later his heart was in his throat.

Fortunately, others heard his cries and ran to perform the water rescue. I can still hear the water sloshing in the thick rubber galoshes worn over my shoes as I rode the elevator up to our apartment. I received an abundance of hugs, but also stern warnings to never, ever, walk on the pond again without permission and supervision. I cried in Grandpa Mitnick's arms and thanked him for "saving" me, although I didn't understand the full significance of his role at the time. Some life lessons are remembered, but the seriousness doesn't register until we're older and wiser.

Mother, Grandma and Me

Thanksgiving Day brought another event to be enjoyed and right outside our apartment window—the Macy's Thanksgiving Day Parade. Julia would hold me up so I could press my face against the window pane. If the window were open, I could almost reach far enough to touch the huge balloon image of Mickey Mouse or of Pinocchio, who was constructed with an enormous nose. Although the parade was short, by today's standards, it was still magical for a little girl. The people, crowded shoulder to shoulder on the curbed side-walks, cheered the loudest when the tall, red-white-and-blue Uncle Sam balloon appeared. The sounds from below my window were deafening.

My fascination with giant balloons was fulfilled many years later when I sailed in a hot air balloon into the wide blue yonder with the clouds. It was a thrilling experience, and although the balloon landed much too close to a freeway for my liking, it satisfied my lifelong desire to fly above the rooftops and higher than any Macy's parade balloon.

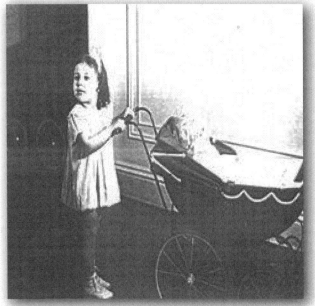

Wheeling my doll carriage in New York apartment

In February of 1937, I was delighted with the arrival of my baby sister. She was as cute as my pretend baby dolls, but she cried continuously. Sandra Hetty Sorkin was a dainty child with dark cognac eyes that flitted from one object to another. I found great pleasure in kissing her chubby cheeks whenever I could get close enough, and after weeks of doing this she would watch for me and coo with pleasure.

As soon as Sandra was old enough, Mother dressed us alike. An old photograph shows us in matching magenta coats and hats, but the photograph doesn't show what I was thinking. I thought my baby sister got more attention than I did. Whenever we were taken for a walk, people in the park would peer into the buggy and exclaim, "Oh, isn't she precious! Look at those eyes! And

 those rosy cheeks!" I'd either lift my face, hoping for the same attention, or hide it in Mommy or Julia's dress. Of course, babies and toddlers need more care; they can't do anything for themselves. But an older sibling who has received all the attention of adults until this moment in time doesn't know that. My jealousy caused innumerable tantrums.

When Sandra finally reached the age of playing house with her own dollies, we became friends and were inseparable. I enjoyed having a live-in playmate. When Sandra graduated from her crib, her "big girl" bed was placed right next to mine, and we shared a bedroom as long as we lived at home. Being the oldest sister brought me a few privileges, which I enjoyed. For instance, I was allowed to stay up longer on special occasions and occasionally skip a nap, but it seemed that my story time with Julia was shortened, so we wouldn't awaken Sandra.

A daily source of amusement for me during the good-weather days in New York was our visits to Central Park's playground and rides on the merry-go-round. Sandra watched from her buggy or Julia's lap, and I felt "special," because I could do something she couldn't. At three and even four, I was still too young to reason about the feelings of sibling rivalry that are a natural phenomenon in families with several children. If I poked Sandra too hard, or tried to make her cry, by scaring her with a couple too-loud boos, I would hear, "Stop it, Carol!" or be sent to my room. In those days, women's journals weren't replete with articles on the why children behaved as they did and how to recognize potential problems or what to do about them. New mothers used their instincts or did what their mother always did.

In 1938, we started to visit Auntie Martha (Mitnick) and Uncle Sol in their summer cottage in Providence, Rhode Island. I jumped at the chance to accompany Uncle Sol to the docks where he'd purchase lobsters directly from the boat owners. We'd take them home in a grocery-sized brown paper bag, and I made sure to walk on Uncle Sol's other side while keeping a wary eye on the still very much alive and unrestrained lobsters that made that bag jump. Sometimes, a particularly rambunctious lobster would find its way out of the bag and head across the kitchen floor. I'd head into the next room as fast as my little legs would take me. Fortunately, the ugly live lobster looked nothing like the buttery white chunks placed on my dinner plate a couple hours later.

On one late summer day of 1938—September 21 to be exact—Mommy, Sandra, Auntie Martha, my cousin Stephen, and I headed for the beach to have one last picnic lunch before it grew too cold. School had started, so we had the beach pretty much to ourselves. The women had their arms full trying to balance a picnic basket of food, a blanket to sit on, shovels and pails to keep Stephen and me busy, and a beach umbrella. For the first several minutes, I scampered after my cousin, who seemed in perpetual motion running through the sand and kicking it up his wake. "Carol, stay closer to me!" Mommy shouted. "You're too close to the water's edge." At one point, she and Auntie Martha moved all our gear further up the beach and away from the shoreline, because the water was advancing too far, too fast. We did this a couple more times, and Martha's complaining increased. Each time we moved, the water invaded the area where she had spread the blanket for our lunch. By the time we had eaten it, the shoreline was disappearing so fast and the waves were becoming so high, Auntie Martha finally said, "Let's pack up and get out of here, Babe! I don't have a good feeling about this. I've never seen the tide come in this early or so ferociously."

The two women quickly collected beach toys, folded up the blanket and rushed us three children back to the car. Luckily, Auntie Martha's instincts had alarmed her just in time. By the time we reached home, it was ominously dark and windy. Uncle Sol had rushed home from work. "A terrible storm is about to hit Providence," he said. "Those winds are supposed to reach 60-70 miles an hour. Gather up all the candles in the house . . . and matches. Don't forget the matches. The power might go off. I'll turn on the radio to hear what they're saying before that goes off, too."

"Is it one of those hurricanes we've read about, Sol? Didn't yesterday's paper say one was supposed to hit Miami today?" Aunt Martha was bustling my cousin and me to the center of the living room. "Stay here, kids. I'm going to get a few of your toys. Babe, get the blankets out of our beach bag. It's already chilly in here."

For the next several hours, we, along with the people of Providence and all those along the upper East Coast, experienced a super storm often called the Great Hurricane of 1938 or, as some news stories labeled it, the Long Island Express. Although I listened with one ear to Mommy and Aunt Martha as they expressed their fears with Uncle Sol, I was much too young to interpret the severity of the storm's rage outside the house. It wasn't often that I had the opportunity to visit with my cousin, and I took advantage of his having to accept me as his playmate.

At that time in our history, the weather professionals couldn't detect hurricanes far in advance or track their pathway; radio broadcasters couldn't issue warnings until they'd received word from authorities or local weather-watchers who could literally see the winds pick up and the flooding begin. No one knew what to expect or how to prepare. I read in one newspaper report that those who were my grandparent's age in 1928 had never experienced such a horrendous storm; many hadn't been born yet and knew nothing about the 1815 hurricane that had struck their same area. My family members were at another disadvantage. Russia didn't have hurricanes. No one in my family knew about their potential for danger and destruction or about the surging walls of water that cause most of the damage.

Not until my young adult years did I read the accounts and then question my mother about the storm, which had also been dubbed the Yankee Clipper. "What I remember reading in the papers, Carol, was that about 600 people died from the storm, most of them from Rhode Island. Another 700 or more were injured. Downtown Providence was hit by massive flooding. The newspaper articles said the storm surge reached twenty feet and slammed into City Hall. You can only imagine the extent of the destruction. It was like a war zone. Several beach communities were completely obliterated. Gone. Disappeared. The people. The houses. I shudder even now to think of it. Telephone lines were down for days. I had no way of reaching your father, and he couldn't reach me. He was beside himself with anguish, not knowing if we were still alive. We were spared, thank God. It was a miracle. That's the only way I can explain it."

Hurricane Sandra (2012) was declared the deadliest and most destructive of the Atlantic hurricane season. As in the 1938 Great Hurricane, it was the ocean surge that caused most of the property destruction, and then the massive flooding that followed weakened the walls of any remaining structures, making them too dangerous for habitation. One major difference in the two storms was that the people in danger in 2012 could watch minute-by-minute, hour after hour of weather coverage on their television sets or iPhones. They heard many warnings from mayors and governors to pack up and leave their homes and areas. Unfortunately, despite what they were told of the danger, there were thousands who scoffed with disbelief and merely hunkered down, refusing to leave their property. Then, at high tide, the forecasted storm surge grew to nine feet and swept over the island communities with a fury that destroyed miles of Long Island and New Jersey and even downtown New York City. People scrambled to leave their neighborhoods to save their children and pets, causing traffic jams for miles.

In 1938, the affected states and cities rebuilt and its citizens resumed life, more thankful for it and wiser about the unpredictability of storms. Perhaps today's citizens, many of whom never read about the former hurricane, have become all the wiser, too.

In the aftermath of the tragic 1938 event, New York City was in the midst of fulfilling plans for its first World's Fair. Officials were determined to remain on schedule, despite the devastation in their neighboring states and the great numbers of dead and wounded. They had conceived of and planned for the Fair as far back as 1934, and worked tirelessly for almost five years to turn a swamp in Queens into a 1,200-acre exhibition site with a theme based on what a future world would be like. All that technology had produced and was in the process of producing would be on display, and the structures would reflect the future in architecture.   The opening date of April 30, 1939, was a mere six months after the destructive hurricane, but it had been selected because the date coincided with the 150th anniversary of the New York City inauguration of George Washington as president of the United States.

Several countries had committed to participating in the Fair, and were in the process of finishing the interiors of their pavilions when the storm slammed into the East Coast states. For the months between the hurricane and the Fair, even more work was available for the huge labor force still reeling from the 1930's Depression. Everyone worked to help clean up the City and surrounding areas in preparation for visitors from every part of the world.

Finally, the Fair opened. There was both a radio and television broadcast by President Roosevelt. Yes, television. The first models had miniscule screens of a mere three and six inches, but 200 of these sets were distributed throughout the Fair grounds. Daddy and his brothers had heard about television while still young men in London. Before they ever immigrated to America, sets were being viewed by a few who could afford them. Records show that by the end of 1938, over 9,000 television sets had been sold in England, but the first one available for public purchase in the United States was in May of 1939. A three-inch model cost $125 to $150 and a five-inch model $195-$250. That was for the picture tube. If you wanted sound, you had to pay extra!

Cousin Freddie, Uncle Myron's son and a young man in his mid-thirties, was eager to see one of these technological marvels. Some family members had already visited the Fair in the first week, but Freddie hadn't been able to attend. He came over one morning to pick me up and took me with him. "It's like visiting a park that's two-three times the size of Central Park, Carol," he said, holding tightly onto my hand while leading us through the crowds. "I'm going to show you a television set. You can watch movies and even cartoon shows on it, just like when you go to the movie theater, only the picture is toy size. Can you even imagine that? And the theme of the Fair is 'World of Tomorrow.' It's like nothing we've ever seen before!" He could see by the look on my face that I wasn't as enthralled as he was.

"Maybe, if we're lucky, we'll even see some royalty. Remember, Carol, our daddies grew up in England where they have a king and a queen. Real ones."

I was still too young to know what he was talking about. In 1939, little girls were left to their imaginations when playing with baby dolls. We didn't have the benefit of Disney princess dolls in all their finery. I do remember that my eyes widened at the sight of the ultra-modern constructions and the masses of people. It wasn't at all like visiting the Central Park zoo, but I haven't forgotten drinking hot cocoa with marshmallows and getting a delicate bracelet with tiny pickle charms from the Heinz booth in the food pavilion.

Much later in life, I read a 1939 New York Times review of the television demonstration Cousin Freddie and I watched at the Fair. It said, "The problem with television is that people must sit and keep their eyes glued on a screen; the average American family hasn't time for it."

We remained in New York another year before my father was lured by stories of the wonderful opportunities for musicians on the West Coast. The movie industry was cranking out films as fast as they could be written, and he was told, by other musicians, that the studios were hiring people to supply the background music. Daddy hoped this meant he'd be provided with steady work and greater financial security. By now, he had developed great confidence in his talent.

After endless discussions with my mother and other members of the family, Daddy felt he was ready to travel to Hollywood and compete successfully. In 1939, the best way to get the family to Los Angeles was to drive by car across the country. Daddy owned a 1936 4-door Buick sedan at the time. There was no air conditioning, so the windows were open during much of the trip, and the sound of the wind rushing past them made normal conversation or listening to the radio impossible. There were no car seatbelts either. My Uncle Sol drove a car with a rumble seat, and I remember mentioning several times during the trip, "Mommy, I'm hot!" It became an oft-repeated refrain during the trip.

My sister and I grew bored with our dollies and were too short to see out the windows if we didn't stand up. Mommy forbade us to "hang" out the windows to let the wind blow in our faces. It was all the more dangerous, because she had the entire floor space of the car stuffed with baskets and canvas bags filled to the brim with toys and changes of clothing and family treasures she hadn't wanted to send with the movers. Then there were pillows and afghan-sized blankets taking up space on the back seat. Sandra fussed or cried much of every day when she wasn't sleeping. Daddy had to stop often to refill the gas tank and to let both of us run off some of our built-up energy. Many times when I napped on the backseat, Sandra would sleep in our mother's arms.

At age five, I was old enough to be curious about some of the things we saw outside, especially when making our gasoline stops. In Arizona, I noticed that the trees didn't look like those in Central Park. "They're called cacti, Carol," Daddy said. "One of them is called a cactus. A saguaro cactus, to be exact. It's the state flower and the tallest kind of cactus in the United States."

"Flower! It looks more like a tree!" I exclaimed. "Why do they have all those holes in them?"

"It's just called a flower, because they produce masses of white flowers every spring and there are so many of them in this state. The taller the cacti are and the more arms they have, the older they are. Some of them are a couple hundred years old."

"Tell me about the *holes*," I insisted.

Daddy laughed. "You're just like your mother, Carol. A million questions. I read on a brochure in the motel we stayed in last night that a special kind of woodpecker and another bird called a gilded flicker chisel those holes with their beaks to make a home inside the cactus trunk.

"Mommy was as intrigued with them as I was. "Don't they need water to live?"

"I can only tell you what I read, Babe. It doesn't seem like it right now, but the Sonoran Desert actually gets both summer and winter rains. The roots of the cacti are evidently very shallow, and spread out in a circle as wide as the stem is tall. They soak up significant amounts of water and store it for the hot summer months. Now, enough of your questions. I want to just enjoy the beauty of the whole vista. I've never seen anything like it before."

The trip was long, and my questions continued, especially when Sandra was sleeping and taking up all the room on the back seat. "Why aren't there any houses out here, Daddy? Why is there so much sand and where is the beach? I don't see any water? Why isn't there any grass? Why is the road so flat and straight?"

"No more questions, please. I can't think straight. Can't you do something, Babe?"

Yes, Mother knew how to shush me up. She brought out the cookies from a container under her car seat. She had instinctively known before ever leaving New York that the long trip would seem endless to young daughters who would rather do anything other than stare out a window. Cookies worked. At least for a short time.

We visited an Indian reservation along the way, and I gawked at people wrapped in colorful blankets. Some of the men wore red, white and yellow feathers on their heads. We had to come to a complete stop on the highway one afternoon when a few wild burros decided to wander onto it. Sandra and I were too skittish to put our hands out the window, and so was Mommy. As soon as the road was cleared, Daddy stepped on the gas.

"Where's all our furniture, Daddy? Did those men haul it away? Where will I sleep?"

"Those men you saw packing things in boxes and crates work for the Bekins moving company, Carol. They do nothing but transport people from their old houses to their new ones. Sometimes it's only across town. Sometimes it's across our entire country. That's what we're doing. Moving from New York to California, from the East Coast to the West Coast, from the Atlantic Ocean to the Pacific Ocean."

"Bekins doesn't have trucks big enough to carry all our household belongings, Carol," my mother added. She tended to speak whatever was on her mind and mine was a receptive sponge. "They pack things up in big crates and ship the crates by train, from big city to big city. When our crates get to Los Angeles, they'll be stored in a huge Bekins warehouse until their smaller trucks can bring them to our new home."

By the time we reached the city of Los Angeles, I was more than ready to see this new home. I was accustomed to living in an apartment high above street level, but Daddy said things would be different. "If I'm lucky and get lots of work, maybe we'll have a house with a backyard in a couple years, Carol. For now, we'll live in an apartment building, but it won't be anything like the one in New York. That's all I know. Auntie Lee found us a place. It's on a street called Romaine."

"Romaine! Like the lettuce? That's silly. Is it green?" I paid more attention to everything I saw outside the open window of our car, looking in vain for a green high-rise building.

Uncle Sol, Auntie Martha and my cousin Stephan had packed up and moved to Florida shortly after the hurricane that all but destroyed their town of Providence, but they eventually moved to Los Angeles, where they lived in the same apartment building my Auntie Lee had found for us.

Whenever I think of the old cliché 'birds of a feather flock together,' I think of the many Sorkin and Mitnick family members who "flew" from Russia to different countries, then to different places in the United States, and, ultimately, to the Los Angeles area. My father's parents, Abraham and Esther Sorkin, remained in New York, as did Uncle Myron and his family.

5

O NCE WE WERE decently settled into our new apartment, my father wasted no time looking for work. He already had feelers out among his many friends in the music industry. Then he heard that one of the movie companies in Studio City in the San Fernando Valley, Republic Pictures, was hiring musicians to perform background music in their films. All it took was one interview, a cursory look at the clippings in Daddy's portfolio of his musical history, half a song on the sax he carried with him, and he was hired on the spot.

I have many memories of the Republic Pictures studios, but my first one stands out. It looked like a circus to me, because literally hundreds of actors called "extras" milled about dressed in every sort of costume. The colors and patterns were vivid, in order to create contrasts in the black and white films. Eyes were emphasized with heavy mascara and fake eyelashes; the lipstick was dark. My eyes were immediately drawn to those in cowboy or Indian attire; however, the Indians weren't half as impressive as those we'd seen while traveling through Southwestern states in the Buick. I saw dozens of horses and covered wagons, and streets of buildings that were only painted panels of wood or canvas. Although I wasn't clear about the purpose of the strange-looking equipment atop enormous wheeled platforms, Daddy told me the men perched on them were operating the movie cameras. He pointed at several people striding past us or across the lot and mentioned names like Gene Autry, Roy Rogers, and John Wayne. He was clearly agog by their celebrity, but I had no idea who they were at the time. I couldn't understand why adults wanted to play dress-up. But these three actors were Republic Pictures' stars in the serial B pictures they produced.

At this time of my life, I was totally fascinated with Trigger, Roy Rogers' horse, more than Roy himself. I loved Lassie, Rin-Tin-Tin, Toto (the Cairn Terrier in The Wizard of Oz), Flicka and National Velvet. Today, when I finally take note of the stars on the screen in the oldies-but-goodies, I can appreciate hearing my father on the flute or other woodwind instruments in many of the John Wayne and Maureen O'Hara films, like *Wake of the Red Witch* and *The Quiet Man*. He even played a solo with Arthur Rubenstein in the movie *I've Always Loved You*. This experience made such an impression on him that when my brother was born in 1945, Daddy named him Donald, Rubenstein's middle name.

On one of my visits to the studios, I watched a scene where the cast had to be helped from a Ferris wheel that had apparently stopped working. The girls had overly full, multi-layered, cumbersome skirts and wild-looking hats, and their bumbling efforts to reach the safety of the terra firma were funnier to me than the original scene.

Although I found this strange world outside our home stimulating and exciting, I balked at the incessant reminders to obey the men who shouted, "Quiet on the set!" Daddy wanted to make sure I understood that meant me, too, and I feared upsetting him or having someone throw me out if I so much as wiggled my feet. "Here's a Hershey bar, Carol. Eat it slowly to make it last and don't get chocolate on your dress."

By now, I expected to be rewarded or bribed for good behavior with chocolate, candy, cookies, cake or ice cream. It was rather like training a puppy to go to the door when it wants to be taken outside, or to sit calmly and wait for you to pour food into its dish. I was the puppy, eager to please . . . and to get my reward. Today, I can draw up a memory of being taught about the scientist Pavlov, and how he trained a dog in his laboratory to salivate when it heard a bell ring, a stimulus given every time it was fed during the training process. This conditioned response became predictable. The drooling was called a reflex. I was being conditioned to believe that anything sweet would calm my anxieties or change my irritation or impatience to calm composure, which is what adults preferred from children. Like puppies, we are eager to please, especially if we got a pat on the head, a "good girl," or a sweet reward.

The thought of savoring the chocolate while it slowly melted in my mouth removed some of the fear I had of being scowled at by a studio stranger. I waited as long as I possibly could, holding on to the Hershey bar and leisurely feeling through the thick paper cover for the separations between sections.

Suddenly, the musicians—including Daddy—stopped the chaotic tuning sounds of their instruments, and I saw that the orchestra director had lifted his baton. Seated in one of the very back rows of the small studio auditorium, I was almost afraid to breathe, the quiet was so powerful. The lights dimmed and the soundless movie appeared on a screen directly behind the musicians. The second the director's hands and baton went into motion, the musicians began their already-rehearsed passages that had been specifically composed to enhance whatever action the actors on the scene required. Drums rolled, cymbals clashed, violins wailed, and Daddy's sax crooned. Music suitable for romance, mystery, chase scenes, funerals, or whatever else was showing on the screen filled the studio auditorium. It was magical.

In my many visits to the studios, one actor in particular frightened me. Much later in life, I learned he was Erich Von Stroham, known best to old black and white movie buffs for his role as Max von Mayerling in Billy Wilder's 1950 movie *Sunset Boulevard* with Gloria Swanson. Mother had met him at a couple parties and told me his role was considered biographical in part, because of his own "pig-headedness" when working with directors on other films. His personal vision of how his role should be played caused too much of the film to end up on the cutting room floor too many times, costing the studio money. A former Austrian director and producer, Stroham earned his fame as a film star of the silent era. I thought he had a strange way of speaking, but it was the sternness in his voice that scared me. I stayed close to my father whenever he was around.

Even while Daddy was working steadily at the studios, he was busy forming his own orchestra. His style of jazz was popular at the time, just as it had been at the Savoy, and he was hired by many of the stars to perform at their private parties. Uncle Harry Sorkin became a mailman when he moved to California, but he occasionally played the saxophone in Daddy's orchestra.

They would practice together in our living room whenever Uncle Harry visited us with his family.

One of my father's friends, Dr. Sam Hoffman (a podiatrist by day), played in Daddy's orchestra. He played an unusual instrument called a Theremin. It's actually not an instrument per se, but an elaborate electronic device with two projecting antennae that can generate tones through two high-frequency oscillators; the pitch is controlled by the performer's hand movements toward and away from the circuit. The better the performer, the more he could produce a steady, continual rhythm. It was invented in the early 20th century by a Russian man, Lev Theremin (1896–1993); perhaps my grandfather had listened to this instrument in Russian recordings and interested my father in it as his own musical interests and talents grew. The Theremin has a haunting and ethereal sound that appealed to my budding musicality. Even now, when I watch reruns of the movie *Spellbound*, starring Gregory Peck and Ingrid Bergman and produced in 1945, I get goose bumps when I hear the Theremin being played.

Dr. Hoffman brought this strange box to our home, and I thought it looked like the X-ray machine in his office and shoe store that measured the length and width of my feet to ensure my shoes fit properly. He let me try the instrument. It was supernatural in sound and easy to play, but Daddy said it was very difficult to master. Dr. Hoffman was highly skilled and performed in numerous other films, using the first synthesizer. In more recent years, I've recognized its haunting sounds in a few other films, such as *The Lost Weekend*, *The Ten Commandments*, *Batman Forever*.

Hollywood loved glamour in those days. The old black and white movies produced during the forties are a truthful depiction of the lifestyle these privileged people lived. Whenever he was hired to perform for one of their private parties, my father would leave home looking like a polished prince, with French-cuffed, stiffly starched white shirts and beautiful initialed gold cufflinks. On rare occasions, he wore tails, but for the most part he didn't project the "penguin" look. Tails were reserved for album covers or very special occasions, perhaps an elaborate wedding or charity ball.

It wasn't only movie stars who dressed to the "nth degree" in those days. Men dressed in suits and ties and women in hosiery, high heels and hats even to have dinner at the homes of their best friends. Certainly to go to church or synagogue, or to the movie theater. It was never "the fashion" to wear denim jeans, even to do the gardening. Mother wore a pantsuit. Sandra and I always had bows in our hair; they were washed and pressed and worn again many times. Mother wore hats everywhere but the grocery store, and loved to make them. She received much her inspiration for creations from Hedda Hopper, who was one of the most famous gossip columnists to ever cover Hollywood stars and events. Mother never missed reading her newspaper column "Hedda Hopper's Hollywood." Hedda was renowned for wearing quite outrageous hats. For years, I have also worn them, whether it's a turban, cowboy or newsboy cap, and never leave home without one on my head. Maybe, just maybe, there's a little bit of Hedda Hopper in me, too.

I met my life-long friend, Adrienne "Dupsey" Greenberg while sharing a bench in the schoolyard of Rosewood Avenue Grade School. Her first words to me were, "You talk funny." I had a New York accent flavored by my father's English pronunciations for certain words. Since Adrienne had an infectious laugh and a mischievous nature, I didn't harbor any ill-feelings over her declaration. We became bosom buddies and were really quite naughty on occasion; for example, we called certain members of our class one evening with the message that all of us were supposed to report to the principal's office by 7:30 in the morning. We provided the names of two other students they were to notify so it would seem more official. Adrienne and I swore ourselves to secrecy over ever telling anyone we had instigated the clever scheme.

The next day, when our teacher had us in her crosshairs, after we'd been ushered by the principal's secretary to our classroom, I simply stared at her with widened and what I hoped were innocent-looking eyes. I didn't dare sneak even the slightest peak at Adrienne. "Which one of you started this prank about reporting to the principal this morning?" she asked, her tone transmitting a seriousness that infused a feeling of utter terror.

Guess who immediately raised her hand? *Dupsey*. "Carol and I did it," she declared, turning down the edges of her mouth like she was about to cry from remorse. Everyone's eyes turned toward me, and I slumped in my chair as far as I could without falling onto the floor. For an instant, I wished the floor would open up and swallow me. Fortunately, our teacher had a sense of humor. We had to apologize to our classmates and our parents were not informed. That's how discipline was conducted in "those days." On the spot and by the teacher, whom the parents respected.

Dupsey was a little shorter than me in our preteen years and always remained so, even as an adult. I liked to pretend that gave me more authority over our relationship. She remained wide-eyed and curious about whatever her future would hold, and although she went through major losses in her lifetime, her ready laugh remained as infectious until the day she passed away. We had been friends for over seventy years and shared everything. We danced at each other's weddings and cried at our parents' funerals.

Dupsey's sister Marsha died far too prematurely from lupus, an autoimmune disease that is currently more manageable because of various prescription drugs, but is still incurable. It is not contagious or infectious; it develops in those with a genetic disposition who are exposed to particular triggers, but the imaginations of many, at the time, created new and inaccurate diagnoses for anyone who was ill for any reason. The word HIV/AIDS was being whispered about anyone in California with a misunderstood illness, and we didn't add fodder to this malicious fuel when Marsha had to receive blood transfusions on a regular basis.

Although our lives led us through many detours and we suffered through our share of traumas, our heartbreaks were always intermixed with terrific belly laughs. I didn't know, when I enjoyed these carefree years that I would rely on her trusted and caring friendship even more when my adult life brought seemingly endless trials.

The United States was at war with Japan, and soon afterward with Germany, when Dupsey and I were in grammar school. Everyone attending

Rosewood Avenue Grade School was instructed to bring a "survival bag" to school daily and to wear the formal I.D. tag around our neck where it could be clearly seen. Because we were on the West Coast, Rosewood conducted bomb drills regularly. Whenever the alarms sounded, we students would immediately stand and file in an orderly fashion into the hallway where we were told to sit on the floor close to the walls and cover our heads with our arms to protect them from potential falling bricks and debris. We remained in this position until an announcement came over the loudspeaker that the drill was over and we could return to class. We were instructed to treat each drill as though it were a genuine bombing attack. It goes without saying that each time the alarm reverberated throughout the school, fear grabbed hold of our hearts.

Japanese ships had supposedly been sighted off the coast of California, so blackouts were initiated statewide. Every household on the West Coast was required to cover windows with blackout shades, because the threat of Japanese ships or planes coming within bombing distance of our shores was too great a possibility. The street lights were turned off and cars drove without their headlights. Traffic accidents were common.

According to Mother, when we discussed "the old days," what added to everyone's jitters was that in February of 1942 an oil facility close to Santa Barbara was shelled by a Japanese submarine.

"Eighty miles probably doesn't seem like such a great distance to you, with today's fancier cars and highways, Carol, and although it took us longer to drive there, but it's much too close to Los Angeles."

The rumors started to fly. Everyone in California saw this as the continuation of the Pearl Harbor surprise attack. No one wanted that to be repeated, but Washington couldn't be distracted by something new at the time. They were too focused on building, training, arming, and then transporting our troops to the ships that would take them into both oceans, and to also prepare for an all-out war on our continent. We understood that its war efforts couldn't include preparing for potential battles in every American town and city, but newspaper articles fueled our concern. Hearsay often replaced research or accuracy."

"Don't you want to pack us up and move to someplace in the center of the country, Mommy?"

"We can't, because the people who hire your father and his orchestra live on both coasts. They are the ones with the money for private parties and dances requiring musicians."

In an effort to bolster national defenses, the government created the Civil Defense Division, and asked citizens outside the military to be on alert and practice life-saving drills, like those the people in England were doing. Signs went up, newspapers and magazines stressed how to go about this, and millions joined in to become air-raid wardens who watched the skies for unfamiliar planes. Every window was covered with a blackout shade or drapery to make the sighting of targets more difficult. Air-raid wardens walked or drove up and down our streets looking for the slightest slit of light that could be seen by a Japanese plane or submarine off our shores.

On winter nights, during those war years, the sun set early. By five or six o' clock, my mother would go from room to room and pull the blackout drapery or shades over the windows. Once, I peeked out to watch an air raid warden pass by. When my mother found me, I received a harsh warning to never, ever do that again. I thought she didn't want me to mess with the shades in case I would accidentally tear them down. I didn't connect war and bombings with window shades. "Why don't you practice your piano lesson and surprise your daddy with a lovely song," she'd say. As long as she could hear the piano, she didn't have to worry about my whereabouts.

Mother planned our meals carefully, writing out her menus for the week just as they do in the White House to this day. This task was routine and necessary, because there was rationing of many food items. "The feeding of our soldiers always comes first, Carol," she would say as I watched her write the grocery list.

"Can we have some Oreo cookies, Mommy?"

"Not this week. And say *'may'* we have, not *'can'* I have."

"How about Barnum's animal crackers or Honey Maid graham crackers?" My list of soul-soothing treats didn't exclude graham crackers, because the honey added a sweet taste.

"We'll see." Mother always said "We'll see," to end my pleading. It was a phrase that left hope and I was usually satisfied with the response.

Even Daddy got into the discussion of rationing, especially when America joined Allies in the European Theater and the food-restriction list grew longer. Washington issued war ration books and tokens to each family on a monthly basis; they were to be used for sugar, meat, lard, butter, cheese, coffee and other items found in every kitchen. Mother would take Sandra and me with her when she went to collect her new ration book. Every coupon or token was as precious as gold during these years.

Washington urged everybody on the home front to plant a 'victory garden' to provide fresh vegetables and herbs for personal use and that of our extended families and neighbors. Even public parks and other city and county properties were utilized for this effort. Golden Gate Park had over 250 garden plots. Posters appeared in public places to encourage participation. The goal was to not only provide fresh vegetables, but to harvest enough to can for winter use, because our trains and trucks had to transport soldiers and munitions.

Mother had a plot dug up in our backyard, and I helped her weed the rows of carrots, radishes, onions and other vegetables on a regular basis. It was a way of life for us. Now, in the second decade of the 21st century, our grandchildren and great-grandchildren are planting home gardens or frequenting farmers' markets to grow or buy the fresh vegetables that come directly from God's green earth and not a greenhouse. They call it 'organic' gardening. In the war years and the decade after it, it was 'good sense' gardening.

In my research, I learned that by 1944, 20 million victory gardens were producing 8 million tons of food and boosting morale in the process. Amazingly, these gardens provided approximately 41 percent of all the vegetable produce consumed by Americans during these years of war. It was not only a family endeavor, but a community one. It brought everyone together for a common cause.

Although I liked to listen in on the adult conversations, and continued to insert endless questions about the subjects of their conversations, I was more impressed by pictures in magazines showing that even Elsie the Cow created a victory garden. At Rosewood, our teachers pointed out that major corporations, like Coca Cola and Carnation, were contributing support in their magazine ads. Coca Cola illustrated how we could entertain in our victory garden, and Carnation provided recipes for using their products with the fresh vegetables we grew.

During these years, and even though Hollywood was thriving, everyone in my family's circle of society friends had to follow the same rules of war. Every owner of a car was restricted to a limited amount of gasoline at each tank refilling, because of the vast amounts needed for war planes, ships and tanks and the transportation of goods. Signs, posters, and radio and newspaper ads asked citizens to drive less. Those who owned a car had drummed into them that less driving also saved wear and tear on the tires. Rubber was in critically short supply. At the time, the United States imported close to 90 percent of its rubber from Japan and other South Asian countries occupied by Japan; naturally, after Pearl Harbor, our rubber supply came to an abrupt halt.

Citizens were urged to collect every scrap of rubber for recycling in the production of tires for war vehicles. Mountains of used tires were stacked up in railway yards waiting to be hauled cross-country to factories. My school collected anything made of rubber, including old garden hoses, goulashes, bicycle tires and even bathing hats that had seen their last bit of use. Mother and I dug in drawers to find those with broken straps or tears.

We also tied every newspaper and magazine from home into bundles and hauled them to Rosewood for paper drives. I helped Mother remove the labels from canned goods and the two ends of the cans she'd removed with the hand-operated can opener. Then I'd stomp on the clean cans to flatten them. When we had filled a box, we'd drive them to the recycling center. We also saved the foil from every stick of gum and added them to a growing ball, which Sandra and I rolled throughout the house. We did the same for every piece of string or twine. Nothing was wasted.

Every month, Daddy would buy a war bond. So would my grandfather and uncles. "What's a war bond?" I asked more than once. My experience with money was in nickels and dimes.

"It's a special piece of paper that represents a promise from our government to pay the amount stated on it when the war is over," Daddy said, finally showing one to me. "It takes a lot of money to pay for a war. Billions of dollars. Think of all the planes and ships and tanks and parachutes that need to be manufactured. And all our soldiers and sailors and airmen need uniforms and food and medicine. We can help pay for them by buying the bonds, Carol."

"I guess so, but I don't get it."

"Here's an example. I can buy a $25 bond for $18.75. In ten years, Uncle Sam, the name we give our government, will give me the full $25. That's called 'earning interest' on my investment. Maybe that's still too hard to understand, Carol. If you wanted to invest some of your allowance, you could give me eighteen cents today, and I will promise to pay you a whole quarter when you're twenty years old. I'll write out my promise on a piece of paper and date it so you'll have proof of my pledge."

I was impressed with the idea.

"Investing for the future is important, Carol. But I'm buying the war bonds for a more important reason. I'm investing in America and what it stands for. Not a single day goes by that I'm not thankful your grandparents left Russia to come to this country."

Soon after this discussion, I learned more about war bonds in school. Rosewood held several drives collecting all the change we could bring from home. Although both Mommy and Daddy gave me some from their pockets, they both insisted I take money from my piggy bank to encourage my personal involvement in the war efforts.

The hallways of Rosewood were decorated with posters showing Bugs Bunny, Donald Duck, Superman, and other cartoon characters buying $.25 war stamps. We were given a special booklet to paste them in. They didn't collect any interest, but if we filled a booklet, we could put the money toward the purchase of a Series E war bond and buy it at the reduced rate.

When we lived on Romaine Street, Uncle Moe spent his money freely on showgirls. He stayed out until dawn, and often I'd hear him sneak into the bedroom I shared with Sandra and flop down on the bed kept there for him. Both he and Uncle Jack frequented the nightclubs on Sunset Boulevard and bragged about their exploits. They were frequently photographed with stars and their pictures appeared in the papers; I particularly remember Janet Blair and Marie McDonald.

Their habits changed as more of their friends left for the war. Then came the day they were both drafted into the army, and they made tearful good-byes to us. Somehow, my infamous Uncle Moe became a captain, although he hadn't attended a military school. He was involved with entertaining the troops. However, many of his habits were too deeply ingrained for him to change into a completely new man. He wasn't accustomed to strictly following the laws. He used his cunning, experience in wheeling and dealing, and outside contacts to buy and sell hard-to-get items to the troops, like cigarettes and liquor. He regularly supplied my mother and aunties with nylon stockings (which were restricted during the war years because nylon was used for parachutes) and lots of chocolate and bubblegum for me, courtesy of Uncle Sam. Sandra and I were the only kids on the block who had bubblegum, and it made us quite popular.

How my Uncle Jack ended up in the Army Air Force (AAF) is beyond my comprehension, because even as a young girl I knew he wasn't military material. When I came home from school one afternoon, I found him on the floor in the living room. He had been injured while parachuting from a plane on his very first mission. He never jumped again. "I hurt my back," he said. "Badly." He received an honorable discharge, and it wasn't long before he was back to his lifestyle of dating showgirls. Evidently they didn't tire of hearing his war stories, and being in the company of lovely ladies distracted him from thinking about his back pain.

Some of my cousins were also drafted and saw action. Jerome went to Germany and served under General Patton. Francis ended up on a ship that was torpedoed; he jumped overboard and was able to save himself from drowning by hanging on to a broken broomstick.

Although my father wasn't drafted, he worked with the American Red Cross, and because he was also a talented draftsman, he was used by Lockheed Aircraft. Its Vega factory was located in Burbank, and its location allowed him to continue with his movie gigs and nighttime entertainment. Many times my mother would pick him up at Lockheed after he'd completed his drafting for the day, and I gawked at the enormous burlap tarp that covered the entire facility. Loving anything having to do with art, and losing all interest in piano playing by this time, I was fascinated by the faux art that covered every inch of the burlap. The camouflage scene portrayed an average neighborhood replete with three-dimensional houses, buildings, trees, shrubbery, and even three-dimensional cars and fire hydrants constructed from chicken wire and then covered with a variety of materials. It stretched over the entire Lockheed factory to make its location difficult to find for Japanese pilots should their planes target the West Coast.

Like all entertainers in Hollywood who hadn't been drafted into the armed forces, Daddy performed at the various USO centers nearby. Had he been drafted, he most likely would have been assigned to one of the bands that entertained troops, like Glen Miller. According to USO WWII history (http://www.ww2uso.org/history.html), Hollywood stars, musicians and thousands of those who worked in the industry, paid regular visits to the more than 3,000 centers serving those in the armed forces and their families. Many entertainers flew regularly to perform at training camps, hospitals, and even overseas battle sites. Bob Hope was one of the first stars to entertain troops with a performance at the March Air Force Base in California, not far from Beverly Hills and Hollywood. He liked it so much that he made it a regular part of his life for the next fifty years, through all succeeding wars. He was always joined by other stars as recognizable as he was . . . like Bing Crosby, Betty Gable, Betty Hutton and Rita Hayworth. The centers were known as "a home away from home."

Since Americans were glued to their radios from dawn to bedtime, every show ended with a pitch for buying a war bond by the show's stars. Daddy participated in several war bond drives that featured at least one popular movie star. Grandpa Mitnick told me that none of them could hold a candle to

Kate Smith, who was one of his favorite singers. When she was featured on a CBS 16-hour marathon broadcast, people bought bonds like they were going out of style. In those sixteen hours, she was credited for selling of $40 million in bonds. After the war, when prosperity returned to our country and television took off, I would see Kate Smith on shows like Ed Sullivan. Even as a teenager, I was touched every time she sang *God Bless America*.

When the Japanese bombed Pearl Harbor I was seven years old, and Sandra was four. By the time America had fought two fronts against Germany, Italy and Japan, and World War II ended, I was eleven. We were young and still liked to play with our dolls, jump ropes, and jacks. But we continually witnessed the apprehension on the faces of the adults in our extended family and heard the anxiety in their voices. Neither Sandra nor I had any real concept of what war was, of course. We were children in a theatrical family. Our parents' social life centered around actors, directors, producers and musicians. They partied, laughed a lot and gathered around the piano to sing, while members of Daddy's orchestra or band tuned in, but their conversation drifted to war themes and what they'd heard from their "sources."

War was what we saw in those newsreel broadcasts that preceded a feature film at the movie theater, like *Lassie Come Home*. It was a continuing drama with bombing of cities and uniformed men and women fighting. The theaters were always packed to the doors. "Don't talk, Carol," Mommy would say. "Those around us want to hear the newsreel."

I asked Uncle Jack about them, since he had been a soldier. He said, "People go to the theater to see them, because they're better than listening to Edward Murrow talk about what's happening over the radio, Carol. There's an old saying, 'A picture is worth a thousand words.' Remember that. You like to paint, don't you? Well, what you draw on paper is what you're thinking about and feeling at the time. If I look at it, I can tell, and I don't forget your painting. It's printed in my mind. Those movie newsreel reports are real pictures of what the family members of those in the audience are going through to save us from having the war fought right here on our homeland. The next time they listen to a radio broadcast, they see a better picture of the war in their minds."

I didn't pay much attention to the newsreels, because I was busy removing the paper from a piece of bubblegum or a candy bar. For me, war was secondary to the feature film, which was usually a musical. It was the singing and dancing and band playing I enjoyed, regardless of what was happening in some far away country.

At Rosewood, many of the rhymes we chanted while jumping rope had war themes, and my classmates would play war and pretend they were orphans. Some of the older kids belonged to an organization that allowed them to do things for soldiers wherever they were located. I was too young to be a member of the Civil Air Patrol, but I thought it would be fun to wear a uniform and learn something called Morse Code.

When my uncles and cousins went off to war in their uniforms, war didn't seem quite as much like a play for a movie. Those in my household talked incessantly about their safety, where they were fighting, and if they would 'make it home.' That's when my anxiety increased. Sometimes I was scared and had nightmares, wondering how I could survive a bombing and take care of Sandra if Daddy had to go to war and Mommy had to work in a factory all day. Many times when he went off to work, I imagined him not returning home. I would practice the piano right after school and try to please him, hoping I'd get at least a pat on the head. Parents lived in a stressful time that of necessity created stressful home atmospheres. If I had been a boy, maybe I could have acted out my bottled-up feelings by playing war; instead, I became more subdued in public and fed my fears with sweets when I wasn't playing with Sandra.

6

DESPITE THE WAR that consumed every part of my life during these first few years of living in Los Angeles, I can't deny that I was also exposed to unique excitement and glamour. I was too young to grasp how very special my life was, compared to millions of children throughout the country. Few children can see beyond today or tomorrow, and most are centered on themselves. Like any child between five and twelve, I lived in the moment.

Sometimes, if I was awake when Daddy got home, he'd bring me toast and warm milk and sit on the edge of my bed and tell me about Ray Bolger, Bert Lahr and Jack Haley who were in the movie, *The Wizard of Oz*, with Judy Garland.

I was about seven years old when Daddy started to play at Ciro's Nightclub in West Hollywood on Sunset Boulevard (1941). On summer afternoons, since school was out, I would beg to go with him to rehearsals. The nightclubs along what became known as Sunset Strip—such as Ciro's, Mocambo, the Trocadero and the Coconut Grove—became familiar territory to me. Each was frequented by the biggest stars in the movie industry (e.g., Bette Davis, Arthur Murray, Carole Landis, Jackie Coogan, Joan Crawford, Cesar Romero, Ginger Rogers, Frank Sinatra and his wife Nancy, Clark Gable and his wife Carole Lombard, and even Capt. Ronald Reagan and his wife Jane Wyman).

At Ciro's, which had a stunning Baroque interior with pale green walls draped in heavy silk and wall booths upholstered in equally heavy silk that was dyed as rose-red as the ceiling paint, I would watch the Jack Cole dancers perform. All the chairs would be stacked upside down on the tabletops to enable workers to vacuum the carpet. Daddy would take me to a table right next to the stage, and I'd munch on a candy bar while eagerly watching and listening, enthralled by the great sounds and fast, drum-beat dancing.

Daddy told me, when I was old enough to care, that Ciro's was absolutely packed from wall to wall every night with those lucky enough to get a reserved table so they could listen to famous performers, like Liberace, Sammy Davis, Jr., Peggy Lee, Dean Martin and Jerry Lewis, and even Sophie Tucker and Maurice Chevalier (whom I can never forget for his role in Gigi). Daddy also took Mommy and me to the recording studio to see Lucille Ball and Desi Arnaz when they first started their radio show. I sat with Mommy for the live performance of Kate Smith and Rudy Vallee, too, but I didn't know who they were at the time. I only knew it was special because of the smile on Mommy's face throughout the performances. I was always told to lie about my age if anyone asked about it, because young children were not allowed in the studio during live productions. Since Daddy was short, no one ever questioned my wide-eyed response. I was, essentially, a chip of the old block. It was critically important to listen quietly, and to clap politely after each performance. Of course, the adults in charge didn't know I was considered a perfect child who knew the meaning of the word "quiet" in the strictest sense of the word. I would watch with great delight as the sound effects engineer worked his magic with a paddle, bell and sticks.

We moved from our first Los Angeles apartment on Romaine Street to a larger one on Arnaz Drive, also in Los Angeles. This time, my father was earning more money so he bought the building, and we had an upstairs and a downstairs. Sandra and I still shared a bedroom. Auntie Martha, Uncle Sol and my cousin Stephen lived in one of the apartments, as did two other tenants.

As a side note, Arnaz Drive was named after a 19th century landholder, Don Jose de Arnaz, and not Desi Arnaz, the husband of Lucille Ball. Although many of the almost 50,000 streets in Los Angeles County are named for noteworthy people as a way of remembering history, these people are, for the most part, local or state officials, or those who have contributed to the community. It's confusing; because so many of the names are the same as those we tie to the movies or to those of such stature as national presidents. In 1967, a Los Angeles Times reporter interviewed Harrison Kimball, who was in charge of naming streets for the Bureau of Engineering. He said, "A person's a hero one year, but then he vanishes from the public eye or becomes a crum-bum in the years beyond. It's an embarrassing situation if the street is named for a developer and then he ends up in the clink."

Mrs. Maybelle Iribe, one of our apartment tenants who had made the building her home long before we arrived on the scene, was a statuesque and elegant lady of French heritage. She was the mother of two daughters, Maybelline and Judith, and a son Paul. Judith was married to the film director Billy Wilder. Maybelline eventually settled in San Francisco and wrote about French cooking. Although I have no memory of how I came to be the possessor of Maybelline's French-English Dictionary, it still resides on a bookshelf in our Michigan home. Her name is penned on the book's flyleaf with the date 1935, and location Palm Springs.

A bigger apartment building came with several benefits. One was a much larger backyard that permitted more play opportunities for imaginative children. One Easter, Sandra and I were given adorable, bright yellow baby chicks and spent hours cuddling them. The vegetable-dye color lasts only a few weeks and comes off as the chicks shed their fluff and feathers grow in a normal color, but we didn't care. We fed them and talked to them like they were baby dolls. As they grew, they had to be kept caged in the backyard and only let out to run about and forage for handfuls of chicken feed we'd toss onto the grass. It was a sad day when we were made to give up our pets. Daddy packed them in their coop and placed it beside us on the backseat of our car for the tearful drive to the estate home of Judith and Billy Wilder near Mandeville Canyon. Our cuddly, peeping chicks had become noisy clucking chickens and were no longer suitable for backyard city lifestyle. "If you were a chicken, where would you want to live?" Mommy asked.

Children don't view issues with logic. We were convinced those chickens would rather be cooped up in our backyard and hear our version of their clucks every day than to roam about a vast acreage in freedom.

Whenever we had an opportunity to visit our chickens, Sandra and I waited at the door a half hour early. "Hurry, Mommy, hurry!" we'd nag in whiny twin voices. On one visit, however, Sandra ran up to the chickens with such cries of delight, her arms waving in the wind, that one of our full-fledged and now independent pets was alarmed by her exuberance. When Sandra scooped it into her arms, it flapped its own wings in fury and protested by pecking her near an eye. Sandra dropped the hen and screeched at the top of her lungs in pain and pure fright. Although she suffered no permanent damage, her bawling continued most of the way home.

We never saw our chickens again. No explanations were needed. Both Sandra and I had lost all affection for such temperamental fowl and wanted nothing more to do with them. However, we learned later that the Wilders divorced in 1946.

Sandra cried often and in long wails and loud howls. Maybe that's what all younger siblings do to ensure they're being noticed. Mrs. Iribe had no tolerance for such outbursts. She would bang on her side of the wall separating our apartments, as if scaring Sandra would get her to stop the tantrums. They didn't. "I don't know which is worse," Mommy exclaimed, in exasperation. "At least Sandra's crying stops with only our nerves slightly jarred. Mrs. Iribe's wall bashing is surely hacking a hole that will require time and money to repair." It did.

It wasn't until much later that we learned more of Maybelle Iribe's background. Her first husband was George Coppicus, a theatrical/concert impresario, but she was an heiress in her own right. Judith was their daughter. After their divorce, Maybelle became Paul Iribe's second wife. Paul was a famed French fashion illustrator and designer. Their son Pablo was born in 1920, and their daughter Maybelline in 1928. The couple separated immediately afterward, a decision predicated upon Maybelle learning her husband was having an affair with Coco Chanel, the equally famous Paris couture designer who "revolutionized" women's fashion in the Twenties.

The Chanel suit jacket style is still classic, as is her simple "little black dress," which is still touted to be an essential part of just about every woman's wardrobe. First Lady Jacqueline Kennedy Onassis, who was known throughout her husband' s presidency as a fashion icon, will be forever remembered for her raspberry-pink Chanel suit, which was actually made for her by the New York City dress salon, Chez Ninon. It cost a fraction of a custom-made Chanel, and at the time, President Kennedy thought it wise for her to wear an American-made outfit to Dallas. Although she made the 1960' s sleeveless sheath dress popular, her pink Chanel suit has become a symbol of her grief upon being witness to her husband's tragic assassination. I never see a photo of her without thinking of Mrs. Iribe.

Chanel was notorious for her outrageously blatant affairs with several men of fame, but became especially known for her totally original and never-to-be-forgotten fragrance, Chanel #5. Although created in 1921, it is still one of the most popular and iconic perfumes. I'll never forget when I was given my first bottle.

Our lives are influenced, in some way and however slightly, by what we have seen, heard, smelled or experienced. I write of my childhood for this reason. I did not choose my family or decide where they should live or with whom they should socialize during those years under their care. Many will say I was lucky or privileged. You have already learned that this wasn't always so. Like most Americans in those decades, my immigrant family members struggled to make a living and a place for themselves in the melting pot we all call our homeland.

Our fourth apartment tenant was Jerry Frank. He looked rather like Johnny Weissmuller from the Tarzan movies, because of his dark hair and strong, muscular body, and if you had seen his apartment décor, you'd have thought he was a real man of the jungle. His carpeting was bright green fake grass. He used the wall near his telephone as an always-ready and easy-to-read phone book, with every often-used number scribbled in indelible ink. In the backyard of our building, a former owner had installed an actual army gun turret. Jerry would routinely perch on it, lost to the world in his fantasies. One Christmas Eve, he hauled a 15-foot Christmas tree up the street, placed it on the front lawn and decorated it. He knew we didn't celebrate Christmas, but the tree was evidently such a bargain, he thought we would enjoy it . . . and we did.

Jerry frequently visited a rabbi mystic, Meyer Davis, on Melrose Avenue in Los Angeles. He told my father about him and kept asking if he'd visited him yet, so Daddy finally gave in. Davis told my father that he would become very famous and that he would have another child—a son; both of these predictions came true. Rabbi Davis had advised Jerry to buy vacant property on South Beverly Drive, saying it would become quite valuable one day. At the time, this area was nothing but empty lots with knee-deep weeds. Today, rent on any business or apartment in that area can bring in $10,000 a month. Jerry did purchase a few lots and became a millionaire. My father, on the other hand, was not tempted.

When I was eight years old, a few of the neighborhood children wanted to put on a March of Dimes talent show in Arnold Resnick's garage. Arnold talked Sandra, my cousin Stephen, and me into participating. One of our tasks was to set up chairs in the backyard for attendees. I was also put in charge of the lights. "All you have to do is hold up that floodlight and point it at the performers," Arnold said.

The floodlight consisted of a round metal dish that held one light bulb. A frayed electrical cord dangled from it with the plug that could be inserted into a wall outlet or another longer cord. We were kids. We didn't think beyond our noses. All we knew was that since our performances would take place after dusk for the paying patron saints, the lighting was critically important.

We started the rehearsal inside the garage, because the closest electrical outlet was the length of the floodlight cord and only a few feet from this practice performance area. "Quiet on the set!" Arnold shouted. "Lights and action!" he added.

Feeling important and visualizing one of the lighting men on the set of my father's musical productions, I held up the flimsy floodlight fixture and clicked on the button just above the dish. Nothing happened.

"It's not plugged into the wall!" Arnold bellowed.

I gripped the dish tightly in both hands, pointing the bulb directly at the scene of action. I didn't want a second criticism. Kids make faces at you, when you mess up, and such visual disapproval made me cringe. My innate shyness required approval. One of the other kids grabbed the cord and pushed the plug into the socket. "Yeeeow!" I yelled, as a mysterious zapping shocked me into the rigidity of a fence post. My mouth stayed open, but no more sound came out. My eyes widened in terror. My hands stayed glued to that silver-toned reflector. My heart raced and pounded like a tympani drum.

"Let go! Let go!" Stephan shouted. "I can't, I'm stuck, ---------------------------

"*Pull the plug. Pull the plug.*" Arnold's face turned red and then white.

I can still experience the gush of electrical power that instigated that startling shock as it raced up my arms. Fortunately, my hands weren't wet, or the experience could have been much worse that it was. I was too young to realize what was happening and how close I had come to being fatally electrocuted. And kudos to the boy who yanked the plug from the socket in a split second. I didn't require an emergency room checkup, but we all got a stern reprimand from Arnold's father. Needless to say, we accepted adult assistance with the lighting before our charity talent event could take place.

It is my belief that this incident in my life was the beginning of a lifetime of my sensing the occurrence of events before they take place. Many have said, over the years, that I have the gift of extrasensory perception, or what is better known as the sixth sense. It was not something that was discussed or written about for the general public in those days, and as a child, teenager and young adult, I thought everyone had it. All I knew was that starting that night, things would happen that I had already envisioned.

We were careful to keep any discussion of politics or religious faith out of our conversation. Since Daddy had been raised in London by his immigrant Russian parents, he was a proper English gentleman in his demeanor and speech. In addition to his notable musical talent, these traits stood him in good stead. As I have already mentioned, my family only attended services at the synagogue for special holidays, like Passover, Hanukkah or Yom Kippur. We were obviously Jews, by name and physical features, but my father's livelihood depended upon his playing for Hollywood's high society, and during most of my childhood years, the world was at war and much of it was anti-Semitic. We were obviously Jews by name and physical features, but for all practical purposes we were not "obviously Jews."

My parents raised us to be colorblind, because some of the finest musicians and vocalists were Black: Dizzy Gillespie, Duke Ellington, Ethel Waters, Billy Holiday, Louis Armstrong, Lena Horne ... the list goes on. They were my father's contemporaries, and their musical recordings were always on our record players, so I grew up recognizing their voices on the radio.

I'll never forget the day I came home from grade school to announce that my teacher was pregnant. "Mommy, Mommy!" I shouted as soon as the front door slammed behind me. "She's having a baby!"

"That's wonderful, Carol," she said. "And so are we. Mommy's pregnant, too. Very soon you and Sandra will have either another sister or a baby brother. Will you like that?"

I nodded. "I guess so." I headed directly for the kitchen and used a couple cookies to soothe my deflated spirit. I thought Mommy was just copying my teacher and my happy news was replaced by her own.

It was a long summer of waiting and waiting, and Sandra (age eight) and I (age ten) had already started school, each in a new class with a new teacher, when our brother Donald was born on September 20, 1945.

Since we were a family that appreciated music above all worldly things, it is fun to remember that the favorite song of Americans that month was "Till the End of Time," sung by Perry Como.

If I had experienced any misgivings about sharing family time with another sibling, it was all forgotten with my first glimpse of Donald. I thought he was adorable. Our Auntie Ida carried him into the house when an ambulance brought him and my mother home. Yes, an ambulance. Daddy was working, and having to sign a zillion documents to see if an insurance policy would pay for such expensive transportation wasn't part of the equation in those days. Mommy needed transportation, and the hospital provided it.

Being girly girls, one of the first things Sandra and I noticed was that Donald had Mommy's gorgeous red hair. "It's not fair," we mumbled to each other. "He's a boy. He should have our dark hair."

Today, as I write this. I'm reminded of a philosophical essay included in Khalil Gibran's 1923 book <u>The Prophet</u>.

> *Your children are not your children.*
> *They are the sons and daughters of Life's longing for it-*
> *self. They come through you but not from you,*
> *And though they are with you yet they belong not to you.*
> *You may give them your love but not your thoughts,*
> *For they have their own thoughts.*
> *You may house their bodies but not their souls,*
> *For their souls dwell in the house of tomorrow,*
> *Which you cannot visit, not even in your dreams.*

Adding one more tenant to our apartment building made no difference to anyone, except to Mrs. Iribe, who continued to bang on the wall whenever Donald's crying became too much for her to endure.

Being a property owner meant tending to the maintenance. Although Daddy wasn't around much and these duties often fell to Uncle Sol, the two of them and a couple neighbors would help each other out. They seemed to enjoy group projects and each other's company. They would walk to the local hardware store as a group, shop as a group, and consult with each other about everything, especially in the after-supper hours, because the others were home after a long day's work.

One evening before bedtime, Sandra, Cousin Stephan and I sneaked through the bushes and peeked into the living room of a neighbor while Daddy and Uncle Sol were inside the house. They were watching men wrestle each other inside a small black box that was propped up on a table across the dark room. I remembered exactly what the box was, of course, and delighted in telling my version of what a television was as described to me by my older and wiser cousin while at the New York World's Fair. "It's like magic," Sandra said. "Do you think we can talk Daddy into buying us one?"

"Yeah," Stephen agreed, while lamenting that he wasn't inside with the guys. "We should get one, too."

Another time, we all went to the Recording Studio in Hollywood to make an Easter recording with the handsome actor John Garfield. I still remember having to practice over and over again the words "Hippity, hoppity, Easter's on its way," from the song *Here Comes Peter Cottontail*. I honestly can't remember if John had a good voice or the studio was merely using him because of his fame at the time. Musicals were popular in the forties, and the Hollywood studios had many of their stars try their hand at singing. Remember John Wayne and Jimmy Stewart? Today, I remember Garfield for his unforgettable performances in *The Postman Always Rings Twice* with Lana Turner (1946), *Humoresque* with Joan Crawford (1946), and the Oscar-winning Best Picture *Gentleman's Agreement* (1947), which became a political football because of its subject matter of anti-Semitism. Tragically, Garfield died of a heart attack when he was only thirty-nine.

Life seemed a lot simpler in those days, especially after the war. I could play outside and my parents had no fear of my being kidnapped, molested or shot. I could walk safely to and from school, and even to the neighborhood drugstore, for nickel candy or a Cheerio ice cream bar. School was still challenging, but nothing like it is today, especially in big city schools. There was no grade-school homework to speak of and my seventh-grade homework took an hour or so before dinnertime, not until midnight.

Even the selling of Girl Scout cookies was uncomplicated. I was never cautioned to avoid ringing the doorbell of a house when the occupant wasn't known by me personally. I was encouraged to be aggressive (not in my nature) and to meet the challenge of selling the most boxes of any other girl in my troop. Why, I even got Mrs. Iribe to buy from me.

On Halloween Eve, I would go with a few kids from the neighborhood in and out of every apartment building in the area, and up sometimes dozens of stairs to ring the doorbell or pound on the door. My fellow costumed and masked revelers would join me in shouting, "Trick or treat, money or eats!" at the top of our lungs. We would be invited into each apartment or home to add an allotment of candy to our already bulging pillowcases. Sometimes we'd be asked to perform a trick for homemade cookies, caramel apples, popcorn balls and witch's brew (usually root beer or grape Kool-Aid).

We didn't need a fancy plastic pumpkin to hold our loot, or a decorated canvas Halloween bag. And our costumes were put together with our mothers' help. We became tramps with patches stitched onto our jeans, and we carried a hobo bag made from a farmer's red neckerchief tied around a stick and stuffed with toilet paper to make it seem full of necessities for traveling the railroad. Once, I became a ghost with a pillowcase draped over my head for the gown; Mommy had cut out holes for my eyes and mouth and used her eye shadow to outline them with smoky circles. Some kids were witches, especially if their mother could sew a simple gown with long flowing sleeves from black fabric.

Today, parents walk along with their children, who are decked out in expensive costumes from a party store, and diligently avoid the houses of strangers. Or, they trade trick or treating altogether at a party sponsored by a neighborhood church or other organization. And no homemade goodies are allowed, not even apples. Only commercially wrapped candy is acceptable, just in case someone who dislikes children or the holiday in general has chosen to bake a drug into the brownies, slip razorblades into the apples, or do some other hazardous and hideous act.

As it happened, we always lived just outside the district limits of the school closest to us. My parents would provide the address of a friend nearby, after gaining permission from them. This deception created anxiety for me. I was always fearful about being discovered and sent home in shame as everyone in the school watched my departure from the classroom windows.

Daddy could never attend P.T.A. meetings or other school functions like the fathers of my friends. If he had a long-term gig playing nightly at a ballroom, he would get home in the wee hours of the morning and sleep until noon. He would eat his breakfast while we ate our lunch, usually dressed in his morning jacket of burgundy velvet with a black satin collar. Priscilla, our dear and much loved housekeeper who lived with us, doted on Daddy by preparing all his favorite foods, regardless of the time of day. Priscilla was born on the same day as Mother, June 17, and we always celebrated their birthdays together. Daddy was invited to dozens of parties throughout the year, but when the annual round of Christmas parties started, Sandra and I were thrilled when one included children. At Gracie Fields' home, we would receive Christmas gifts from Santa Claus himself.

New Year's Eve was one of my father's busiest evenings. Private planes would wait at the airport to fly him to another party, sometimes in another time zone. One year, he had five such parties scheduled. Usually, Mother stayed at home with us. Sometimes other members of the family would come for dinner, and then leave in time to watch a fireworks demonstration somewhere in the city.   Daddy's hectic and ever-changing schedule meant he often used sleeping pills. He said he found them necessary to quiet the music that reverberated repeatedly in his head, especially as the clock hands reached four o'clock in the morning.

Perhaps surprising to many, our parents never cursed. They raised my siblings and me to be careful in our speech. "Such language is not ladylike. A gentleman never fouls his language with words from the gutter." To this day, neither my sister nor I ever swear. Our home atmosphere was more serene in that respect.

When I was about eight years old, Grandma Dora Mitnick died and my grandfather, Benjamin, moved in with us. Because of that, I got to see more of Uncle Moe and Uncle Jack. They would come to visit Grandpa. "Do you need anything, Pa?"

"I'm fine," Grandpa would say, gesturing with a hand as though shooing them away.

After another five minutes of chatting about the weather, the war, or his health, my uncles would leave. No discussion ever ensued about their 'work' activities outside our home or their substantial income sources. It was as though the less he knew the better for him. For all of us. We met their various girlfriends and listened to accounts of parties and movie premiers and other social engagements.

Uncle Jack was much more social and fun than my Uncle Moe, who had a very intractable face and appeared mysterious and a little scary to me. His manner discouraged any foolish nonsense, and we kids learned to never question him, and I mean never. In a moment's notice, he could pick himself up and leave the house without a backwards glance. Both Mommy and Daddy would give us that 'look' parent's give that silently transmits the warning to behave and zip up. I rarely had to be given the 'look,' because I would be on guard as soon as Uncle Moe entered the house. When I was older and had better developed my artistic senses, I decided this was his way of protecting us from his real nature . . . that of a gangster.

Both uncles lived in an apartment on Willaman Street, only a few blocks from the rest of the family. Both were socially friendly with the Hollywood "in" crowd that included Cary Grant, Dean Martin, George Raft and Janet Blair, to name only a few with more recognizable names. If Mommy took Sandra and me to visit Uncle Jack and Dean Martin's manager, Mack Ray, was there, we girls would hide in a closet and not come out until he left. This giant of a man (compared to the Sorkin and Mitnick men), with an angular face that was unlike any we had ever seen, would tease us. We found his teasing intimidating and couldn't warm up to him.

On one occasion, when I was about ten years old, Uncle Jack hired Sandra and me to help him with a special task. "These are called lottery tickets, girls. They're from a country not far from here called Mexico. I'll give you each five dollars to carefully cut them apart and tuck into these envelopes. Watch me." It took us a couple hours, but we finished the project to his satisfaction . . . and to ours, when we pocketed the money.

Uncle Jack had been married to a gorgeous model before I was born, but she died. I believe this tragedy and the depth of his sadness kept him from ever marrying again.

My bachelor uncles' lady friends were always dressed in the latest fashions and both my mother and I checked them out very carefully. The men wore custom-made suits, shirts with French cuffs, monograms, and gold and diamond cufflinks. Uncle Moe's favorite fragrance, Zizani, was in a silver bottle on his dresser and we girls were warned not to touch it. He always smelled nice, and I knew when he had been in a room, because the fragrance lingered long afterwards.

Sandra and I would sometimes be gifted with hand-me-downs from my uncles' friends, once, a movie projector from George Raft. Mack Ray always had chocolates or candy handy, and if anything got the two of us out of the closet, especially me, it was the offer of a treat. Anything sweet gave me a jolt of courage.   My uncles were also on close terms with members of the Las Vegas mob, including Bugsy Siegel and Mickey Cohen. Once, Uncle Jack asked Bugsy for a ride back to Los Angeles from Vegas trip. "Can't do it this time, Jack. Sorry. I'll catch up with you later. Come to the house." Apparently, Bugsy knew there was a contract out for him and didn't want to place Uncle Jack at risk. I was riding in the backseat of Uncle Jack's car a couple days later, when Uncle Moe flagged him down. "They got Bugsy," he said, glancing at me and not elaborating. This took place in late June of 1947. Much later, I learned that Uncle Jack felt enormous relief that he hadn't made that visit to Bugsy's home, although Bugsy was assassinated at the Beverly Hills home of his girlfriend, Virginia Hill, not at his residence or in his car.

My uncles were wide apart in their own car preferences. Uncle Moe had a personal driver to tote him around town in a black Cadillac sedan. He considered having a driver part of his society image. Cadillacs were a sign of success in those days, and he never changed car brand or color in his lifetime. Besides, black was the color of limousines. Uncle Jack wasn't that particular. At the time of his death, he was driving a Ford Pinto.

The day my father bought home his first Cadillac was a memorable one. We all ran outside to see it and Sandra and I begged for a ride around the neighborhood. Daddy's secret dream was to someday own a Rolls Royce, and although he used the gold-colored key with the RR engraving as a lucky charm kept in his pocket, he never bought one. I still have that key and at one time in my life came close to buying a used Rolls, but the passenger window wouldn't roll up. I took this as a sign that I shouldn't buy it.

Celia, Mother's sister, was a lovely and gentle woman who made her living plucking hairs from the eyebrows of movie stars, and any other facial hair they had that might be seen on the large screen. It was trendy to pluck every hair from natural eyebrows and then draw in thin, highly arched replacements. Think of Marlene Dietrich, Bette Davis and Ann Southern. Those who wanted to emulate these women provided Auntie Celia the opportunity to run a thriving business. She was kept so busy; she never had children and spent her free time crocheting hats and sweaters for all her nieces. Happily, I was one of the recipients. I adored Auntie Celia and often wondered if she was lonely. I was so accustomed to a houseful of family and relatives and her apartment, just off Sunset Boulevard, was always so quiet. Interestingly, I learned that her next-door neighbor, Dolores de Acha, was the mother of Desi Arnaz. On one of our visits to Auntie, we met Desi Arnaz when he was visiting her. Dolores was a small—boned, short woman with a strong Cuban accent, just like we were accustomed to hearing from Desi in the radio shows and later television shows that made him and his wife Lucille Ball so well-known and loved worldwide.

Auntie Martha, like my mother, was a great cook. Both sisters were in their kitchens in every spare moment trying out new recipes or attempting to replicate ones they'd enjoyed at five-star restaurants or someone else's home. They had a fierce cooking rivalry throughout their lifetimes, and were always trying to outdo each other to gain bragging rights. The aroma of Mommy's famous cinnamon buns was intoxicating to me. Today in the shopping malls, a whiff of the commercially prepared Cinnabons never fails to remind me of hers. I was her official taster and more than happy with this task, because it meant I got to lick the frosting spoon.

After the war, we all took a long, deep sigh of relief, along with everyone in the country. Factories that produced nothing but war products and uniforms reverted to their former product specialty. Women workers returned to their homes, making jobs available for all the veterans who were eager to resume a degree of normality once again. The economy switched into high gear, and people started to move to the city suburbs and build homes . . . row after row of them, all similar in appearance and size. One-story ranch-style houses with big yards. Gone were the victory gardens. Now, women prided themselves now in creating lovely flower gardens.

Although Daddy had worked steadily during the war years, his growing fame as an orchestra leader meant an increased income that provided ample money for store-bought clothes for Sandra and me. Mother was not ready to give up her sewing machine, however, and continued to create 'twin' outfits for us, especially fancy party dresses, often using Vogue patterns. She had a great eye for color and design, traits that she passed on to me, although I used them for my artwork. Mother's second 'home' became the Home Silk Shop, owned by the dressmaker, Mrs. Neely, whom she had used for years to keep her as stylish as the stars.

Southern California worked hard at restoring its former unique beauty. The Valley and Encino areas groomed or replanted row upon row of orange trees, especially along the boulevards, and Beverly Hills capitalized on its already famous use of palm trees. Running parallel to Beverly Drive in Beverly Hills, Rodeo Drive was originally a bridle path. It wasn't unusual to see beautifully dressed riders trotting their equally beautiful horses beside us as we cruised up the boulevard the first couple years we lived in Los Angeles. Hollywood equestrians would ride the trail and then lunch at the Beverly Wilshire Hotel. But the city wanted to limit horseback riding, and encouraged the use of bicycles instead. By the time I had graduated from high school, the bicycle path was removed and the center median became a lush green lawn. Today, Beverly Drive is still embellished with the famous palm trees, but the small homes that lined the street have been replaced with elegant gated and guarded manors.

Soon after, Daddy, the maestro, started his own orchestra; he was playing for Pasadena society parties. Early members of the orchestra included drummer Phil Rale, bass and trumpet player Irving Parker, and pianist Freddy Karger. My father played his saxophone and other reed instruments. Soon they were booked for the annual Navy Ball, Photoplay parties, and the All Nations Ball, to name only a few.

The following text appears on the back cover of the first record album featuring only Daddy's orchestra, and describes his life as a musician. It was written by Cobina Wright, who first earned fame as an American opera singer under the name Esther Cobina, and later became a Hollywood actress who appeared in movies like *The Razor's Edge* (1946). Daddy and the rest of us in the family came to know Cobina best as a party hostess extraordinaire and a syndicated gossip columnist. She and Daddy became friends over time, as she hired him to provide music for several of her parties.

TO ALL DANCE LOVERS *by Cobina Wright*

It is only seldom that anyone arises in the entertainment world who has the power to exhilarate and excite an audience. In his chosen field of dance music, such a personality is Barney Sorkin—the foremost society dance orchestra leader on the west coast. The "dancey" sounds he creates with his saxophone and orchestra are the difference between a just "so-so" party and a wonderfully gay and successful affair. Whether it is a debutante coming–out party, a wedding reception or a charity ball, no society matron in southern California, anxious for her party to be envied and enjoyed, decides on a date before first consulting with Barney to see if he is available and to get his ideas on plans for the party. Yes, weddings, balls and other social function have been postponed and their dates set to fit in with his busy schedule.

Not only Hollywood, Beverly Hills and the Pasadena society "crowd, but those in other parts of the country also look to Barney and his music to spark their parties, and with the advent of the jet age, travel is becoming a greater part of his routine.

Recently, he was called upon to play for one of the largest wedding receptions on the East Coast. The entire orchestra was jet-flown from Los Angeles to play for the wedding of Michele Myers in Rye, New York, after which the band winged its way to Wilmington, North Carolina, for the bridal dinner and wedding reception for George Matthews and Betsy Kelly, and back to Los Angeles for the Symphony Ball. Then another flight to Evanston, Ill., this time a bridal dinner-dance and wedding reception for the Bill Seeds; following the newlywed couple to New York for the bon voyage party aboard the Queen Mary.

During the holiday season, Barney again takes his orchestra to New York for Mr. and Mrs. Ricardo Gonzales for their annual Xmas party. And in February, to the ball in Palm Beach, Florida, dedicating the Henry Morrison Flagler Museum, formerly the internationally known Flagler residence, the famous Whitehall. But of course, it is on the Hollywood scenes and its environs that Barney and his wonderful dance rhythms are always in demand. In the spring of 1959, when the Duke and Duchess of Windsor were visiting on the West Coast, two lavish parties were given in their honor, and Barney, naturally, played for both of them; one was held by Randolph Hearst at the famous Romanoff's in Beverly Hills, and the other by me, at my home. You know, I never, but never, give a party unless Barney is there to furnish the music.

When Edwin Pauley honored King Hussein of Jordan with a sumptuous party during the monarch's visit to Los Angeles, again it was the music of Barney Sorkin that made the dancing feet go round and round. And so it is with all the society set, from Mrs. Norman Handler in Los Angeles to the society luminaries in Beverly Hills, whether it is the Leonard Firestones honoring Henry Ford II and brothers Benson and William, or Mrs. Ray Stark "partying" Aly Khan,

or any other preeminent society function, if you recently saw pictures in Life
Magazine.

In this album, Barney manages to convey the feeling of both beautiful melo-
dies and danceable rhythms, played in the style that has so captivated the elite of
Hollywood and Beverly Hills. You can imagine yourself at Mrs. Buddy Adler's
(Anita Louise) party to welcome Ingrid Bergman, or a party for Lauren Bacall.
He played for the Spinster' s Ball, Photoplay Annual Gold Medal Awards
Dinner, Red Book Movie Awards and in the Persian Room of the Beverly Hills
Hotel for a limited engagement.

Over the years, I've read many articles and a few books about how our childhood experiences help shape who we become as an adult. Of course genes help
determine our personalities and many of our traits, like whether we're more
likely to be an introvert or an extrovert, a giver or a taker, or a math whiz. A
science genius or a gifted teacher. But much of the time, whether or not we're
able to communicate well with others is based upon our birth order and the
quality of the interactions we have with our parents. Having a musician for a
father and seeing and hearing my uncles play their instruments with him at
family gatherings certainly influenced my early musical talent, but so did the
artistic talents of my parents, both different and yet providing me with the
innate ability I had to draw on paper what I was seeing and feeling. I grew up
in an era when children were to be seen but not heard in adult gatherings. We
were 'cute,' but didn't have anything important to offer in the way of conversation. We were told how to behave, when to say 'please' and thank you,' and
how to thank our host or hostess for "the lovely time." Such politeness and
show of good manners were expected.

Sandra and I played together for years and then became friends as well as
sisters somewhere along the way. Since our brother was several years younger,
we tended to treat him like one of our baby dolls, and then we thought he was
too rambunctious, forever upsetting our 'let's pretend' play and demanding
attention. We thought he was a pest, and we more often than not shooed him
away. It was hard for him to be the only boy in the family, especially when his

father was trying to sleep after a late night or rushing from the house to get to a rehearsal and later to a party gig. A boy can only be told so many times to hush and keep his voice down. He couldn't expend his excess energy with games of catch or baseball with his daddy.

I think Donald held back his feelings, as I did when I yearned to receive my father's approval after hours of practicing a piano piece, or drawing a particularly beautiful picture (in my opinion). Thankfully, I was able to appease some of my angst by accompanying Daddy to his rehearsals. The more I attended, the more I grew to know and enjoy the musical numbers. I knew his band and then his orchestra members by name and tried hard to act in a way that would please him and, in that way, be invited to accompany him again. Although I'm certain Mother had no understanding of it while raising us three children, she taught us that our choices and actions had consequences. She also knew that my watching her cook and sew was the best way for me to learn. We can read hundreds of recipes but not know how to bake a cake until we've tried our hand at it. I tried, but usually ended up with flour all over the counter. Of course, that was frowned upon during the war years, when every teaspoon of every ingredient was worth its weight in gold.

One major sorrow about my early childhood and grade school years, it is that I didn't receive enough praise. Lots of reprimands, lots of instructions, lots of discipline, but not enough of the kind of praise that would have helped me develop a stronger self-esteem and more confidence. I wanted to please both of my parents and to be liked by my siblings and all my relatives. A few more pats on the head or my back, a little more verbal applause in the form of compliments would have gone a long way in assuring me that I was loved despite my failings or inability to live up to expectations.

Instead, I was given cookies, candy or ice cream.

And I loved those sweets. Really love those sweets.

Lest I be too hard on my parents, I must add that I also learned, over the years, that most parents do their best, using their own experiences as guides and what they see others doing with their children. Stress, finances, moving across country, dealing with a society that was totally foreign to them, and a war that engulfed the entire world and involved anti-Semitism in much of it was enough to cause my parents many sleepless nights and concern about what tomorrow would bring.

That my family was not personally touched by the horrors and permanent wounds of that war is a blessing that can never be forgotten. My uncles and cousins came home to us. And like every American family that was eager to see what the future would bring, Daddy worked even harder and was reward-ed for it, and Mother did what mothers do when their spouse is away from home for hours and even days at a time—she kept the home fires burning and raised us children. The public benefited from my father's efforts. We benefited from them and from our mother's efforts.

7

IN 1949, WE moved into our new home on Motor Avenue, near Beverly Hills. At that time, it seemed like Daddy was spending a fortune, but in today's currency value, the purchase price of $45,000 is not much more than the cost of a medium-sized sedan or the down payment on a home. Motor Avenue was not paved at the time, but our home was near 20th Century Fox Studios, the center of Daddy's work life. From my classrooms at Beverly Hills High School, I could watch the filming of movies on the back lots and imagine what the camera men were seeing. I had stood right next to numerous camera scaffoldings on visits to the studios with my father, and I found this experience a means of holding a conversation with other classmates whose parents might not be in the movie business.

Beverly High was not your average high school. Many of the students in my classes were delivered in limousines. The floor of the basketball court covered an Olympic-sized swimming pool and was mechanically rolled back for swim practice and events in between basketball practice and games. Whenever the school had student productions, the audience included several producers, directors and agents from the movie industry who were scouting for future stars.

Beverly High is where I became serious about my talent for painting. The teachers inspired my imagination and stimulated my creative interests. They taught me techniques and the magic of color. I couldn't get enough of it. And the introductory classes in art history fascinated me. I learned about the various art movements and the contributors to each style, from the Renaissance works of Michelangelo and Raphael, Mannerism of Greco and Cellini, Baroque style of Rubens and Rembrandt, the Romanticism of Delacroix, Realism of Daumier, Impressionism of Monet, Manet, Renoir, Cassatt, and Degas, the Cubism and Futurism of Picasso, and the Abstract Expressionism of Pollock, de Kooning, and Warhol; the last four were making their names in the art world during my school years.

Art was by far by best subject. Perhaps because I felt I could compete successfully with my peers and in the art world where one's appearance didn't matter. Talent did.

Dick Chamberlain and I had a couple drawing classes together. He was quite a talented artist and later in life returned to it, but at the time, he seemed to prefer the idea of becoming an actor. He had what Hollywood loved in those days and still does . . . rugged good looks, a sculptured face and perfect physique. He fulfilled his destiny and became a favorite American actor, especially of television miniseries like *The Thorn Birds* and *Dr. Kildare*.

It was in one of my first art classes that I first met Joanie Jacobs, who became a life-long friend. Joanie loved art as much as I did. Our friendship grew as we chatted about our families, boys, school, music, the movies, our favorite stars, and everything else girls talk about while using our creativity through dozens of in-class assignments and projects. While I admired Joanie for many reasons, her equestrian-lean physique and Bridget Bardot blond hair were near the top of the list. In that way, Joanie and I were total opposites. I couldn't quite shake my seemingly inborn inferiority complex about being short-legged and not naturally svelte. Of course, it didn't help that I made use of the school's vending machines, which were more than willing to cough out chocolate bars as long as it was fed enough coins.

Joanie was the only child of Ruth and Melvin Jacobs; Melvin was a self-made man who experienced tremendous success in all his endeavors, made an abundance of money, even during the war years, and bestowed much of it on his only child.

The Jacobs were more than generous with me as well. They treated me like another daughter. One time, a good friend of Mr. Jacobs, Colonel Tom

Parker, bragged about a young singer he was representing, whom he felt was set for stardom. Joanie got to meet this singer when she accompanied her father to a meeting with Parker. The young man was Elvis Presley.

Joanie and her family were Jews who didn't practice their faith on a weekly basis either, and somehow, Joanie got involved with a Christian Science congregation. She invited me to attend the Wednesday evening healing classes with her. I was fascinated with what I was seeing and hearing, as many people shared a personal demonstration of their faith. I didn't realize how much of an effect the doctrine was having on me at the time, and continued to study with Joanie until we got to the part of Christian Science that involved giving up any kind of medical treatment. I had already experienced how necessary doctors are to restore our bodies to health when my mother had been saved from death by the doctors who treated her for bacterial meningitis. I thought of all our soldiers during the war years who needed medical care and surgery of all kinds. Knowing this was a spiritual challenge I could not meet, I found one excuse after the other not to attend future Wednesday meetings, until finally Joanie gave up on me.

We did continue to share our love of art and fashion, however, and our friendship flourished all through our years at Beverly High.

Another thing we enjoyed was dancing. At public functions, we danced like the adults; mostly the foxtrot, waltz, two-step, and other dance styles that allowed conversation while on the floor, swaying to the music. It was what our grandparents and parents considered mannerly and acceptable in public. Although we loved the music Daddy and other big bands had been playing for years and that had made dozens of musical stars, like Frank Sinatra and Bing Crosby, we preferred the new sound and new beat of the jitterbug that our war veterans had danced to in ballrooms and dance clubs throughout England and France.

The jitterbug, of course, had been popular among certain population groups in the United States since the mid-1930s, with Cab Calloway's jitterbug music and movie to spread its joy of life to every state. It combined movements from the free and easy style of the deep South's lindy hop and the East Coast's swing. The melodies and lyrics were as easily sung and understood and relatable as the music of the thirties and forties, but the faster beat was more appealing to every teen, whether from a small town or the most populated city, especially those of us who wanted to get a little wild and crazy while away from home.

I had already graduated from high school when most of the great music of bebop, doo wop, the lindy hop and rock 'n roll was being recorded. Music that made the top of the charts was still sung by the likes of Tony Martin, Doris Day, Johnnie Ray, Pattie Paige, Eddie Fisher, the Ames Brothers, and Peggy Lee. It still catered to adults or the entire family, because most households had only one record player, maybe a console in the living room. It was still the big band sound, smooth and romantic. A couple could dance in their small living room, without knocking over lamps.

After the war, however, companies focused on creating new products, not parts for tanks and airplanes; they experimented with innovative models of phonographs, even producing radios for cars. Better phonographs meant better quality records, and faster speeds created better, clearer sound. The usual 78 rpm records we played on my parent's console, with one song per side, changed to 33 1/3 rpm records that held whole albums of songs, and finally the 45-rpm speed.

The 45s recorded only one song on each side, too, but they were more affordable by teens on an allowance or working at a drive-in restaurant. Not only that, we could play these records in our rooms behind closed doors using a small phonograph manufactured especially for this new money-making phenomena. We could even take our phonograph and record collection to a friend's house for a slumber party and practice our dance steps.

Joanie and I started collecting 45s, like everyone else at Beverly High, and compared our favorites. We'd play these favorites over and over again. My most vivid memories of how this music effected my teen years are those of my two high school proms. At my junior year prom, held at a local country club in June of 1951, we danced feverishly to Elvis' recordings of "You Ain't Nothin' but a Hound Dog" and "Don't Be Cruel." But anything too energetic was frowned upon by the school authorities as well as our parents, which was exactly why we liked it. At my senior prom in June of 1952, which was held at the famous Coconut Grove, we danced to "The Glow Worm" and "Kiss of Fire." Girls often danced with girls, because boys weren't as willing to move with abandon to the music. We had a 60th High School reunion a couple of years ago and my date for the prom Sanford asked me, "Carol why didn't you finish your steak?" Can you imagine how my life might have changed if I had finished my steak!

With my friend Dupsey; dressed in my high school graduation blue gown – 1952

I graduated from Beverly Hills High School in June of 1952 with an art scholarship from the Los Angeles Art Center. Richard Chamberlain and I were the only two who received this scholarship from our school, but he went on to Pomona College, considered a highly academic college and suitable for his intelligence and goals. He graduated with a degree in art and theater arts; the school eventually awarded him an honorary doctorate.

In a way, earning this award did its part in building some of my self-esteem and providing validation for my interest in art rather than music. During the summer months, I grew to accept the notion that maybe I was on my way to becoming a professional artist.

That is, if I could just stop comparing my work to that of others and believing mine came up short.

Once I was a high school graduate and eighteen—the age of adulthood—I found my life expanding beyond the movie and music world of my parents. It was exciting, but at the same time scary. I enjoyed it more, but because I was still basically shy and insecure, I experienced trepidations about starting out on this new chapter of my life. What if I were a failure at everything I endeavored to do? What if I couldn't make 'adult' decisions after refusing help from my family and went flying down the wrong road? Goodness knows, this had already happened to many classmates from Beverly High before they ever saw graduation day.

My habit of listening in on the conversations of adults at family events and social parties came to my rescue those first couple weeks of art school. I learned that my classmates shared some of my characteristics, and they could put into words what I had felt for so many years. "We're the artistic type," was the reason they gave for not only every stroke of the brush, but for every mood swing. "I'm a loner, just like most artistic people. Think about musicians; they have to practice for hours to excel at what they do. Think about writers, who spend most of their waking hours at the typewriter. Or sculptors, composers and even comedians. They live in their heads and work by themselves."

"I'm an introvert, except when I have to be an extrovert. Then watch out. I'm wild!"

I nodded to myself, tucked the logic into a drawer of my mind, and then heard the words come from my own lips when they suited the occasion.

For the most part, I thoroughly enjoyed attending classes at the Art Center, and put everything I had into improving my eye for line and color and my skills for transposing what I saw onto the canvas.

Although art consumed most of my time, I was also becoming more interested in boys as dates and not just best friends. I found myself flirting with classmates and enjoying the reaction I received. I dated a little and, in the process, found myself quite timid in the love department. I would quickly end any relationship when the boy wanted to move beyond kissing and hugging. Even the hugging bothered me. I was constantly battling my weight and felt self-conscious about my looks. I started to buy over-the-counter diet pills and didn't stop using them until I was in my early thirties. This was the beginning of my serious inner battle with food in general, and with anything sweet in particular. Anything that would soothe my continuing and aching lack of self-confidence. I imagined myself being the subject of jokes, but couldn't stop feeding my fears.

It didn't help that my appearance seemed to be the subject of my entire family's discussions. I was either getting heavier, or I wore too much make-up, or my hair wasn't right for my face and figure, or I wore clothing that was too baggy. It went on and on, and as much as I tried to please everyone, my efforts never seemed good enough. I wanted to believe no one realized the inner pain and anxiety their criticism caused me. My dear Auntie Ida, who also struggled with weight, was my only ally. "Don't listen to them, dear," she'd say. "You look lovely."

The party scenes at our Motor Avenue home increased during my teen years, and by now had become a regular occurrence. I was more aware that the preparation for each party was as elaborate and extensive as the results. They took hours of planning and, in those days, invitations were always extended in writing, on fine velour. At our house, preparations on party day would begin with the gardeners mowing the lawn and pruning the trees. Then, the Abbey Rental trucks would arrive to set up white canvas tents and white tables and chairs. The catering staff would arrive early, laying out linens on the tables and added centerpieces of flowers and candles. They'd organize a dozen or more over-sized chrome (to look like silver) serving trays and prepare the chafing dishes with Sterno cans to keep hot food hot.

Once the guests started to arrive, the uniformed staff would pass around tiny hors d'oeuvres, each one more eye-appealing than the others. Then came the carved roast beef, shrimp, lobster, and sliced chicken breast with a special fruited sauce to use with pilaf. There was always an array of fresh vegetables, fruit, cheeses and desserts. Although the buffet table groaned with the extensive menu, the portions guests served themselves were small so they could sample a little of everything. However, in those days, calories and diets were not a subject in conversations.

My siblings and I were not allowed in the kitchen on party days, not even as teenagers. "It's off limits after four o'clock, Carol. You know that by now." My mother would scowl at me as I headed for the dessert trays for fear I'd eat too many and she'd not have enough for guests. She knew full well about my "weakness" for sweets, as she had willingly contributed to it.

An elaborate bar set-up took up one whole side of a tent, replete with a bartender and bottles of scotch, vodka, gin and several aged bourbons. Champagne flowed. What was a Hollywood party without champagne? By the time several guests had been served cocktails, a few members of Daddy's orchestra would arrive and start playing in another corner where a portable dance floor had been installed. A rented piano was always included in this arrangement so that Freddie Karger could play (Freddie later became the husband of Jane Wyman). They would perform several numbers from their usual repertoire, but always include the most popular chart-making numbers of the year, like *Mona Lisa, Tennessee Waltz, My Foolish Heart* and *My Heart Cries for You*, all from 1950; and *Unforgettable, Too Young* and *Charmaine*, from 1951. My senior year, *Because You're Mine, Anytime* and especially *Singin' in the Rain* were favorites. The last number would invariably get more of us teens on the floor as we tried to emulate Gene Kelly and Debbie Reynolds, without all the uninhibited abandonment, to prevent careening into older (or slightly inebriated) dancers. All the numbers Daddy's band played were geared toward providing easy-on-the-ears background music, while guests mingled and talked and checked out who else had been invited to the event. But they were danceable and even singable by anyone who dared to compete with the original recorder of the song, who might be a guest that night.

I felt rather isolated from the others at these parties, which included not only Daddy's social and business friends, but also my parents' personal friends. Most of these elaborate parties included my uncles and their dates and other family members who might want to attend. It didn't matter. My mind was always thinking about the 'what ifs.' What if I approached someone with an inane comment and saw eyes roll? What if I got nothing but a fake smile or groans? What if guests saw me coming and mumbled to their partners that they'd have to make nice, because the Sorkin's were their hosts?

My parents tried their best to make me fit into the shoes of a young society debutante, but I didn't feel comfortable in them. I'd more likely than not hover in the background with a soft drink in my hand, watching, singing the words of the music in my mind, and imagining my own someday-lover.

Lest I give the impression I was a totally unhappy young woman and remained so my entire life—ungrateful for the far above average lifestyle lived by most Americans—I must mention that I was fully aware of the blessings that didn't seem uncommon while they were being experienced. Like most of us, however, it's not until we have lived long enough to acquire a higher degree of introspection that we understand how people and events and our reactions to and interpretations of them contribute to who and what we are. The lifestyle of my family, during the years that had their greatest impression on how I would perceive myself in comparison to others, contributed in many ways to my social insecurities. How can any ordinary girl compete with movie or music stars for attention and appreciation of talents that weren't a part of their personal world?

At one of my parents' parties in 1953, Frank Sinatra was the subject on everyone's lips. He had just made a celebrated comeback, after losing his recording contract a couple years prior, by winning an Oscar for his role as Maggio, an Italian-American soldier in *From Here to Eternity*. I had met Sinatra at a theatre once, in my grade school years, and was surprised to find him no taller than my father, only much thinner. It was in 1943, when he was just beginning his solo recording artist career as a crooner, and we were surrounded by screaming girls called bobby-soxers. I had a hard time hearing him. He shook my hand and leaned over to tell me he had a daughter Nancy, who was younger than I (by five years) "but just as cute." (In 1966, Nancy recorded *These Boots Are Made for Walkin'* with her father and it became a national hit.)

The Maestro (right), presenting movie stars at a party

The Hollywood scene in the fifties was so different from what is considered the norm in today's society. Women wore dresses and never jeans or slacks when outside the home, even if they'd worn slacks while working in factories during the war and were only headed for the grocery store. There was a return to femininity, fashion, and a great sense of what was proper in public. This attitude was fostered by the fashion industry, which was eager to return to brighter colors and more flattering designs after the war years, when it seemed obscene to do so. Hollywood embraced the change and the increased proliferation of fan magazines contributed to the belief that a 'lady' needed to wear gloves and hats to church and social functions, and a tight girdle to smooth out bulges in the sheath dresses with longer skirts that competed with the full-circle skirts worn with crinolines favored by the younger set. Remember poodle skirts?

One of the many memorable evenings I had as a young woman on my own took place at the Beverly Hills Hotel. I was invited to join a few friends for dinner, and we kept remarking about why the waiters were hovering around the secluded table of a couple across the room. Suddenly, three violinists strolled through the room and stopped to serenade them. We could only see that the man was casually attired in a suit jacket and a white shirt without a tie, and the woman was dressed in what appeared to be a suit. We finished our meal and were about ready to leave when the fussed-over couple rose from their table. It was Howard Hughes and Jean Peters! She wore a soft grey suit with a white orchid on the lapel. We gaped at each other and made faces, saving our exclamations for when we reached the hotel lobby. Hughes wore white sneakers and no socks and the shoe laces hadn't been tied. They dangled on the floor. My friends and I elbowed each other as discretely as possible and laughed afterwards, wondering what would have happened if we'd hustled after them and accidentally-on-purpose stepped on the laces.

Another time, my father was playing at a party give for the producer Ray Stark, who was married to Fran Stark, Fannie Brice's daughter. She didn't seem at all pleased that I was there, as it was a much older crowd, and some of the guests might feel intimated under the watchful eyes of a teenager. At least that's what I believed she felt. I tried to be inconspicuous as possible, which wasn't difficult for me.

One of my favorite New Year's Eve parties was held at the Bel Air home of oil magnate Arthur Cameron. I invited my lifetime friend Dupsey to attend with me, so I wouldn't have to spend such an exciting evening alone, and we exclaimed over and over again at the extent of the magical décor and glitter in one home and for one party. Arthur's girlfriend, Ann Miller, was there, as well as Caesar Romero. Dupsey said, "Push me into him, Carol. I want to stare up into his Latin eyes." When the occasion came up, I obliged her. She was absolutely stunned that I'd literally do such a thing, as was I, and we laughed about if often over the years.

I wasn't unlike any other star-struck teen during this era, and I toyed with the idea of becoming an actor. I was asked by the director William Castle to take a screen test, but both my uncles, who were well acquainted with the foibles of Hollywood, convinced my father to nix this idea as soon as the discussion came up.

After staying on the dating scene for many years, Uncle Moe finally married the woman he'd dated the longest. Helen Franklin was an interior designer who decorated the Acapulco Towers in Acapulco, Mexico, and the Miramar Hotel, in Palm Springs. Helen was not like any other woman I'd met before. She was slightly taller than Uncle Moe, especially when she wore high heels, a very attractive blonde (the hair color of choice in Hollywood; think of Marilyn Monroe, Lana Turner, and Betty Gable), and always immaculately dressed, but many would describe her as being eccentric. She was certainly unconventional. For instance, she was the only person I'd even known to have a professional floor-model hair dryer in her home. She was fastidious about washing her hair at 5:30 a.m. every day, and she used the time under the hood to write notes in her business journal about client projects.

Since Uncle Moe seemed to have an endless supply of money and had no trouble making California connections, Helen was able to furnish their Spanish-styled home (once owned by Eva Gabor) with the most extravagant décor. Interior decoration was her special talent. She had exquisite taste that was admired by their circle of influential friends, who included the then president of Mexico, Miguel Aleman. Although Helen filled their home with artifacts from Europe, she had many from Mexico because of her connections. She had been born and raised there and, obviously, spoke fluent Spanish.

As I grew older, I saw that Helen attained clients not only because of her unique talent, but also because of the influence of Uncle Moe's friends and associates. His name brought in the Hollywood crowd and they wined and dined with the likes of Tony Martin and his wife, Cyd Charisse, and even the renowned mobster attorney Sidney Korshak.

Speaking of Korshak, he was a labor lawyer who had done considerable business with the Chicago mob, but had moved to Los Angeles to gain more anonymity and became a legendary "fixer" for many of Hollywood's movers and doers. His brother, Marshall Korshak, had also been part of the Chicago political machine, and gained his power and prestige by getting into city and state politics, even serving as a state senator.

Auntie Helen hated children and adored pets, which she didn't mind picking up after, even though she insisted upon a spotless house. The better I got to know Helen, the more I understood that she preferred animals to people because of her childhood years in Mexico when she had witnessed the awful abuse of animals. When there isn't enough money to feed the children, no one worried about whether the dog had been fed. There were no veterinarians, and unneutered animals proliferated freely, which meant there was an abundance of strays roaming the streets. Helen and her dear friend and compatriot Betty White devoted much of their time in Hollywood to the rescuing of abandoned dogs and providing veterinarian care and safe kennels until they could be adopted by loving new owners. Helen also kept the windows of their home free of screens, so that when she opened them she could lay bird seed on the sills.

I got along very well with Helen, because we shared an interest in the arts. The more my techniques improved while in art school, the more impressed she became with my skills in a variety of mediums. She and Uncle Moe both knew that I painted in oils and could use some extra money. They also knew that I could keep secrets. For these reasons, I became a valuable commodity.

"Carol, I need a favor quickly," Helen would say in a phone call. I knew exactly what this favor would be. She wanted me to copy a painting or drawing that would only be in her possession for a short time. Her modus operandi was to remove the artwork from a client's home, after suggesting it needed reframing. She hired me to create works that certainly challenged me at the time and seemed questionable on most such occasions, but the projects provided me with spending money and suited her purposes. On these occasions, I noticed new things she'd recently purchased. Valuable and stunning and eye-widening. One day, I saw a pile of dog droppings on the gorgeous dining room carpet and, after calling it to her attention, was amazed that she never flinched. I had to surmise it was not a rare occurrence. She did, however, always have me set up my easel on the back veranda, just in case I was careless and permanent oil paint would mar the floors. Aurelia, her lifetime helper, would make lunch for me.

I reasoned that my painting for Auntie Helen was not unlike painting a copy of a masterpiece on a class assignment to a museum. I was given the opportunity to copy original works by Chagall or Picasso, or maybe Diego Rivera or Orozco, sometimes on loan to Helen from a gallery or from the home of a client, including Kirk Douglas and Debbie Reynolds. Helen didn't want to reveal her motives to me, but I remember hanging the copy I'd painted from "Debbie Reynolds' collection bed. The two of us worked to steady ourselves while standing on the bed she shared with Harry Karl. lifting the fake painting into position. "Great job, Carol," Uncle Moe would say. "You're a genius. Think of it this way. You're learning the techniques of the masters. Someday, you'll be one yourself, and I'll be first in line to buy one of your originals. You can put that in writing, and I'll sign it."

"Your uncle and I fell in love with this painting, Carol," Auntie Helen would say. "We simply must have a copy of it in our home." Sometimes, she'd say, "Your uncle said he simply must have a copy to hang in his yacht."

I looked at this as an artist would . . . as an event. It gave me immense pleasure to see whether I could study each brush stroke and color shade on the original and reproduce it on a clean canvas. On one particular occasion, I was left to myself to examine and dissect and touch an original Chagall. It was a watercolor of flowers in a vase. Upon close observation, I was surprised to see that Chagall had used strips of tape cross the entire paper to prime it, rather than using a gesso. It was a new technique I had never tried before, but I tried my best to copy it piece by piece by piece.   The result? Helen didn't know which watercolor was the original, once I had finished. I wondered if this influenced her decision about whether to place the original on the wall of her client or on her own. I have no hesitation to believe that Uncle Moe would have made the decision for her, and maybe even sell the original. It would have given him immense pleasure to know his house was as richly bedecked of original works of art as were those of greater wealth . . . or that he had yet another way to fatten his wallet.

A Diego Rivera painting offered me another art challenge. It was painted on raw brown canvas, and Rivera hadn't used one bit of primer before laying on colors. The subject was of a child holding a bright orange in his hand. The canvas seemed to be almost transparent when held to the light, and it was screwed into the wood frame used to keep the canvas taut.

As I mentioned earlier, Uncle Moe always carried a wad of money on him. Whenever I finished a project, he would reach into his pocket and pull out a few hundred dollars for me. He did this even when I hadn't just finished an art project. His favorite words were, "Do you need anything? Buy something. On me." He was generous to a fault with everyone in the family. Perhaps this was a Mafia character trait that covered up for failings in other areas of his life. Either that or a purposeful gesture of giving things to those who could someday do things for him out of a sense of obligation.

Uncle Moe, as was Uncle Jack, was driven by a thirst for power. In my mother's later years, I pumped her for information about his friends. "Did Auntie Helen know about Uncle Moe's associations or where he got his money?"

"I don't think she did, Carol. If she suspected what he did for a living, she never mentioned it, and I never saw her look worried about anything. Her addiction was for what his money could buy, including a social life with those whose names appeared in the daily newspapers. None of us questioned your uncles. We didn't want to hear the truth and we didn't want to put them on the spot to lie to us. What we didn't know didn't hurt us."

According to an article that appeared in the *New York Times* after my uncle's death in 1996 (*New York Times*, Jan. 22, 1996, by author Robert McG. Thomas, Jr., who elevated obituaries to an art form), my Uncle Moe, like Sidney Korshak, "had never been indicted, despite repeated federal and state investigations. And the widespread belief that he had in fact committed the very crimes the authorities could never prove made him an indispensable ally of leading Hollywood producers, corporate executives and politicians."

When Helen and Uncle Moe dined with the Hollywood glamour crowd, she usually dressed in black and wore a cocktail ring with a huge round diamond. Yet she never carried money in her purse. She charged purchases to her business, or to Uncle Moe. Whenever I accompanied her on shopping trips for her design business, she invariably asked me for parking meter coins. "Will you drop them into the meter for me, dear? They will dirty my gloves, and then I'll make a smudge on my dress."

Uncle Moe and Helen had an unusual marriage, but they adored each other. He had the connections for her clients, and she had an incredible eye for design that made them happy and him proud. I would often see Uncle Moe give money to the workers on the sly. "Do not tell Helen about this," he'd say to me. Helen would say the same thing whenever she found another dog or some other animal to rescue. "Don't tell Moe about this. He thinks I spend too much time and money on my secret love."

Sometimes, when they had to be away, I stayed at their home to feed their beloved black spaniel Jet and the Hill Mynah birds that mimicked their voices perfectly. Both Uncle Moe and Helen had told me about their birds' capabilities. "They are capable of mimicking any voice or sound they hear and learning as many words as you want to teach them, Carol." What I found the most fascinating was that the birds would talk like either of their owners, seemingly when they chose to do so. They never failed to put a smile on my face.

When I was about eighteen years old, both my mother and I came down with the chicken pox. Her case was much more severe than mine, and she was essentially bedridden for a few days. Since I was quarantined, but able to move around, I answered the doorbell one evening right after the dinner hour. It was Uncle Jack, with a young woman beside him. "Hello, Carol. I would like you to meet someone quite special. Myrtle Aronsberg, my niece Carol Sorkin."

I showed them into the living room, apologized for staying at a distance from them, and made an excuse for my mother's inability to entertain. "Would you like something to drink?" I asked.

"No, no, that won't be necessary, Carol. I was driving in the neighborhood and wanted you to meet Myrtle. I met her on the pier in Santa Monica last month and haven't been able to get her out of my mind. She is an enormously talented singer. I' m going to make her a star."

Myrtle and I peered at each other, both shy, but raised to be polite. We were about the same age and both had dark hair and eyes. She was much more petite. Myrtle's name was changed to Gogi Grant: Gogi after the restaurant in New York, and Grant after Uncle Jack's pal Cary Grant offered profuse compliments of her singing.

Gogi went on to sing *The Wayward Wind*, and was the voice of Helen Morgan for the *Helen Morgan Story*. She appeared numerous times on television and in Las Vegas. I don't know why Uncle Jack didn't marry her, because they obviously were in love. Today, she is still performing in Palm Springs, California, in her eighties.

I survived the chicken pox, as did my mother. I continued with my painting and with the praise of various teachers and classmates, grew increasingly content with my life.

Then everything changed.

8

O H, HOW I have been dreading writing about this chapter of my life. Even after so many years, it is painful to remember. I can philosophize now and understand how the decisions we make can have a profound effect on our future life . . . especially the momentary missteps that come with youth and innocence and affect our ability to mature with confidence. We can forgive ourselves and move on, but that doesn't make the memories of such events disappear. I am a grown woman with a fabulous life today, but I remember with clarity how a single traumatic experience caused me such mental and emotional distress, it shook the very ground I walked on.

It was so painful; I was ashamed to share it with anyone. I lived with a sense of shame and self-doubt for months. It haunted me day and night and almost destroyed my interest in maintaining relationships with members of my family and friends for fear I'd say something and reveal something evil about myself.

Coming "of age" for a girl in the fifties was as difficult as it was for young women from any previous decade, especially when hormones are raging and the desire to be a self-reliant adult is so strong. I definitely found it complicated. Young women then tended to be less aggressive and more subservient, because they had their mothers and grandmothers as models. I was raised to be a conservative, well-mannered and upright girl, one who wouldn't bring shame to the family (even though the latter rule didn't extend to a few men in our family). Beverly Hills High School students were more progressive in their thinking and the boys were more than willing to let their own hormones rule their bodies. They were as aggressive then as they are today. How far is the girl willing to go? Was their mantra, I learned very quickly that the best way to avoid being tested was to remain a buddy, not a date.

Timid as a child, I remained so as a teen. This mindset carried over into my young adult years. In particular, I didn't want to be touched by a fellow, because I felt fat. I had reached my sixteenth birthday and "never been kissed," and that continued kiss less state remained until after graduation and art school. Talk about being naïve! My mother and several of her friends tried their best to introduce me to young men, and occasionally I went out on blind dates, especially if I would be part of a foursome or group going dancing or to a movie. There was safety in numbers.

One lovely summer evening, I readied myself for another of these blind dates, not really looking forward to it, even though a friend had arranged for it. "A man I know is going to be in town this weekend, but I already have plans," she said. "Please, please will you go out with him? He hates to dine alone."

I hesitated, not really in the mood for chit chat with a stranger. On the other hand, maybe it was better to have dinner with a stranger than to stay home and doodle on an art pad. "Okay," I said. "But you owe me big time!"

John Doe arrived exactly on time. He was older than former dates (about thirty) and that took me aback. He was certainly more mature than I was. By far. He lived in Chicago and was in Los Angeles on business, but he knew Los Angeles well. "I have to come here pretty often," he said.

He was attentive, affable, gentlemanly and a dusty blonde with sparkling blue eyes. I was fascinated.

"I've made reservations at a small restaurant near my hotel," he said, once he'd escorted me to his rented Lincoln Capri convertible and taken his place behind the wheel. He chatted about his love for the city and state and its access to an ocean. "We have Lake Michigan, which can seem like an ocean at times, but it's not the Pacific."

I listened and offered a few shy smiles.

The maître d' led us to a booth near the back of the dimly lit restaurant. We talked about my interest in art and, of course, about Daddy's career as an orchestra leader. It was a subject I could comfortably discuss. I finally relaxed enough to enjoy my meal and our conversation about the changing music scene.

And then the subject drifted to sex.

I twisted the napkin in my lap into a knot and peered at people seated near us at tables and wondered if those in the booths backing both of us could hear. Uncomfortable, I wanted to excuse myself and run. I could take a cab home. There would be lots of them near the hotel. I sneaked a look at my watch. It was still early. We'd been together for less than three hours.

"I'd love to have you meet a friend of mine," JD said. "She lives in an apartment only a few minutes from here. I think you'd like her."

Flashing him a quick peek from under my hooded lashes, I decided my imagination had gone haywire. He was looking at me with nothing but kindness. "All right," I muttered, thinking anything was better than continuing our current conversation. If I didn't like the girl, I could always call a cab from her place, and he could remain behind to visit with her.

We drove to a street in West Hollywood and parked in front of a two-story apartment building. JD took my hand and led me up the stairway to the second floor. As soon as he knocked on the door, it was opened by a pretty girl. Well, to be honest, she was far more than pretty. She was Vogue gorgeous. Slender, but voluptuous, with voluminous bleached-blonde hair that tumbled over her shoulders ala Jayne Mansfield. She held up her face for a kiss from JD on a rouged cheek and then smiled at me, her bright red lips curving over amazingly white and perfect teeth.

She couldn't have been more than a couple years older than I, but I felt like a dowdy dowager in my conventional navy dinner suit, even though it came from an exclusive Beverly Hills shop. JD introduced us and we shook hands.

"Please come in and make yourself at home." She gestured toward a couch and a nearby club chair. Chattering about the balmy weather and JD's trip from Chicago, she offered us both cigarettes from a box on the coffee table.

"Thank you. I don't smoke," I said.

She and JD lit up their Lucky Strikes and she poured scotch from a decanter into the glasses she had on a tray, offering one to me.

"Thank you. I don't drink," I said.

"Oh, I'm sorry; I don't have any soft drinks." She and JD clicked glasses and sipped the straight-up scotch while smoking. Then, she unexpectedly reached for a photograph album on the end table next to her. "You might enjoy seeing these pictures of me."

Every photograph showed her in a risqué outfit or none at all. The kind of photos I'd seen on wall calendars in the dressing rooms of male movie stars or in the two Playboy magazines' I'd seen art students pass around class.

My palms were wet with perspiration by the time I had flipped through several pages, and I was finding it difficult to breathe naturally. This from nervousness, not arousal. I closed the album and caught JD's eyes. "Please take me home," I said quietly, knowing my face was flaming red. I refused to hide my cheeks from the four eyes gazing intently at me. That would make me look even more immature than I felt. I rose from the chair and fumbled for my purse.

"Okay, no problem," he said. "But first, come into the other room with me. I want you to see something."

I politely followed both of them, my feet dragging. The room was a dimly lit bedroom, with cranberry red bedding. As soon as I entered, JD locked the door. My heart skipped a beat. Before that action and what it might mean took root in my already muddled brain, he had kicked off his shoes and whipped off his clothes. Our hostess did the same. She rubbed her naked body against his and he laughed with delight. I backed against the door and fumbled for the lock. Ending their lip-smothering kiss, JD reached for a chair and pulled it close to the bed. "Sit here, Carol," he said. "This won't take long."

If I hadn't done as directed, I would have fallen to the floor in a dead faint. My legs felt like wet noodles, my stomach was roiling, and I could feel tears stinging my eyes. I blinked several times, hoping none would escape and make a trail down my cheeks. I already looked like an adolescent in adult apparel. He took two steps and reached for my arm, pulling me toward the chair. I couldn't bear to look at him. His nakedness wasn't the same as the hired male models for our art classes.

He rolled onto the bed and the clearly experienced girl-model proceeded to kneel in front of his spread legs. What they were doing should be done in private. I wanted to close my eyes and shut out the deplorable scene. I lifted them only slightly to an area of the room a couple inches above the tableau. All the time he was otherwise occupied, JD kept looking at and talking to me, making sure I wasn't shutting my eyes. He moaned several times. I was horrified and humiliated. I had never seen anything like what I was being made to watch and hear.

"What do you think, Carol? This could be us. I wanted a long evening of sexual pleasure with you, but it became clear during our dinner conversation that you were unlikely to oblige me. I thought this is the next best thing. It's fun and sure feels good. We could have a threesome, before we head for home. Interested?"

Frozen in the chair, I couldn't find my voice. My skin crawled with a zillion stinging vermin. I felt dirty. Soiled beyond repair. I contemplated dashing to the window, breaking the windowpane and leaping to my freedom but thought I might fail in my attempt and be at the mercy of their laughter. My only saving grace was to look at the scene as objectively as I would Titian's famous paintings of nudes. His Rape of Lucretia flashed before my eyes.

In a daze, I was barely aware of their re-dressing or of JD leading me back to his car. All the way home, he kept talking to me as though nothing untoward had occurred. At the time I had no awareness that this whole scenario was routine for him and that my innocence formed the very core of his excitement.

I remained mute. As soon as his rented vehicle stopped in front of our home, I bolted from it and dashed to the entrance as though being chased by ravenous wolves. I slammed the door behind me, locked it tightly, and sank to the floor with my face hidden in my drawn-up knees. That's when I finally let go and cried like I had when my grandmother died. My heart had broken then. My innocence had died this night with no warning. I would never be the same.

I kept this secret locked up, never telling anyone for four years, not even the purported *friend* who had fixed me up with John Doe. Guilt weighed heavily on my mind. I believed the whole ugly incident was my fault. I must have said something, done something, behaved in some way that conveyed a message to JD that he had my permission to take such liberties. I felt violated, foolish and very ashamed; and yet, I had never been physically touched. How could I have the authorities charge him with sexual abuse?

Throughout my entire adult life, my heart has ached whenever I've read an accounting of a child, teen or adult who could no longer hold inside the pain suffered when being sexually, physically or psychologically abused by another human being. I have understood them being frightened into silence or feeling too ashamed to speak up. They felt powerless.

JD continued to call me whenever he was in Los Angeles. He'd ask, "Are you ready to have some fun, Carol? I'd sure like to see you again." My mother would happily hand me the phone, so glad I had found someone who was persistently pursuing me. She even provided a phone number where I could be reached, if I wasn't at home. When a friend or her parents answered their phone, I couldn't refuse to take the call just in case it was JD. Dozens of times, I wanted to tell Mother, "Never hand me the phone when he calls. Never give him a phone number. Tell him I'm dead!"

This was my first introduction to sex. I thought if I didn't talk about it, then it wasn't real. It hadn't happened. When my conscience would say, "It happened, all right. Deal with it, Carol," I worried that if I related the incident to anyone in my family, JD would be taken care of . . . Mafia style. So I kept silent.

One night of innocent trust was all it had taken to transform me into a different person. I hadn't learned yet that I had a voice and would find personal power in speaking up. Any self-confidence I had previously gained vanished after this dreadful incident. I wouldn't let any nice young man get close to me. Sadly, the inability to trust stood in my way of forming a romantic relationship. My fear and anxiety over what it might lead to produced a frigidness that became a real turnoff to a potential suitor.

After almost four years of dealing with even a dread of phone calls and slamming the receiver back on the hook whenever John Doe's voice reached my ear, I finally demanded that he stop calling me. That's all it took. Firmness. No explanations required. He stopped. From what I've learned over the years, there are certain men who are aroused by simply engaging in sex talk over the phone with a stranger. Some find their victims by randomly dialing a phone number; some see a newspaper photograph of a local woman and look up her name in the phone book. Nowadays, young women are more educated about the activities of perverts. In the fifties, there was no Internet and women's magazines did not discuss such things.

Food became my panacea. Not alcohol or prescription drugs. Not just any food, either. I preferred something that was sweet and felt like a treat. I had been using sweets to make me feel good about myself and mend a broken spirit since I was a young girl, and the effect had numbed the pain for the moment only. Sweets are what we call "empty calories" today and such calories, for most people, just add on pounds. Subconsciously, that's exactly what I wanted. The more weight I gained, the less chance any man would take a serious glance at me. Second helpings. Dessert for sure. Daytime snacks. Evening snacks. And chocolate in all forms: bars, brownies, ice cream and especially Whitman's Samplers.

My father was now playing nightly at the Beverly Hills Hotel and the life he and my mother led continued to be actively social. It was expected that they would entertain; the guests at parties would hear Daddy's music and hire him for their own parties. Mother was kept busy planning both indoor and outdoor events. Dinners, buffets, lunches, cocktail parties, anniversaries, birthdays. All anchored in food. I stayed in my own self-imposed prison and refrained from entering wholeheartedly into any event, except for the sampling of a little of everything on the menu. On one of these occasions, I wore a cape over my dress to conceal an expanding waistline.

Of course, my behavior caught the attention of every member of the family. "You're just in your early twenties and I swear you live like you've got one foot in the grave!" "You've become a hermit, Carol. Why don't you go clubbing with Dupsey this weekend?" "You're such a stick-in-the-mud, sis. It would be more fun to attend a funeral than to hang around you these days."

"I happen to enjoy my life exactly how it is!" I'd retort. "Parties are frivolous. I want to dig deeper into my art work." Next to food, working on an art project provided some of the inner comfort I craved. I could lose myself in it for a few hours at a time.

Of course, one by one, my friends were beginning to marry. Girls married young in those days. Many right out of high school or in their early twenties. I attended their showers and dinners and ceremonies, going through the motions of being deliriously happy for them. The desserts were stunningly beautiful to behold and absolutely divine to eat.

My odd behavior at social events, accompanied by mood swings continued. Finally, my parents became frustrated enough to suggest I seek medical help. They both confronted me one evening when no one else was at home. Daddy was in his maestro attire, ready to leave for a party. Mother glanced at him and he nodded. "We both love you dearly, Carol, and only want the best in life for you. We're concerned about your health. We've decided I should make an appointment for you with my own doctor or seek his advice on what to do. We hope you'll agree. What will it hurt to have a thorough checkup?"

"Fine, do whatever you want," I said, secretly hoping the doctor would give me prescription drugs in high enough dosages to erase certain thoughts or at least numb my negativity about life's seamy reality.

I was sent to Mother's physician at Scripps Clinic in La Jolla, California, and put through a battery of tests. With the results in front of him, the doctor folded his hands on the desk and examined me closely. "Your physical exam and the blood test results indicate you're in fine physical shape, Carol. Is there something in particular bothering you? What's going on that has your parents so worried?"

At first I merely shrugged, but after some encouragement, I finally shared one thing. "I don't feel good about myself. It makes me sad."

He advised me to see a good psychiatrist and gave me a name of one he thought would make a good fit. By this time, I was desperate to be helped and agreed. My parents were shocked at the doctor's advice, but pleased that I was willing to do something, anything. In the fifties, most people who were sent to psychiatrist were thought to be crazy . . . a schizophrenic, pyromaniac or kleptomaniac. Not someone with food, mood or anxiety disorder. All of which I had.

During our sessions, the psychiatrist worked at breaking down my wall of resistance. I would talk in circles and still could not spit out the words of the scenario that had caused my mental distress. Finally, I realized I could trust him not to repeat what I told him. He would keep my secret. In a halting voice, I revealed what had happened to me. As the words spilling forth, it felt like a heavy yoke was being lifted from my shoulders. He didn't express shock. He didn't blame me for being so gullible or suggest that I should have taken a cab home from the restaurant and none of this would have happened to me.

With the psychiatrist's encouragement, I finally told my dearest friend Dupsey and then, later, with Dupsey's urging, my mother. She was in her room dressing for a luncheon date. I was sitting on her bed watching and simply blurted the disgusting story. Mother stood rock still, clutching her throat to muffle guttural groans, and staring at me with widened eyes that spoke of her own horror. When I had finished, she rushed to the bed and pulled me into her arms. We sat there rocking and crying.

I didn't beg her not to tell my father about the cause of my unhappiness, but I know she did. He never mentioned it to me. I'm sure the devastation he felt was as deep as my own, and he suffered from the same malady I had. If the words weren't spoken aloud, maybe what happened to his oldest daughter wasn't real. For a gentleman who was raised in England, the subject matter wasn't suitable for mixed company.

Slowly, I started to create a new life. It began with eating less and losing some of the excess weight. Over time, the girl in the mirror appeared quite attractive. I was older and wiser and felt better equipped to face society again. Laughter burst forth from my lips with welcome sounds. My social life was more enjoyable, and I found it easier to chat with young men without drawing into my former shell.

Family friends in Beverly Hills, the Riches, hired me to create and address the invitations for their Parisian-themed party. It promised to be a fabulous event. My father's orchestra would provide the music, of course, and Mother and my siblings would be there.

By now, I had met someone and invited him to be my escort for the evening. Dressed in a French-inspired silk brocade cocktail dress with a stylish full skirt that emphasized the narrowness of my waist, I felt truly lovely and accepted his compliments with a mixture of nervousness and grace.

The Riches had gone all out to ensure every guest had fun. They had life-sized, circus-style boards of a man and a woman in the Parisian fashion of the early Twenties, with cutouts to insert your face for a photographed remembrance of the party. The tent was filled with maroon balloons and the waiters presented wonderful French appetizers as a prelude to a dinner menu that was sure to be memorable. I greeted friends and their parents with some of the delight I'd seen my mother exhibit at such functions for many years.

Then, the lights dimmed and the music began; Daddy and his orchestra started to play the lively French can-can, revived to popularity with the 1954 French production of a musical by that name everyone applauded. Then the backdrop drapery rolled back and out came five beautiful can-can dancers, high-kicking in time to the music. They were dressed in the 1890's style with the long skirts, layers of petticoats, and black stockings held up with visible garters. They swished their skirts while kicking and gyrating suggestively. My escort pulled me through the assemblage of cheering party guests to reach the area closer to the stage. I remembered reading in an art history book that the famous painter Toulouse Lautrec had once described the dance as "La vie est belle, voila le quadrille!" Life is beautiful; here comes the can-can!

Grinning and clapping with everyone else, I glance at Daddy and he winked at me. He hadn't said a word to any of us about this wonderful surprise. When I turned back to enjoy the dancers, my breath was literally snatched from me. I felt instantly faint and my legs threatened to buckle under me. It can't be, I thought. This isn't happening.

She was the middle dancer. The bodice of her tight costume revealed the voluptuousness of her breasts. I could see hints of her bleached blonde hair under the edges of the black wig styled in vintage fashion. It was that girl. The friend of JD. The same girl who had assisted him in locking me in her bedroom while she performed her real specialty. Not dancing. Not modeling. Sex acts.

I was almost blinded by the flashbacks of the most horrifying night in my life. I was back in that room, a prisoner and victim of unwanted and unexpected sexual assault. The rest of the evening was spoiled for me. My escort asked me repeatedly what was wrong. "I must have eaten something that didn't agree with me" I said. "Would you mind taking me home?"

Within the next twenty-four hours, I lost control once again and restarted the cycle of self-punishment. I couldn't look in a mirror. I dreaded having to leave the house. Would I run into her again? Had she recognized me? Had she told JD she'd seen me at the party? Would he start calling me again?

At a time like this, I couldn't think logically. She was the one with the problem, not me, I reminded myself. It didn't matter. I started to eat again. Mindless eating of anything within an arm's reach. It was safer to be plump than a drug addict or alcoholic. Hollywood and Beverly Hills had enough of them and none ever seemed happy.

Once again, I buried myself in my painting and even opened my own studio. I entered art shows and contributed to a few group exhibits in galleries on La Cienega Boulevard.

All the while, I kept up the food compulsion and my dating celibacy.

One day, the stove in my studio kitchen wasn't working right. I smelled gas. I called the gas company and asked for someone to check the gas line for a possible leak. A repairman arrived a couple hours later, and I took him into the small kitchen adjacent to the workroom. When I was working on a project, I didn't bother with makeup and usually wore my customary artist's smock, which covered a lot of sins. I was frumpy. I knew it. The girl in the mirror reminded me of that every morning. But I didn't care.

The repairman kept looking at me from the sides of his eyes, while he asked questions about the stove and gas smell, and I felt my skin crawl.

He worked on the stove, keeping me in the room by continually inquiring about how long I had noticed the gas smell and if the stove flames ever fluttered when I lit it. I wanted to return to the larger space of the studio and wait, but remained rooted in place to answer the questions. Suddenly, he stood up and put his arm around me. I sank to the floor and sobbed, begging him to leave me alone. This stranger looked at me and backed off, visibly frightened by my reaction. "I'll have the company send you the invoice," he said as he fled from the kitchen. He was gone before I ever rose from my knees.

Once again, I felt worthless. What was wrong with me? I shouldn't have stayed in the tiny kitchen. Because I hadn't left immediately for my studio, I gave the impression I enjoyed the repairman's company. I spent the day hunched over my art table feeling miserable. Seeing the psychiatrist again wouldn't reveal anything I didn't already know. I had failed him, too.

I started to take over-the-counter diet pills, tired of the constant feast or famine battle I fought. Despite taking the pills, I lost the incentive to do anything but feast.

My artist endeavors were my saving grace. An increasing number of my paintings sold and I continued to exhibit at various art shows. I was doing the best I could, never losing faith; but, the demands of my family were disheartening and it was difficult to look put together and act normal around them. They saw me as a daughter, sister, niece, cousin with numerous talents, but not seeming to mature into a self-confident adult. My life was unstructured and risky. And I wasn't completely self-sufficient. Although I had seen Mother scrimp to get by during the war years, I was too young to think about budgets and paying utility bills and saving to buy myself a car. I was still basically living on the generosity of my father and pretending at being independent.

I was plagued with questions about my capabilities. Maybe I wasn't cut out to be a working artist. Maybe I wasn't good enough to earn acclaim. Maybe my problem was that I didn't want acclaim; then my name wouldn't appear in the newspapers and JD and that girl wouldn't see it. Maybe I wasn't charging enough for the work I managed to sell. Maybe I charged too much. Maybe I should get a studio in a better part of town. What if I did and no one ever entered the doorway and word spread that I wasn't any good? Should I paint like Renoir, El Greco, Picasso or Jackson Pollack? Did buyers prefer landscapes, cityscapes, a still life of fruit or flowers, or just colors thrown at a canvas with no definable object? Should I paint what art critics raved about in articles, or stick to what I enjoyed?

I yearned for solutions. My friends were busy with their own lives and I was too private to discuss my personal problems with them anyway. Pretending was practiced to an art form in Hollywood. Many evenings, I'd lie on my bed and read. One day, I read T. S. Eliot's 1915 poem *"The Love Song of J. Alfred Prufrock*," and several lines spoke directly to me:

> *There will be time, there will be time*
> *To prepare a face to meet the faces that you meet;*
> *There will be a time to murder and create,*
> *And time for all the works and days of hands*
> *That lift and drop a question on your plate.*

For at least that moment, I pinned my hope on those lines. Good things come to those who wait. I would meet my Prince Charming and feel safe in his presence. I would improve my painting skills and welcome publicity and accolades. Patience would bring solutions to all my questions.

Mural I painted in sister Sandra's house

9

A FEW WEEKS later, I was introduced to a young man, Alan Ferber who instantly reminded me of George Segal, the actor; they shared similar blond hair, great smiles and infectious laughs. As a potential suitor, however, I wasn't drawn to him. There was no spark. No subconscious reaction of flirtatiousness on my part to capture his interest in me.

No one was more surprised than I was when he had me laughing within the next five minutes. Spontaneous laughter that felt good. I loved to laugh and hadn't found anything worth the effort for a long time. Encouraged and enjoying my response, Alan remained at my side, putting me at ease with his witty repartee. I responded in kind, and before long, he had chipped away at the wall of self-protection that usually kept me on edge in public, especially when left alone with a man of any age.

Alan suggested lunch, then another. Quite rapidly, we became friends. We walked areas of Beverly Hills, and I found myself chattering about my life as a daughter of a well-known orchestra leader and about my career goals as a budding artist. He seemed to care about me and listened without censure to my confessions of public shyness and insecurity regarding my looks, body shape and weight. He even sent me to Meryl Norman for skin treatments. He ordered for me in restaurants to ensure I was eating healthy foods and in proportions that would help me lose weight. Soon, he was selecting clothing that would flatter my figure and coloring.

In other words, Alan slowly gained control of my life. I depended upon his gentle candor and relaxed way of facing the world and didn't object. I wanted—needed—someone to care enough to shower me with the attention I had craved all my life. I was twenty-one and ready for "a steady" date.

If I knew then what I know today, I would have recognized this wasn't a healthy relationship for me. It took away the need for me to make my own decisions. But, I felt safe with Alan, and safety while in the company of a handsome man was essential. Besides, I received verbal and tacit approval from family members and friends, who were already thinking of wedding bells.

Over the next three years of off and on dating, Alan and I became close friends; then he began to court me with flowers and more personal attention. He hugged and kissed me, tenderly, not passionately. All the while, he kept saying, "Carol, there's something I have to tell you." This went on for months.

Alan was not a very demonstrative man. Although this was one reason I felt so secure in his presence, my need to know why outweighed our maintaining an unspoken understanding. That's when I had an "aha" moment. On our very next date, I approached the subject hesitantly. "Alan, I think I know what you've been trying for weeks to tell me. You . . . you like men. You know. In that way."

The look on his face told me he was startled at my boldness and yet relieved. "Yes, Carol," he said, fighting for the right words. "You're right. I have been struggling with the urges for years and only a few people know this about me. It may seem as strange to you as it does to me, but I have fallen in love with you and want very much to marry you, if you'll have me. I believe we have something quite special. We're good for each other. I enjoy being with you and talking with you. My life would seem empty without you in it."

Still naïve about human behavior, those last few words lit up a very dark hole in my soul. Alan was the total opposite of most young men in my dating circles. I rationalized that if he were a latent homosexual and he loved me, I obviously had the ability to change his conduct. At the very least, he was unlikely to cheat on me with other women. He understood what I had been through with John Doe, and had been compassionate, thoughtful and helpful in restoring my self-confidence. His loving attentiveness had also changed my public image to one of being desirable, and this stemmed the tide of negativity from members of my family and those in their societal circles.

Alan had found a bird with a broken wing and set about to heal it. I was now hopping about, but not quite confidently enough to fly on my own. I was flattered by his continual complements and impressed with the details his rapt attention encompassed. Soon, I fell in love, and within weeks, Alan formally proposed. We were officially engaged. Within a week, we had set a wedding date, and my excitement grew along with that of my mother and every relative eager to participate in some meaningful way. Even Uncle Moe.

Alan's mother, Edna Ferber (not the author), had attended so many showers and weddings of her friends' children that she welcomed every offer one of them made in way of payback. Although she never mentioned it, I believe she was enormously relieved to know her son would no longer be the target of gossip and unspoken innuendos. Five bridal showers produced a showroom of china and silver in the dining room of my parent's home.

Alan traveled up and down the California coast representing a menswear line. He was successful in this line of work and wrote me letters during his absence with enclosures of magazine pages illustrating dresses and suits he thought were perfect for me, noting why the style, shape and color would flatter my figure, hiding the least attractive areas. He would even suggest what accessories, if any, would enhance the outfit. I was grateful, of course, and more eager than ever to please him. I bought several of his choices. He noticed and praised me. I was the luckiest young woman in the world and very much in love.

When Alan was in town, we dined at a wide variety of restaurants and clubs and he watched everything I put in my mouth, even commenting casually on how much salt I used. I called it love. Today's young people call it OCD; enough articles have been published about obsessive-compulsive behavior to educate even the very young as to the visible symptoms that often demonstrate this disorder. Millions were avid fans of Adrian Monk, the brilliant ex-detective of the San Francisco Police Department, who not only suffered from OCD, but had 312 phobias that kept him housebound, unless the police chief needed his brilliant expertise on a murder case. The show, Monk, was on the air for eight seasons between 2009-2012.

I wasn't bothered by how obsessive Alan's behavior was towards me, because we were both people with obsessive tendencies. If anyone had observed us together and suggested that I should be furious about his make-over criticisms, I would have been offended and highly defensive. After all, I was twenty-four, an adult who knew my own mind.

We finalized our wedding plans amid great excitement. I was going to have the most gorgeous wedding money could provide, because it would involve

my father making a command performance. All of the people he had conducted business with over the years—from the florist, photographer, caterer, cake
baker, to the hotel management—were involved in producing a noteworthy
extravaganza. They bent over backwards to please both my mother and me
to ensure a fairytale wedding that would receive the finest reviews from every
newspaper. Beverly Hills and Hollywood thrived on favorable mention in the
gossip columns.

Every other week for the next couple months, I went for a fitting on my
gown. I was on a rigid diet now, determined to look Vogue beautiful in my
exquisite lace and satin wedding dress, knowing that hundreds of eyes would
be on me. I would be the object of conversation the entire evening and later when photographs appeared in the newspapers. I posed for formal studio
photographs in advance and worried that I still wasn't able to live up to the
Hollywood image of a bride.

Betrothal Is Told To Friends

Mr. and Mrs. Barney Sorkin of West Los Angeles have announced the engagement of their daughter, Carol Elaine Sorkin, to Dan Ferber. Mr. Ferber is a son of Mr. and Mrs. Harry Ferber of Hollywood.

Miss Sorkin graduated from Beverly Hills High School and attended the Los Angeles Art Center and USC. The bridegroom-elect attended USC and was affiliated with Tau Epsilon Phi fraternity.

The couple's betrothal was told at a family party, given by the parents of the bride at their home. The wedding will take place this month.

Our wedding took place on July 27, 1958, in the Crystal Room of the Beverly
Hills Hotel with all the ambience, elegance and glitter expected of a princess. It
was a perfect setting for the beginning of a perfect new life as a wife. There were
over two hundred guests in attendance, dressed in their finest. Daddy's ten-piece
orchestra played the customary wedding songs, Gogi Grant sang for us, and my

bridesmaids carried bouquets of water lilies to match their gorgeous blue dresses. I was bursting with happiness as the blushing bride and my husband-to-be was as handsome and charismatic as Prince Charming. The hotel management gifted us with an engraved silver cake cutter to commemorate the occasion. It still occupies space in my silver flatware drawer, but is never used.

As expected, photographs of the wedding appeared in the local papers and became the talk of the town the next morning by those who attended the gala and those who wished they had been included on the guest list. Mother saved copies for me to occupy pages in my new white leather albums. I was now Carol Sorkin Ferber. A married woman who could decorate her own house in her own style and entertain guests of her own choosing. The thought of how I could accomplish this without the input of my husband never occurred to me.

Every member of my extended family attended the wedding. Since the ceremony took place in July, the dress code for men was white jacket and black pants. There isn't a man of any age who doesn't look spectacular in this attire. Thankfully, the Beverly Hills Hotel was air conditioned in 1958!

Alan and me at our wedding reception

My beautiful dress

Newlyweds Take Cruise To Far East

Following a wedding ceremony and reception in Crystal Room of Beverly Hills Hotel, Mr. and Mrs. Alan Ferber left for a honeymoon tour of Hawaii and the Orient.

The former Carol Elaine Sorkin, daughter of Mr. and Mrs. Barney Sorkin, selected a Cahill gown of Chantilly lace over pleated silk organza for her marriage to the son of Mr. and Mrs. Harry Ferber.

She was attended by Sandra Sorkin, her sister, and Mrs. Jeanne Hiller. Ferber's best man was Donald Slate. The bride attended UCLA, USC and L. A. Art Center. Ferber was graduated from USC and is a member of Tau Epsilon Phi.

Returning from an extended cruise, the couple will divide time between homes in San Francisco and Los Angeles.

The morning after our marriage, Alan and I flew to Hawaii. During our honeymoon at the Hilton Head Resort, he continued on his campaign to remake me. Every morning, my breakfast consisted of plain sunny-side up egg on a plate decorated with orchids to make it seem more enticing and even romantic. We walked the beaches, danced to the hulas, and attended a luau. It rained for an hour or so almost every day, but we utilized these brief interludes to shop in the hotel mall and discuss the best location for our first home and the style home we liked best.

The ocean was so blue and clear against the breaking waves and skyline; the panorama inspired me to buy canvas, oils and brushes so I could paint my version of it and of Diamond Head Mountain in the distance. While I painted, Alan went off by himself. I didn't question his whereabouts or activities, because he always returned with flowers or a gift or a suggestion for our next adventure on the island.

Each night, Alan offered his opinions regarding which of my honeymoon outfits worked best for me and why or why not. He advised me on which dress made me look thinner and how to wear my hair and makeup. He'd tuck an orchid in my hair, or a lovely tuberose blossom that has a beautiful scent much like that of a gardenia. Before dinner, a fresh Micronesian ginger lei would arrive, often braided into a work of art more spectacular and fitting than any necklace of gems.

The magnificence of the Hawaiian vistas and the romance of these gestures obliterated any budding feelings of resentment over the earlier judgments about my flaws. We traveled home to Los Angeles by ship with my three-by-four-foot Diamond Head painting crowded into our small cabin space. It was a five-day journey, and I luxuriated in the pampering offered by an attentive staff. And Alan. We both looked forward to our new life together and laughed often over even ridiculously inane things.

We drove to San Francisco to establish our first residence, not only because it made sense as a base for Alan's sales territory, but because the ocean and mountains and 'old city' grandeur created endless stimuli for an artist. I visited every hardware store along the way. I love gadgets and some of my favorite haunts are those containing aisles of them. It was an exciting venture and I gave it my full attention, producing pages of sketches of what I envisioned for various rooms. Alan, of course, believed he knew all about wall and fabric colors and interior decorating and took great joy in planning even the most minute details for our new home, usually overriding my viewpoint. He seemed to forget I was a talented painter with a palette of color and my own vision of my first home as Mrs. Ferber.

I tolerated Alan's obsessive behavior, because I felt he genuinely wanted a wife, friend and lover. To our delight, we had a healthy sex life. His business territory as a clothing representative grew to reach most of California, and we traveled up and down the coastline, enjoying the time alone between his meetings with clients.

We ended up purchasing a charming home on Cloud View Road in Sausalito that overlooked the San Francisco Bay. Situated near the northern end of the Golden Gate Bridge, it had become a shipbuilding center in WWII, but quickly developed into an enclave for the wealthy and artistic in postwar years. If I couldn't be happy in such a gorgeous place, there was no place on earth for Carol Sorkin Ferber!

Surrounded by so much inspiration, I filled my time at home painting murals throughout the home, which I kept immaculate in case we had 'drop by' visitors. By now, I knew Mrs. Ferber senior quite well, and it pleased her to find even my cupboards well organized. I was proud of our home and enjoyed entertaining, even if it was a neighbor for morning coffee or afternoon tea.

Alan traveled so much, it became difficult to know where he was and for how many days. It wasn't long before I learned he was a regular at the bath houses in San Francisco. I could tell when such a visit would occur, because he would become sullen and withdrawn. He apologized profusely and promised to change, but his urges got the better of him. As a married man, he was now tattered by his guilt. Thankfully, AIDS was not yet prevalent, and I never had to deal with that concern. As his guilt grew, however, so did his tendency to judge and critique me. Praise for anything about me became scarce, despite what I did to support his business endeavors, the compliments given by family, friends and Sausalito neighbors on our home, my murals . . . whatever.

When our easy laughter had dried up and we began avoiding each other's eyes, we decided to see a marriage counselor; the counselor advised Alan to stop picking on me and accept me for exactly who I was. There would be more promises and more setbacks and more apologies. With the erosion of our marriage, I lost my appetite. Any excess weight I had left melted off my body, but despite looking as glamorous as Alan had dreamed of my becoming, he was now afraid I would put the weight back on and started on a new line of critiquing me.

When I was spending more time in tears or in staring out at the Bay or in pretending to be asleep when Alan got home, I gave up and called my father to come rescue me. He immediately flew to San Francisco and hired a cab to drive him to Sausalito. I left Alan a note that I was leaving him, but didn't mention my destination. I packed some clothes and a few of my belongings, took my adorable white Westie, Mr. Boo, and drove back to Los Angeles in my black and white Rambler with Daddy by my side.

Alan was devastated. He called everywhere to find me. I didn't care whether or not he would be worried about me. I wanted some peace. What surprised me most was how long it had taken me to understand that our marriage was doomed from the beginning. Torn between two worlds, Alan would never be capable of loving me for me. As long as we were only friends, he had been able to have a relationship with me. But marriage had made him feel both guilty and trapped.

He flew down to Los Angeles and we met again, but our discussions got nowhere fast. "Nothing will change, Alan," I said, finding it easier to assert myself than ever before in our relationship. "This is as painful to me as it seems to be for you. But, Alan, I have so much more inside to give to and share with my lifetime partner, and I want a chance to prove that. You can't offer me such an opportunity. I will feel incomplete."

Even in those days, divorces could get messy when money and property were involved. Ours required a hearing in court months after our separation before the final divorce papers could be signed. Still young and naïve about such things, I was shocked when Alan declared I was such a messy housekeeper it was impossible for him to ever bring home business cohorts or friends. Mother muttered "what utter, nonsensical slander" under her breath several times, and I found my eyes stinging from unshed tears as the hearing progressed. At only twenty-six years of age, I found it surreal that I was in court having to defend my integrity. I was painted in the most derogatory terms, but not once did I bring up Alan's homosexuality being the problem in our marriage, to protect him against gossip in the workplace and with his clients . . . and just in case his parents didn't know for certain.

In the course of our short marriage, Alan's parents and I had become co-owners of a men's store in Azusa, California. I didn't feel I should share in any of this business, as it wouldn't have been fair to them. This was their lifetime dream, and I was happy about its fulfillment for them. The actions of their son shouldn't wipe away this dream.

However, the rest of the settlement I found most unfair. Fortunately, I had sold my diamond wedding ring to buy a good attorney. Upon hearing my story, he said, "Well, Carol, what you should have is a recording of the statements that aren't true." I didn't know he was joking.

One of my dearest lifelong friends, Gerry Goldstein, became my willing accomplice and drove me to Azusa. With instructions from my sister's husband Charles, he explained how to conceal a microphone under my dress and carry the small tape recorder in my purse. Well, small in terms of what such a piece of technology was in those days. When I walked into the store, I saw Alan's father behind the counter. He welcomed me with a forged smile. "I am so sorry I had to lie about everything in the hearing, Carol. I know you can understand how difficult it was for me and for Alan's mother. This has taken a great toll on us both."

Almost in the next breath, he shocked me with another confession. "It has been a long several months for us all, but Mrs. Ferber is thrilled that Alan has remarried."

"Alan has remarried?" I glanced at Gerry from the sides of my eyes and swallowed my astonishment before I could say more. California law required a newly divorced person to wait a full year before remarrying. Alan and I were not legally divorced.

I believe it was critically important for Alan to find a new bride. There were few openly gay or bisexual men in America in the 1950s; few outside

Hollywood knew that Rock Hudson was gay until he was dying from AIDS. I had never mentioned the subject in the hearing, but now, I hoped the news of his 'too early' marriage had been caught on tape so I could use this subject in court.

On Wednesday, June 29, 1960, I proceeded to make some sort of history. All of the California major newspapers carried the story of the "Wife Wired for Sound." The electronic age won me a second divorce trial. Needless to say, Alan was painted as a bigamist, and I became the recipient of a decidedly better settlement.

Winning this small victory gave me some satisfaction, but I couldn't deny the fact that my experience with men was having a far deeper effect on my psyche. Nibble by nibble, I returned to my lifelong habit of finding comfort in food, especially if it contained sugar.

Wife Wired for Sound

Wins New Divorce Trial

—Herald-Express Photo

WINS NEW DIVORCE TRIAL—'WIRE TO WIRE'
Carol Ferber, 26, Shows Electronic Recorder She Used When Mate's Father Told of Previous Trial

The electronic age won a new divorce trial for 26-year-old Carol Ferber today, all because she was wired for sound when she talked to her father-in-law last month.

Carol charged there were irregularities in the divorce trial before Superior Judge Arthur Crum in April, and to prove it, she brought to court a tape recording of a conversation with Harry Ferber, Azusa clothing store owner, and father of Carol's husband Alan, 29.

The older Ferber admitted departures from the truth in his testimony on behalf of his son, according to Carol's attorney, Bernard B. "Bunny" Cohen, who asked and obtained teh order for the new trial. Judge Crum had granted both the husband and wife a divorce and equally divided some $50,000 worth of property.

MICROPHONE

Carol, daughter of society orchestra leader Barney Sorkin, said she secreted a tiny microphone in her dress and carried a recorder in her purse when she visited Harry Ferber last May 10 in Azusa.

"I even took a girl friend along to check to be sure the wire wasn't showing," explained Carol. She got a good recording, and the judge listened attentively as a voice identified as the father-in-law frankly admitted it was necessary to "create" grounds for divorce.

"But there were so many lies," Carol's voice protested.

"Sure, I admit it," the other voice replied, explaining they were only "white lies."

ALL AN ACT

On the tape, Carol also objected to her husband's witness-stand statement, "I'd like to cut her out like a cancer." Her father-in-law, commenting on this, purportedly said:

"That was an act. The whole thing was an act. It was an act to get the thing over with. . . ."

The elder Ferber revealed on the tape his son had remarried, even though there was no final divorce.

Carol's parting shot on the tape was: "All's fair in love and war. We battled, and I'll be seeing you."

However, neither of the Ferbers was in court for the new trial motion, which Judge Crum granted with the remark that Harry Ferber "virtually stuck his foot in his mouth."

The court ordered the recording impounded in the county clerk's safe to be available for any future proceedings, and though the word "perjury" was freely used by both court and counsel during today's hearing, no prosecution at the moment was suggested.

DOMESTIC WOES—Artist Carol Ferber as she appeared for court hearing to complain that her car had been repossessed due to divorce troubles. —Times photo

10

The artist is nothing without the gift, but the gift is nothing without work.

—EMILE ZOLA *(1840-1902)*

DESPITE THE MIXTURE of feelings that came with the final signing of my divorce, the financial settlement was enough for me to consider a trip to Italy for advanced study of art. After several months of preparation for this adventure, I felt psychologically ready to embark upon uncharted territory and actually looked forward to a change in environment and less introspection about my problems and shortcomings.

One thing I knew. I had been blessed with an artistic eye and the ability to translate what I saw onto canvas or some other medium. Having talent didn't mean what I produced could pay the rent, however. I needed an improved knowledge of art history, the techniques of the greats, and the development of a painting passion and discipline that goes with commercial success.

Dupsey encouraged me to accept the challenge. "You'll never have such an opportunity again, Carol. You're single and can go anywhere you want. If you stay here, you'll find a million things to distract you, and if things don't go as well as you'd like, you've got a dozen relatives ready to make decisions for you. In Rome, every decision is yours. If you decide to come home sooner, rather than later, you'll be welcomed with open arms, but you'll be wiser and stronger and know whether or not a career in art in what you really want."

As most parents are, regardless of the age of their children, mine were concerned about whether it was prudent for a young woman to travel alone to Europe. While they supported my stated goals, they had several reservations, some expressed through only raised eyebrows and sighs. When Paris, a Greek friend, declared he had been planning a trip to Europe and would accompany me on the same flights to Rome and take me under his wing, as it were, their concerns lessened. So did mine.

There were no Concorde's in 1961, and I had not flown from one continent to another. The thought of a long plane flight over a deep and wide ocean gave me the heebie-jeebies. Not even the thought of what my ancestors on both sides of the family had endured on their travels from Russia to the United States via ships brought satisfactory encouragement.

Paris put forth his best argument about my accepting the inevitable. "Flying everywhere on the continent and just about anywhere in the world has become the preferred way of travel for those in business and the jet set, Carol. Think about it! Your father flies with his band to gigs on the East Coast and has for more than a decade, and most of Hollywood's stars and Beverly Hills people of means travel the world for public appearances or vacations."

"Yes, but—"

"For heaven's sake, Carol, Pam Am has been flying its Boeing 707 on nonstop flights to and from New York since 1957 and to both London and Paris since 1958. So has TWA. I thought we'd take a nonstop flight to New York and then a transatlantic fight directly to Rome. It's either that or a flight over the North Pole to London, a nineteen-hour flight from LA. The jaunt from here to New York will take about nine hours and we can stretch our legs a little before the ten-hour flight to Rome. What have you got to worry about anyway? I'll be right by your side."

"Remember what happened to Amelia Earhart?"

His look was blank for several seconds. "Wasn't she the first woman to pilot a plane over the Atlantic?"

I nodded. "She's been a role model since I read about her in school. She accomplished dozens of firsts and earned well-deserved fame, but that wasn't enough for her. She wanted to be the first person to fly around the world at the equator. No one, not even a male pilot, had accomplished this feat. Despite all her years of experience involving hundreds of flights, her plane went down in the Pacific Ocean."

Paris shook his head. "That plane was what? A two-seater, one-propeller model? Times have changed since we were toddlers in the Thirties. We're flying in the jet age. And, by the way, if Earhart is such a role model, why don't you develop some of her gumption? And what has being a pilot got to do with being an artist anyway?"

"Amelia wanted recognition in what was a man's world, Paris. It still is, you know. A man's world. Especially in art. Other than Mary Cassatt and Kate Greenway from the 19th century and Georgia O'Keeffe from the 20th century, does the name of any other female artist come to mind and fall trippingly off your tongue?"

Paris peered up at the ceiling while thinking. "Not a one."

"There you go. That's my new goal. Not to become world famous or even nationally famous, but to see if I have what it takes to buck the system and become respected for my talent in the art world and hired by more than my Uncle Moe to produce works of art. If I work at it, you might visit a museum someday in the future and see one of my works."

Once aboard the Boeing 707, in March of 1961, I set aside my unfounded fears, chalking them up to being more nervous about whether or not I could achieve my goals without an immediate backup system of family and friends. The plane had four jet engines—a couple right outside our window—but it was reasonably quiet and Paris and I could hear ourselves talk.

Although we had almost twenty hours in the air and had to sit perfectly upright most of the time, we still dressed as though we were attending an important business meeting; Paris wore a suit and tie, as did every man onboard, and I wore as comfortable a dress as possible to coordinate with my heels, purse and hat. Yes, hat. Women still wore hats and gloves and girdles in the early sixties, for the sake of fashion, convention and modesty. There were no pantyhose or Spanx. Garters in the girdles were necessary to hold up hosiery, and hosiery was also a must. Women suffered in silence.

Long before we reached the New York International Airport—or Idlewild, as it was known until renamed the John F. Kennedy in 1963 in honor of our 35th president—I was ready for pajamas and the ability to at least prop up my legs on a hassock. I had already kicked off my heels and could feel my feet and ankles swell with edema from inactivity. If I rested my head on Paris's shoulder, I could tuck up my legs under me and share a blanket. That was one advantage of being genetically short.

Paris's reason for traveling abroad was similar to mine; only it involved acting. With a face like "Adonis" and a body to match Paris should have no problem. He loved performing and was determined to live his dream life by becoming a movie star. He thought he'd have a better chance in European films. I enjoyed his company and became increasingly grateful for his willingness to be my travel companion. Especially after his pronouncement to my parents that he'd help me find a safe apartment suitable for a painting 'studio' as well as a bedroom—one with basic comforts, a private bathroom, and a location that was within walking distance of a grocery store and other shops and restaurants.

My hope was that Paris would hang around until I had familiarized myself to my immediate surroundings and to what Rome had to offer for someone with my limited experience in anything 'foreign.' That being said, Paris was a suave young man with plans of his own, and they came first. Shortly after we landed in Rome, he hugged me, wished me well and took off. I found myself totally alone, unable to speak or understand Italian, with no place to live and no friends to call for help.

"You'll do fine, Carol," he said, when my eyes filled with tears. "Go to that bank up ahead of us and exchange some U.S. dollars for lira. The teller will be able to speak English. Ask for apartment suggestions in the area of Rome you've marked up in your Fodor's travel guide for Italy. Get it in writing and show it to a cab driver. You can do this. And if it would make you feel better, spend a day at a downtown hotel. The concierge will provide all the information you need. Oh, and by the way, this airport is about twenty miles from Rome. Most passengers will take busses to the train station. I think it's better for you to take a taxi . . . so be sure to get enough lira to pay cash."

The first Italian word I learned—other than pizza, spaghetti, lasagna, and vino, which I already knew—was scoozi, after someone bumped into me on the way to the luggage department. I assumed it meant "excuse me" and used it countless times in the coming weeks, because Paris's unexpected desertion was the first of several disasters. At least to me. For instance, my shoe heel broke as I scurried to find that bank. I stood in the middle of the terminal with the heel in my hand muttering scoozi to everyone while gesturing with my free hand to learn if there was a shoe repair shop in the terminal. What was I thinking! Fortunately, I had tucked a few pair of shoes in my luggage and could make an exchange.

With the assistance of several kind strangers and my Fodor's travel book's useful phrases section, I found a pensione (boarding house) on Via Emilia Ochento Uno. I don't know if it still exists, but I do remember it was across the street from a nightclub, certainly not the greatest location, but it had the space I needed and a few amenities I thought I couldn't do without, like the private bathroom. It became my temporary home away from home.

After getting settled and strolling up and down a few blocks in each direction, I learned what was available to me. A week later, I realized taking bus tours of the city or walking was too limiting. I was completely enchanted with the old city and wanted to explore regions on my own. It was difficult to comprehend that Rome was well over two-thousand years old. The United States was a mere toddler in comparison.

My sense of freedom was definitely curtailed without a car. It didn't take much to convince myself that I needed one. Off I went to buy one. First, however, I called home for fatherly advice.

"Hire an attorney to go with you, Carol," Daddy said. "If you have to, call the U.S. embassy for a recommendation. You want an honest broker who can communicate with you in English and translate accurately. An Italian attorney will take you to his uncle or cousin. Set a limit on what you'll spend. No deals of a lifetime. They usually aren't. Stick with an Italian-made model in case it ever needs repairs. Garages are more likely to have parts or be able to get them quicker than those for foreign vehicles. And Carol, you'll need an

International driver's license. Find a nearby automobile club. The license is good for one year."

I followed Daddy's advice and learned from my attorney, who could speak quite fluent English, that to buy a car in Italy, I had to produce my passport and driver's license, but also a certificate of residence from Los Angeles. Fortunately, one of my well-traveled friends at Beverly Hills high school had informed me of this, and I had one tucked into my billfold.

I still ended up with a gorgeous 1957 silver Lancia Aurelia with tan leather interior, fancy wheels and a stick shift. Of course it was a "deal" and "a real steal." But how could any young, recently divorced and ready-to-try-out-her-wings in a foreign country lady resist such a beauty? I paid in lira, sat through a laborious explanation about the licensing, ownership papers, the rules of the road, the importance of the car horn, and off I went.

For most of the next few days, I drove for miles while taking in the beauty of the country, which was more mountainous than I had expected. If only digital cameras and smartphones had been invented in the sixties. Mine would have become an appendage to a hand because around every corner I saw the view as though on canvas and wished I could snap pictures or call home.

It wasn't long before I made my first friend, Pino, the shortened version of Giuseppino. We met quite by accident over the telephone, where his job as an overseas telephone operator meant he handled most of my calls to California family and friends. Eventually, he billed me for less time, resulting in more calls at more reasonable rates. "Bravo, Signorina Carolina," he would say with each progress I made in my new life. Actually, he called me Carolina Zucchini, and that is how I gave my name when meeting many new Italians. Too many of them pronounced my surname as Sorkini. They knew zucchini. Pino's other job was translating Beatles' music into Italian, or as he called the world famous English band, Beatalas. To this day, I consider him a blessing in my life. He was a dear, gentle, and kind man, exactly what I needed while in Rome. I imagine he is now translating for Michael Jackson and Elvis in heaven.

The evening hours were the most difficult for me from the very first night I spent alone in my apartment. Rome came to life after dark. The nightclub's music, live or recorded, kept on relentlessly until three o'clock in the morning. I imagine that's why my room was so reasonably priced for its size. Since its windows faced the street, I spent what seemed like hours watching people come and go until I was so tired; I could have fallen asleep to trumpets blaring right next to my bed. I love the music of Italy, but after midnight it became less enjoyable and more annoying.

Nevertheless, I came to enjoy the location of my pensione and met some fascinating people. Aggravating ones, too. Italians are opinionated and verbal and argumentative about anything for which they hold strong beliefs or feelings. I had strong beliefs, too, but usually withheld them, still hung up on my need to be liked and at least included in group conversation as a good listener. In the back of mind lurked the theme of The Ugly American, a book about American arrogance that became internationally successful in 1958. I did not want anyone to put me in that category. I had also learned in less than a week that Italy was a masculine society where toughness and assertiveness were signs of machismo. Paternalism ruled; few women worked outside the home, and just like in my home, were in charge of cleaning, cooking and child raising. But, for all their blustery machismo, Italian men treated women with gallantry, at least in public. No one called me Carol until I gave them my permission. I was Signorina.

After wandering the halls of several galleries and art museums, I made the decision to become more adept at lithography. Although I was already familiar with the lithographs of several 19th century artists, like Goya, Degas, Van Gough, and Toulouse-Lautrec, it was those of 20th century artists that interested me most. In particular, those of Chagall, Dufy, Miro and, of course, Picasso. They were contemporaries. Well, at least they were still living and bringing prestige and acceptance to lithography as a fine art. I signed up for a class and bought my art supplies, eager to begin the preparation for my new career. I poured over books showing examples of those whose works I admired.

I was particularly interested in all works by Marc Chagall, because he was born in Vitebsk, Russia, the same as my father's parents. When they were already immigrating to the United States by ship, he was about ten years old.

During WWII, he fled to New York, and soon held his first retrospective at The Museum of Modern Art in 1946. By then, my family was already settled in Beverly Hills and Daddy was becoming renowned as a band and orchestra leader. Chagall was a prolific artist and one of my favorites all through the sixties and seventies while I was struggling to make a name for myself locally. In fact, Chagall received national coverage in newsprint and also on television in 1964 when he created a window for the United Nations building in New York, and again in 1967, for several murals for the Metropolitan Opera House, also in New York.

It didn't take long for me to realize I would not accomplish much in a classroom with other artists. As I said, the art world in 1961 was still mostly male-dominated, and Italian men had a penchant for flirting with anyone wearing a skirt. As soon as I took out my drawing pad, I would hear a chorus of "pssts" from the closest pests. Honestly, I found it exciting and flattering and fun those first few days, but I was still too bruised from my relationship with Alan to encourage a new one. Plus, there was the language barrier. I had a long way to go in that regard. I preferred to wait until I could understand what these male artists said to each other about me, after they learned I was practically illiterate in Italian.

Within two weeks, however, I had made a couple artist friends who weren't interested in whistling, winking, blowing kisses, pinching or in any other way bothering me. Once I had learned the process of lithography, they suggested I work at my apartment and find an artist agent to represent my finished prints. This wasn't an easy task, but by the time I had moved all my setup to the pensione, I found a renewed eagerness to improve my craft and produce enough lithographs of sufficient quality to sell for a profit. I used the traditional specially prepared limestone for the surface of each of my images, which I drew and painted directly on the stone, trying out various lithographic pencils, tusche sticks and paste or pens.

I limited myself to using only one to three colors, because the process for color lithography is so complex; I fully understood that it was based on the fact that oil repels water, which is why I used the 'greasy' tusche products. The images I created with these special inks or crayons would repel the water applied to the stone by the printer and then accept the oil-based ink colors. I kept things simple, too, because it was clear to me that I still lacked full knowledge of color theory and multiple pressings or multiple stones for each color. If I kept my designs uncomplicated, but creative and in my unique style, I would produce better results.

While I was creating my pictures on the stones, I stopped off a couple times each week to watch the printmaker at Il Ticolotore make several impressions of other artists' work before suggesting a collaboration with me for mine. He was careful and accomplished as he went through the wetting, inking and pressing the stone for each lithograph; it didn't matter if a particular piece was only in shades of black and gray, or if it had several vivid colors and shading effects that utilized separate stones for each color. Always, the artist was present. Again, we had the language barrier, but Italians talk with their hands and I was able to communicate adequately enough to enjoy the conversations.

This work-at-home arrangement wasn't ideal, but satisfactory in that I could measure my daily progress. In no time at all, I had a few pieces that earned my personal approval. My sweet landlady often showed her neighbors and friends my work, and on more than one occasion, I returned from a shopping trip or excursion for more art supplies to find a bouquet of roses protruding from the bidet "from an admirer," my landlady would say, her eyes sparkling.

I finally took my first couple stones to Il Ticolotore creating only ten copies, because that was all I could afford. With great hope and crossed fingers, I signed and numbered the copies and mailed one of each lithograph to Associated American Artists in New York. After creating a lithograph, the stone is always destroyed, but I kept and still have one of the originals.

It took me a while to adapt to the customs and pace of life. Wine was served like water, not vintage, but varieties suitable for daily drinking at home. Not only was paying for things in lira rather than dollars confusing, every minute away from my work seemed to take longer than I had expected. It was difficult to make myself understood and to understand Italians from every walk of life and with different accents (just as a Texan might have difficulty understanding the accent of those from Brooklyn or New Jersey and vice versa). Most talked too fast.

In the meantime, I was continually getting lost in the city, and my beautiful Lancia Aurelia was misbehaving. I would find myself driving in the middle of traffic and my supposedly fast and easy-to-operate car would come to an unscheduled stop. I learned to keep an empty wine bottle in the car in case I needed to run to a fountain for water to pour water over the radiator. When my horn went out in the middle of a shopping center, it created a calamity. A horn is an absolute necessity in Italy; almost as much as the petrol. I learned to shout back at other irritated drivers who were repeatedly honking at me, "Niente claca . . . no horn!"

I saw all of the famous Seven Hills of Rome several times while being lost. And I kept parking in bus zones and eventually received a warrant for my arrest unless I paid my fines. Italians consider your manner of dress important and judge you by your appearance. I chose my finest hat and fancy dress and went to visit the chief of police. After I had answered all his questions to the best of my ability and fluttered my eyelashes a few times, he tore up my tickets and asked if I would like to have lunch with him. Sometimes it works being a woman in Italy; at least it did for me. Many of the men who ogled women were married, however, and that knowledge kept me on guard. To my surprise, I was never pinched on my rear end until I reached New York.

My friends back home assumed I would have a mad and passionate affair while in Rome, but I didn't. Aside from constantly itching from some allergen in the air and always getting lost in translations, I found my life there both intriguing and memorable.

I waited and waited for what seemed like an eon to hear from the New York gallery. Of course, the mail system in Italy moved slower than the proverbial molasses in spring. Ordinary mail was expensive and my friends told me it often took two weeks for a letter to reach its destination in a nearby province, so I should be patient. To collect letters at the local post office, I had to produce proof of identity and I went there daily to see if a special envelope had arrived.

Notice in the following four examples of lithographs how the use of color and detail evolved over the decades. Three of them were used as posters to advertise events or causes and the final one of the baby to create income for the artist. I would have loved to attain the skill of Charlotte Becker in her lithographs, but I could only produce such detail on canvas. I was young. I wanted everything to happen yesterday. Becoming really good at anything often requires years. And persistence. And more of that patience.

I will never forget the example set by Vincent Van Gogh. Recently, one of his paintings sold for $149.5 million at auction. He created more than 800 works of art in his lifetime. But here's the sticker: while he lived, he sold only one painting. One. And that was to a friend for mere pennies. Despite experiencing no other sales, Van Gogh never gave up.

Several of my most memorable experiences in Rome involved visits to the Sistine Chapel. On my first visit, I was utterly mesmerized. In awe. I had read The Agony and the Ecstasy about the process involved in painting the ceiling. The Hollywood movie of the book, starring Charlton Heston as Michelangelo and Rex Harrison as Pope Julius II, showed Michelangelo spending hours on his back while executing every brushstroke himself. I was told by artist friends that the design was, in reality, drawn on huge sections of canvas laid out on the floor and then measured into squares to get the proper perspective. Only when Michelangelo was satisfied was each piece hauled up a ladder to reach the floor of wooden scaffolding and positioned in place to see how it looked. Then the painting began and he spent the next four years of his life perched on this scaffolding with brush in hand.

According to A&E's History website, Michelangelo himself designed the wooden platforms of the scaffolds that would hold him and his assistants and "that allowed them to stand upright and reach above their heads." The

platforms were attached to the walls with brackets, which is why the very long ladder was needed to get them from the floor to their working level.

In reading about this magnificent work of art since my Rome experience, I have learned that Michelangelo considered himself a sculptor and wasn't interested in accepting the commission when it was offered to him. It evidently took considerable pressure to convince him it

was a worthier project than continuing with the sculptures for a Cardinal's eventual tomb.

When I visited St. Peter's Cathedral (St. Pietro Basilica), where Michelangelo's celebrated sculpture La Pieta is housed, I was fortunate enough to see it up close and observe the utter beauty of what many consider his greatest work of art. When no one was looking, I gently touched it and felt the smoothness of the marble. The details of Mary's youthful (rather than matronly) face as she held her dead son and of his totally limp body in her lap were so emotionally moving, it is impossible to ever forget. That someone could purposefully attack this masterpiece is unthinkable, but it happened in 1972, and now visitors to St. Peter's must view La Pieta from behind bullet-proof Plexiglas. This sculpture is the only work that Michelangelo ever signed; his signature is on the sash directly across the front of Mary. When I went back to Rome a few years ago and viewed the Pieta from a 50-ft. distance, I felt sad, it was not the same. The sculpture had been coated with a wax like finish and looked plastic.

If you like dates and historical time periods like I do, you may find it interesting to note that Michelangelo was in his twenties when he created La Pieta, finishing it in 1499. In 1492, Columbus left Spain to sail the Atlantic and "discovered" America when his ship veered off course. And I was there in Rome "finding myself" and learning more about art, artists and lithography, also in my twenties. I was certainly in the right place. According to UNESCO, more than forty percent of the world's great works of art are found in Italy.

Deciding a change in scenery would be good for me; I rented an apartment away from the heart of Rome and the nightclub, and began painting on canvas. By pure luck, I was accepted as a renter of the small apartment directly over that of my landlord's. The family lived and worked in the same building, which was not uncommon in Italy. Maria was a hardworking mother of an adorable son Genereno, who became the model for one of my next lithographs, which I again took to Il Ticolatore. The whole young family treated me like a member of theirs.

This was no small decision on their part. By now, I knew that Italians take their time getting to know strangers, regardless of where they were from. They never invite you into their home for even coffee, until they come to know you. They will invite you to have coffee or lunch or dinner in a café or restaurant first. Then, when you are trusted, you are accepted with open arms.

Despite the warmth of their friendship and hospitality, I grew increasingly anxious about my future as an artist and, finally, homesick. I decided to give up waiting for an answer from Associated American Artists and go home... "I'm going to leave Italy in a couple weeks, Maria," I told her one morning in early July. "I've been mulling over this decision for some time now and find myself eager to see family and friends again."

Two days before my departure, she gave me a going-away party. Because her family slept in the dining room, they had removed their beds and brought in a large table for a buffet. She invited a few neighbors and artist friends and others with whom I had developed a speaking relationship. It was one of the kindest and most selfless expressions of caring I had ever experienced and no one could ask for a more wonderful arrivederci Roma.

Those first three weeks of July were inordinately busy for me. There was a strange sound emanating from my auto. "Oh no not again", it was the final straw, my beautiful Lancia Aurelia became a pain in the neck and I sold my Lancia and bought a new, tan 1961 Valiant to be shipped to America. By now, my two most trusted artist friends and even Pino offered me advice on this choice. "I've read all about the Valiant," Pino said. "It's revolutionary. Not just a copy of what we produce in Italy in the smaller auto line. She's got great handling and enough soundproofing from the floor up to the roof to provide a quiet interior. She's got power and high-efficiency and grand style. Magnifico, Signorina Carolina."

There were other memories I brought home with me of my time in Rome. For instance, although it is petty, I thoroughly enjoyed and became addicted to my weekly hair salon appointments. It was easier to hire someone to take care of this need than for me to deal with the less than ideal circumstances of washing my hair in the apartment. The salons were not at all like the ones I'd visited in the United States. I didn't walk from the stylist's station to the sink; the sink rolled to me! Several of the apprentices weren't older than twelve, but completely dedicated to learning the trade.

I also marveled at the magical expertise of the seamstresses and tailors. I could select a pattern, type of fabric, and color choice one day, submit to a dozen measurements, and pick up the finished garment the next day. Obviously, a team of workers had spent the entire night on the project. And the sewing and fit was topnotch.

This photograph of me was taken during my stay in Rome, 1961, by Lawrence Montaigne, who went on to become a well-known film and television actor (perhaps most known for his role as Vulcan Stonn, a paramour of Spock's intended bride T'Pring, in the Star Trek episode "Amok Time," a role he reprised in 2006 in the unofficial mini-series Star Trek: Of Gods and Men), but who held many jobs before this success. Although he was born in New York, he was raised in Rome and learned several languages during his upbringing and education. This aptitude served him well when he returned to Europe in the late fifties, after experiencing disappointment with his film career, and found work in Rome dubbing Italian films into English. That's when I met him. He had also opened a small photography studio and freelanced as a photojournalist for Globe International.

Although I was in Rome for months, I became proficient enough in the Italian language to translate for incoming Americans. I left on the first Alitalia flight to London on July 28, 1961. When I arrived there, I had to take a plane to Madrid first to catch a flight to New York. Once I knew I was on home turf again, I wasn't interested in doing anything but board the next plane to Los Angeles. It was 1:00 a.m. the following morning when it taxied up to the terminal. Daddy was there to meet me; he had driven to the airport directly from one of his gigs. He plied me with questions all the way home, and I didn't mind one bit; for once, I had his rapt attention.

11

The greatest challenge is life is discovering who you are.
The second greatest is being happy with what you find.

NOT LONG AFTER I was back into the routine of life on the fast lane in
Beverly Hills, with lunches ,brunches ,teas and dinners where I was plied
with questions about my art study in Rome, I rented a studio on National
Boulevard in West Los Angeles and started to sell my work. I finally heard
from "Associated American Artists", they ended up purchasing One Hundred
Lithographs, and that were sent all around the world. How different my life
might have been had I heard from them while living in Rome-But I have
learned, Nothing by chance.

My friend Joan Jacobs introduced me to several artists who have become
well-known over the years. She was in love with Everett Ellin, who later became a curator for Guggenheim and various other museums, and their relationship offered her occasions to meet them and familiarize herself with their
work. She lived in a Bel Air cottage overlooking the Santa Monica Mountains
and had already started an impressive art collection. The walls of her cottage
had become a min-gallery. I looked forward to every opportunity to see what
new pieces she had acquired. For instance, I'd find an Andy Warhol next to a
Jasper Johns and my jaw would drop. She kept telling me, "Attend the shows
and buy pieces by these new artists, Carol. Trust me, they will be famous
someday and you'll see the value of what you collect go sky-high."

"First of all. Joanie," I said, "I can't afford even the lowest price, and
secondly, why would I want to buy a painting of soup cans or American
flags?" During this same period, I met Edward Kienholz, who was gaining

significant attention for his unique creations that depicted what he called the wreckage of our society and the debris or clutter generated by our man-made culture of excesses. Ed wasn't interested in following the more acceptable goals of the Pop Art movement. Rather, he wanted to get in our faces with works that revealed our inhumanity, racism, bigotry, or wastefulness. He created disquieting tableaus using castoffs and throwaway objects that were ugly and gauche. He acquired masses of negative reviews, but even critics, who declared his junk art vulgar, were fascinated to see his next work.

Occasionally, Ed and I worked on pieces together, and he gifted me with a sculpture of a coffee pot with a melted timer inside. He was responsible for some of the most outrageous and social statements of his time, yet he was a genuine, gentle bear. He drove a truck with EXPERT painted on it. In 1957, he and Walter Hopps started the famous Ferus Gallery in Los Angeles, which launched the careers of many notable local artists, but also East Coast artists, including Donald Judd, Frank Stella, Roy Lichtenstein, and Andy Warhol. In 1960, while I was in Rome, Ed had his first solo exhibition at Ferus.

On La Cienega Boulevard in Los Angeles, Barney's Beanery had been the hangout for anyone having to do with movies—film producers, directors, actors, screen writers and musicians, since the late twenties. In the forties, movie stars made it their go-to place. The food and drinks were great, pinball machines and a pool table provided opportunities for downtime, but most of all, no one bothered them. Stars could come without makeup or designer clothes and relax. It became a fifties hangout and a home base for budding authors and Pop artists who were creating the new wave of innovative avant-garde artworks. My father and his band members often hung out there, and when I returned from Rome, I found myself doing the same. That's where I met Ed.

The Ferus Gallery was on La Cienega, as were many other galleries. I haunted them, along with throngs of other art students and art aficionados on what was called "Art Walks." They took place once a month on a Monday. All the galleries were open, and we could wander from one to the next and share critiques of the Pop Art movement in general.

Although I tried my hand at what they called funk art—which was meant to expose viewers to its emotional, spiritual and idealistic themes—I found some of it too weird for my taste and knew I had to find what worked best for me.

I went on to have a one-man show at the David Hale Gallery on La Cienega Blvd and soon had works accepted for an exhibition in the Museum of Modern Art in San Francisco and various other gallery shows. Although it was difficult to refrain from comparing what I painted to that of artists whose careers were launched through consistent exposure in the La Cienega Boulevard galleries and promotion by their owners, I found a steady enough business to keep me occupied, not always through paint on canvas. I still worked at honing my lithography skills in order to sell prints at prices more people could afford.

I was hired to paint Italian scenes on twenty-one doors for a home in Trousdale, Beverly Hills, and then began work on a painting depicting the Crucifixion. To this day, I'm not completely sure what motivated me to tackle such a difficult subject; most likely, the works of old masters in the Rome galleries. At one of the local shows I attended, I met Maureen O'Hara's brother, Jimmy, and he posed as Christ in the painting. Since the canvas was 4 feet by 7 feet, I had to stand on a chair to reach parts of it.

One day, my Uncle Jack came to the studio and saw me balancing precariously on the chair. He exclaimed, "Jesus!" I was pleased that he recognized the personage I was painting. Maureen kept this finished "masterpiece" for me in her house, while I remained uncertain about its final home. No, she didn't offer to buy it from me. Perhaps she found the thought of her brother posing for Christ on the canvas too unsettling, as she was a devout Catholic.

Maureen's mother, Marguerita FitzSimons, of Dublin, Ireland, was staying with her at the time, as well as her brother Jimmy and daughter Bronwyn. Everyone was very kind to me, and I was impressed with Maureen's loving care of her mother. She was amazingly down-to-earth for being such a famous movie star and had a knack for making every visit enjoyable. Whenever Jimmy and I would go out with her, she seemed more like a small-town housewife, especially when wearing a babushka to cover her gorgeous red hair, but this form of disguise was seldom effective in hiding her identity from the public.

The months of August through October passed quickly and I was enjoying myself once again in familiar stamping grounds. However, I was earning what Uncle Moe called "pocket change" and still lived at home with my parents.

The first week of November, 1961, the entire Los Angeles area was suffering from yet another hot, windy week with almost zero humidity. It wasn't unusual for this time of year, and we always dreaded the coming of the notorious Santa Ana winds that swept over the city from the desert on the other side of the mountains.

One day—November the 6th to be exact—someone reported a brush fire and it made the news. Reporters added that the grass in the canyons was exceedingly dry, because of the severe drought we had experienced for several years, and there was the danger of even such a seemingly small fire spreading.

They spoke the truth. The Santa Ana wind whipped up a roaring fire that sent hundreds of hot embers into the air for miles. By dawn of the 7th, a billowing cloud of dark smoke filled the sky and blocked out any hint of the sun. Like everyone else in the city, I stayed glued to the television set and couldn't leave the house for my studio regardless of my plans for the day. My parents were worried. Many of their friends lived in the canyons. All too soon, their fears were justified. The news reporters said the winds had reached 65 mph and the fiery embers had landed on the wood-shake roofs—common at the time—and ignited them, causing the houses to burn from the roof to the ground lightning fast.

The flying embers created fires in the next canyons and the still punishing winds fused them over a ten-mile stretch, creating no end of difficulties for the rescue teams and 2,500 firefighters. It wasn't until noon the next day that they finally contained the fires. By nightfall, the local newspapers and television broadcasters provided the depressing statistics. Over 300 police officers had guided more than 3,500 Bel Air residents from their homes to safety, an evacuation that is still recorded as the largest in Los Angeles history.

Each hour brought new information that caused endless tears and empathy for those who had suffered such trauma. In Bel Air alone, 484 beautiful homes were destroyed and another 190 severely damaged; in all, over 16,000 acres had been burned to nothing but black ashes.

"Unsettling as this is," Daddy said, "the firefighters were able to save 78 percent of the homes." He had spent hours calling friends who had homes in the area and learned that the home of Otho Lovering, Paramount Studio film editor, had burn to the ground and destroyed all his career keepsakes.

My mother and I wrapped arms around each other as we heard the names of so many others who had been guests in our home. The houses of actor Burt Lancaster, western singer Tex Williams, and actress Zsa Zsa Gabor, whose home contained valuable jewelry, furs and paintings, were completely destroyed. Other celebrities' homes had been threatened or damaged, including those of Bobby Darin and his wife Sandra Dee, Cary Grant, Ginger Rogers, Greer Garson, Red Skelton, Kim Novak, Alfred Hitchcock, Marlon Brando, Robert Stack, Jascha Heifetz, Peggy Lee, Maxene and Laverne Andrews, and Robert Taylor. A reporter on one broadcast said that Miss Novak had rushed home from a movie studio, climbed the roof of her $200,000 Bel Air house and turned the hose on the property. Even the former Vice President Richard Nixon, whose house was on Bundy, had climbed to his roof with a hose, as did Fred MacMurray.

That's when I heard a name that had me gasping. "Maureen O'Hara, who had also taken a hose to the roof of her house, said it had been miraculously saved."

"I've got to go see her!" I leaped to my feet. "I was just there last week, Mommy. What if my . . .?" I couldn't finish the sentence. A painting by me was worthless compared to what she had lived through. Many of her neighbors and friends had lost everything and the lives of firefighters and rescue teams had been at unending risk. Still, when you're young, it's hard to let go of even such a selfish thought; the painting had taken months to create and I was proud of it.

No one was allowed into the burned area for more than a week if they weren't the property owners or members of the family. Unfortunately, at times like this, looters showed up by the carful and already overworked police had remained positioned at each end of roads leading through the canyons to ask for identification.

I called Jimmy to inquire about his sister and mother. In the course of our conversation, he mentioned the painting. "Don't worry, Carol. It's safe and sound. I saw it myself. No damage."

I was relieved because I didn't have a single photograph of it. Later, when Jimmy drove me to his sister's house, Maurine assured me the destroyed homes could be rebuilt and the owners carried sufficient insurance. "But money can't buy memories or replace one-of-a kind treasures," she said.

My painting was gifted to President John Kennedy and received by Evelyn Lincoln, his personal secretary, during one of his visits to Los Angeles. I like knowing it is housed in the Kennedy Library in Waltham, Massachusetts, and although I had read that our presidents receive multi-thousands of gifts during their terms of office and, by law, can distribute those they don't intend to keep to other organizations, I like knowing that my painting was kept.

About 1998, I called the Kennedy Library and was granted permission to bring my husband, Ian, daughter Lisa, her spouse Tim and little Taylor (in a stroller) at the time to see my painting. The curator took us down to the treasured rooms where we had the tour of a lifetime. I pulled open drawers to see Jackie's hats wrapped in tissue paper. Lisa accidently bumped the stroller into John Kennedy's rocker, and we viewed many gifts given to them by foreign diplomats and presidents. I asked, "What did President Kennedy treasure the most?" The curator said, "The brown leather jacket he wore in the service."

Crucifixion: Sorkin. Hanging in the John Fitzgerald Kennedy Library

As I mentioned before, I was accustomed to Uncle Moe calling with a request to paint a particular canvas for display on his luxury yacht. Or so he said. Usually, I had to copy one he brought with him. One day, Helen called me. "Carol, would you have time to paint a wall mural in Sidney Korshak's cabana at their Bel Air home?"

"Of course, I do, Helen! I'll make the time." I was thrilled for the opportunity. Often, such projects brought me additional business from a client's friends and friends of friends.

After discussing their vision, I sketched a rough drawing of my interpretation. When it was accepted, the Korshaks made arrangements for their driver to pick me up and take me home again on a daily basis until the project was finished. The driver kept the sedan in spit-spot condition, both inside and out. He would use a whiskbroom on whatever I was wearing that day, supposedly to clean it of lint or debris that might rub off on the car seat; of course he never missed whisking it over my breasts, and I'd see his lips twitch to keep from smiling.

The kitchen staff made lunch for me, and I would return from the house well fed and ready to paint more of the ivy that climbed on vines up the cabana walls.

Uncle Moe was very involved with his Acapulco Towers apartments in Acapulco, but despite many invitations to vacation there, neither Mother nor I had accepted. To this day, I have no idea exactly which of the many copied paintings Uncle Moe passed off as the originals, but knowing his ways and lifestyle, I have a hunch it was most of them.

One lovely afternoon in 1962, I was enjoying a visit with Joanie at a coffee house on Sunset Boulevard when I was approached by an interesting-looking man. "I hope you will excuse me for staring at you," he said. "Are you by any chance the Greek actress Aliki Vougiouklaki?"

Jonie and I exchanged smiles, amused by his audacity. That opening line was one we'd never heard before, and it was flattering to me, to say the least.

"Would you mind if I sat with you for a couple minutes? I am in your lovely city to meet with a friend, Plato Skouras." He looked directly at me. "It is my strong belief that you and Plato could become fast friends. May I give him your phone number?"

It had been far too long since I had been amenable to such a thing as a blind date, but how often does a girl meet a Greek bearing gifts? Paris was my last Greek friend and he had disappeared in Rome. I gave this perfect stranger my phone number, never expecting to hear from either him or his friend.

Plato Skouras called the very next day, and we had no trouble chatting for an entire hour. I invited him over for cocktails, hoping one or more of my parents would be home to meet him. They were, and we found him quite wonderful. He had recently been in Rome filming his fifth independently produced movie, St. Francis of Assisi.

Over the next few weeks, Plato and I learned that we shared similar points of view on several subjects, and we became more than friends. He took photos of me while I was painting in my studio and offered helpful critiques of my work. Soon, we were seriously dating, and he took me to a whirlwind of social dinners and parties and, of course, to whatever movie opened in the city over the next several months.

When my father was hired to provide the music for a party thrown by Jean Flagler Matthews at her 93-acre estate, in Rye, New York, I was invited to attend. She had been a guest at my wedding to Alan, because she had developed a trusting relationship with Daddy as the maestro in charge of musical entertainment at all her charity and social events when she was in Hollywood and Beverly Hills. He had even flown his orchestra to Palm Beach when she bought and restored the mansion of her grandfather, called Whitehall, renaming it the Henry Morrison Flagler Museum. She had celebrated the opening on February 6, 1960, with a Restoration Ball, which was acclaimed in most newspapers nationally as Palm Beach's society event of the season. Daddy said that literally thousands of people had attended the museum's opening, and the ball had been a massive success. I visited Whitehall many years later and saw a framed black and white photograph of Daddy and his orchestra on display with the program of the ball and other remembrances.

Plato surprised me and flew from LA to be my escort at Jean's party. Ironically, he was born in Rye and his parents still owned the family home there. They also lived in Bel Air, because his father, Spyros Skouras, had been president of 20th Century Fox since 1942 and was still in the process of producing Cleopatra with Elizabeth Taylor and Richard Burton.

Daddy had told me on the evening of our first meeting Plato, that his father Spyros was the wealthiest movie mogul in the country, that he and his two brothers either owned or controlled most of the movie theaters nationwide at one time, and that he was the producer who had found and signed up Marilyn Monroe.

"Skouras was the cofounder of the Greek War Relief Organization during WWII, Carol, and actively worked to raise hundreds of millions of dollars in both cash and aid, especially when a famine brought on by the Nazi occupiers left the Greeks destitute and starving. He's given credit for single-handedly saving millions of lives. He is such a hero in Greece that when King Paul and Queen Frederika visited the United Stated in 1953, they made a point of visiting Spyros at the Fox Studio to thank him in person."

"My parents insist that you spend the night with us, Carol. I do, too," Plato said when I arrived at in New York. "Then I can spend more time with you rather than on the road driving to and from a hotel." I agreed with his logic, but I was also eager to visit his home and see the neighborhood where he'd spent his childhood and teen years.

As we drove through the winding streets of the suburban community only minutes from the City, I found similarities with Beverly Hills, but the country setting for the Tudor style homes was much more in harmony with the landscape. "This area has become known as the East Coast Hollywood," Plato said. "I'm sure you already know that in the forties and also in the fifties New York was considered the headquarters for motion pictures, not Hollywood. My family isn't the only one that has found this area perfect for raising kids, it has the solitude when they need it, and it is convenient for entertaining anyone and everyone having to do with film production. Albert Warner and Barney Balaban also live out here. See that house over there? That belongs to Johnny Weissmuller."

"Tarzan? And the Warner of Warner Brothers and the Balaban of Paramount Pictures?" I asked, feeling like a tourist on one of the buses that drove through Hollywood.

Plato nodded. "Remember the Audrey Hepburn and Humphrey Bogart film Sabrina? Some of it was filmed on Balaban's place right over there." He pointed out the windshield at a gorgeous property. "And that's the place of Vivian Green who inherited all the Greenhaven property and was instrumental in deciding how it should be developed. He's our neighbor."

Plato's mother, Saroula, was gracious and made me feel warmly welcome. She mentioned having met my father several times at functions on the West Coast and even my mother. Her home was lovely and comfortable. I spent an inordinate amount of time cleaning up after myself to ensure no speck of makeup remained on the marble countertop of my private bath and that no chair was pushed out of place. The problem was mine; I was still insecure and eager to please and to be liked.

In 1962, I was having lunch with Plato and Jack Thomas, who had been the screen writer of St. Francis of Assisi. The two were planning a trip to Egypt for a new film. I learned that it was another documentary called We'll Bury You. "It's an informative look at the history of communism in the West, Carol. We'll begin with Karl Marx, and then Lenin, Trotsky, Stalin and even include the famous 'kitchen debate' between Richard Nixon and Nikita Khrushchev," Plato said.

"I remember reading about that. The two argued stridently about the merits of communism versus capitalism while Nixon was hosting a tour of the model kitchen and home set up for the American National Exhibition in Moscow."

Jack laughed. "That's the one. They were finger-pointing and throwing barbs at each other as to what smelled worse, sheep or pig manure! Nixon wanted to emphasis that the average American could own a great house and have the modern equipment in the kitchen to cook all the food they wanted. Khrushchev argued that Russians built houses to last longer and didn't need or want costly technical appliances for daily living."

I knew several of Plato's previous independently produced film had been documentaries, but I had no clear understanding of why they needed to go to Egypt to do this particular one. Jack's wife Casey—better known as Jimmy Cagney's daughter—was going to stay alone in their cottage situated at the end of the vast Cagney property and not travel with her husband.

"I'd consider it a great favor if you'd stay with Casey while I'm away," Jack said. "Would you mind? Plato said you're living with your parents right now and might enjoy a little time on your own. It's a great place. You could still go to your studio or paint up there. The views are spectacular."

"It can be quite frightening living up there alone, because there's a lot of wild life in the mountains," Plato added. "The grounds are enormous. About six or more acres.

I was ready for another adventure and agreed on the spot. "It's up to Casey, of course," I said. "She may have other plans."

The Cagney home was located high above Coldwater Canyon and had a 360-degree view of the valley and mountains.

I knew the general area because it wasn't far from my sister's home. Although I expected the house to be palatial, it wasn't. Jimmy Cagney and his wife were unpretentious people and Jimmy, especially, liked his privacy. In fact, he had a passion for farming. He owned a couple farms in New York and became a hands-on agriculturist and even raised cattle and Morgan horses. He and his wife enjoyed the peace and quiet of the countryside, preferring it over the Hollywood scene. Although the house had several bedrooms, there were still small guest dwellings, the groundskeeper's quarters and a six-car garage. The most impressive thing to me was that they had their own gas pump.

Jimmy Cagney in Coldwater Canyon home office; view of the main home

Casey was as unassuming as her parents were. To her credit, she was raised to be practical and hardworking. She worked all day at a bank, which meant I was alone most of time, unless I went to my studio or home for more clothes and to visit my mother. After she left the cottage in the morning, I fed the Cagney dogs and played the piano. Every time I stopped between pieces, I imaged I could hear a shaking sound outside one particular window.

"I forgot to warn you there are diamondback rattlers on the property," Casey said, when I mentioned it to her that evening.

"You have to be kidding," I said, working to remain calm while hearing the thudding of my heart in my eardrums.

"Unfortunately, it's true," she said. "Be careful and pay attention to the behavior of the dogs whenever you go outdoors. They won't go anywhere near them and will back away if they sense their presence. The snakes usually eat lizards and frogs and other such things and stay out of sight. We've all lived to tell the tale, so I wouldn't worry."

I called Dupsey that very night. "Look it up in your set of encyclopedias," I said. "I need to know what they look like. I've never seen one."

She returned my call an hour later. "Listen to this, Carol. The diamond-back rattler is the longest specie in the whole country and can be as long as seven feet. It's supposedly aggressive and easily excitable . . . and it's notorious for its fatal bite!"

By now I could feel the blood draining from my head to my feet and quickly curled up on the bed before I could fall on the floor. What if there was a rattler hiding under the bed!

"That's not all, Carol. Now don't spaz out on me. The diamondback has fangs that can fold up into its mouth. Isn't that gross? If I were you, I'd tiptoe around that place. This article says if you agitate the snake, the speed of its strike is so fast you can't even see it coming."

I shuttered at the thought. "What am I going to do, Dupsey? I promised Plato and Jack I'd stay with Casey until they get home from Egypt."

"Well . . . if the Cagney's and all those other people who live up there don't have for-sale signs in their yards, you probably don't have anything to worry about. Just don't leave dog food in bowls outside. That's like free food to hungry rattlers."

"Great. You're so helpful."

"Listen, my friend, you asked for information and I gave it to you. Don't kill the messenger."

The message from the messenger was enough to set off my binge eating again. I pigged out on Cheese Doodles and anything sweet. Bags of candy. Boxes of chocolate. I had already spent months wining and dining with Plato and my belts were growing tighter. When Casey brought out the buttered popcorn, I ate my fill. When she baked a dozen cupcakes, I scarfed down my six in two days.

Dupsey's advice came to mind only a couple weeks later. I had pulled open the kitchen door to carry out the filled dog-food bowls to the far end of the patio and after accomplishing my task was already thinking about having lunch with my sister. As I headed back to the kitchen, I don't know who was more surprised, the snake or me. We scared each other. Within a nanosecond, the diamondback had slithered into the cottage. There I stood my knees about to fail me as I smothered a scream that would have alarmed everyone in the canyon.

There was no way I could go back into the house and the rattler was unlikely to come out. Even the dogs knew something was amiss and, although they stared at the open doorway with perked-up ears, they made no move to investigate.

I waited and waited some more. There was no such thing as a remote or pocket phone in the early sixties. I couldn't make a beeline for the main Cagney residence, because I didn't have a key; besides that I was now afraid to step one foot into the grass. Of course there wasn't a human being in sight. No groundskeeper. No pool cleaner. Finally, determining I had no other choice, I planned a scenario. I would walk slowly and quietly to the door, stop and peer into the kitchen to see if I could spot the viper, and cross my fingers that it hadn't lingered there and was bound for an exploration of the cottage. I prayed for Divine Protection as I proceeded with my plan. My object was the telephone near the refrigerator.

When my hasty eyeball-only inspection of every inch of the kitchen revealed no movement, I dashed inside and to the counter. I dialed the O for the operator and asked for the Beverly Hills Fire Station serving Coldwater Canyon. "It's an emergency!" I shouted, panting so hard I could barely squeeze out the words. Then I sprinted for the back door, slamming it behind me. The dogs hadn't moved. I waited with them on the patio for the arrival of my rescuers.

Happily, the experienced firemen came in a very few minutes. They searched the cottage, found the diamondback, and assured me I could sleep in peace.

On several evenings, Casey and I explored her father's vault of movie treasures and watched a couple old films together. I'll never forget the thrill of seeing them through new eyes, after hearing so much about this extraordinary actor from his daughter, especially personal stories about how well he cared for his mother and the financial generosity that has surely set him apart from anyone we'll ever know. From the time of his first paycheck, he had sent her a third of his income.

I kept in touch with Casey for a couple years after the weeks we spent together, but life has a way of getting in the way of lingering friendships. We tend to become Christmas card correspondents only. I did learn, through Dupsey, that the screenwriting and producing career of Jack William Thomas went belly up when he returned to Egypt in 1964 and spent all his film royalties. Broke, he took a job as an LA probation officer for a few years, and with his talent, used these experiences as perfect fodder for juicy and "gritty" fiction for Bantam Books, mostly about wayward teens of the 1970s—books that were gobbled up by readers in five languages. Jack went on to become what dozens of reviewers would call "one of the finest American pulp fiction writers to ever stomp the terra." He and Casey had two children during this time.

By now, my friend Joanie had become Joan Jacobs Ellin, so it came as a surprise when she and her family invited me to attend the 1964 Cannes Film

Festival with them. Her father, Melvin Jacobs, was president of Technicolor International at the time. It was a magical trip and not at all like the penny-pinching one I'd experienced when on my own in Rome and determined to stay within my personal budget. We stayed in the luxurious Carlton Hotel in Cannes, the Son Vida in Palma, Majorca—which is the capital city of the Balearic Islands in Spain and offered us a fascinating fusion of history, architecture and vibrant nightlife—and temporarily in the President's Suite of the Hilton Hotel on the Thames in London. We were wined and dined and romanced, and I was utterly enchanted by the beauty that soon filled dozens of blank canvases in my mind.

Either Mr. Jacobs or our hosts paid for everything, and Joanie and I enjoyed dressing in our finest. I was grateful and wise enough to know it was a trip of a lifetime for a non-movie star. My ego inflated more than it should have when I was introduced time and again as "the famous American artist, Carol Larkin." I still have a photograph that appeared in the Cannes newspaper where my name was spelled Caril.

(De gauche à droite.) M. Ed Ettinger, Vice-Président du Technicolor International Group, Miss Joan Jacobs Ellin, la célèbre artiste américaine, Miss Caril Larkin et M. Melvin C. Jacobs, Président de Technicolor International

In 1965, my parents were still helping me out financially, but my lifestyle no longer suited theirs when I had friends over many evenings and weekends.

"It's time for you to get a real job, Carol," they said on more than one occasion. "You're a very talented artist. We can't deny that, but your efforts have become an expensive hobby you can't afford for the lifestyle you want to lead. You're throwing away your future. You're an adult. It's time to make decisions that will make you more independent. You'll only do that if you move out again."

They were absolutely right. If Casey could work in a bank, I could find meaningful work, too. I had been procrastinating. What if I failed? Again.

The stress was enough to cause another sugar craving.

12

Blue skies are coming. If you're brave enough to say goodbye,
life will reward you with a hello.

ABOUT THIS TIME, I learned about a job opening at the Broadway
Department Store on Wilshire Boulevard that seemed custom-made for
my artistic eyes and interests; one that involved fashion and display work. I
applied and was hired.

It was a dream job. I was placed in charge of the store's display windows,
floor displays in the women's clothing department, and fashion shows. When
anyone says, "I started at the bottom," I can echo the statement. I literally did.
In the basement of the store. This was where my office was located in order
to be near the storage areas for manikins and other display necessities. There,
I poured over Women's Wear Daily, Vogue, and Harper's Bazaar issues from
cover to cover, only a few of the monthly fashion journals that arrived on my
desk.

Unexpectedly, I was given complete freedom to do whatever I deemed
best. I put on seasonal fashion shows and created Parisian-styled scenes using the store's fabrics and whatever else would make the windows and floors
attention-getting. The purpose was always to bring buyers into the store and
keep them there long enough to make purchases.

The props and set designers were the real champions. We had fun and
games in the basement, including the feeding of a few stray dogs brought in
from the streets, popping popcorn on an iron, and making the sales people

search for a particular creation that didn't exist until it was designed on the mannequin.

I sensed that Management was grooming me to move up the corporate ladder. I was summoned to the men's department to meet with manger Charles Crystal about incorporating men's fashion into the window displays and using my "magic" on in-department presentation of new arrivals. Over the next month, it seemed that I was making an increasing number of 'necessary' visits to confer with Charles 'unnecessarily.' Most of our sessions were spent in chatting about inconsequential things having little to do with fashion or window dressing.

Charles and I started to see each other regularly during and then after work. At first, it was his flirting and complements that lured me into his web. Then, as we came to know each other better, it was his underlying pathos. Charles had lost both of his parents at a young age, and his mournful and poignant persona begged for my consolation. His penetrating dark eyes were in direct contrast to his pale skin, and he seemed almost fragile. My heart melted. I felt sorry for him.

Our lunch dates increased to almost daily occurrences. It seemed natural that we'd have dinner together, at least on weekends. I couldn't help noticing that Charles was generous to a fault when it came to tipping our waiter. Although he wasn't a man of financial means, he would greet me with a pie, a fancy desert or cookies whenever he picked me up in my apartment. Yes. Sugar-filled, irresistible sweets. Since they were my weakness, I was impressed by this uncommonly kind gesture.

Charles was the complete opposite of Alan. He actually thought I was perfect the way I was. He didn't try to change one thing about me. He didn't judge my appearance, my clothes, hair, makeup or weight. For the first time, I was accepted exactly the way I was by a suitor. Lucky me.

During one of our first conversations at the store, Charles had mentioned his brother was a real estate appraiser and he planned to follow in his footsteps. "It's a far more lucrative profession than the one I'm currently in, Carol. Once I learn the Beverly Hills area well, it'll be easy to transition into becoming a realtor." Since I had always admired ambition in my family members, I saw his as an attribute, even though he had already exhibited unlimited potential in retail and could advance in responsibilities quite rapidly. Anyway, who was I to criticize a change in career direction?

I was living on my own, but finding myself in the same position as other employees in the department store. I lived from paycheck to paycheck. I'd already spent the settlement from my divorce and was determined not to turn to my parents to augment my salary. Unfortunately, I hadn't thought ahead before renting a one-bedroom apartment near Wilshire Boulevard in Beverly Hills. The rent was $185 a month. My paycheck was about $80 a week or $320 a month. Car expenses and insurance, food, utilities, telephone and a dozen other expenses meant I was always down to the last penny. On more than one occasion, I poured water on my morning cereal, because I was out of milk.

Ivan Treisault and his wonderful wife lived in a larger apartment in my building and his mother lived in the apartment above mine. Ivan had been a busy character actor in Hollywood most of his adult life, often playing foreign villains from the mid-forties through the mid-sixties in everything from Notorious (1946), The Bad and the Beautiful (1952), Silk Stockings (1957) and Barabbas (1962), to Von Ryan's Express (1965). Since my entire family loved movies from the time we first arrived on the West Coast, I was confident I had seen all of Triesault's films.

Now, he was retired and spent part of his time tending to the yard work. For some reason, and despite my repeated requests, he didn't trim the bushes closest to my bedroom window or the weeds that grew out of the mower's reach. This meant I had to continually deal with creepy, crawly visitors.

A favorite family treasure that occupied a prominent position in my apartment was a wonderful old player piano. I had collected about 400 piano rolls. My favorite one, "I was in Blue Grass up to my knees". All I had to do was insert one, start pumping the bellows and enjoy a wide variety of music while watching the keys keep perfect time. Despite having quit piano lessons when I reached my early teens, I still enjoyed tinkering on the ivories.

One evening, I was pumping to a favorite song while pretending I was accompanying the musicians. Suddenly, a good-sized cockroach scooted across the keys and disappeared into the dark recesses of the piano. I freaked out, imagining a colony of them creating a home and multiplying by the hundreds. What if I forgot it was there? What if one or more of the loathsome creatures crawled out from between the keys just as I sat down to play and flew into my lap?

My irrational fear of all bugs had grown during the days I rented a studio to do my painting. Too often, as the hours grew into evening and I worked by lamplight, the water beetles would crawl out of the woodwork. I vacated that studio as soon as my lease was up. Dupsey had told me an old adage. "A cockroach never gets justice when a chicken is the judge."

Now, my panic alarm sounded and led me to do a foolish thing. I called a piano store the very next morning. "I need to sell my player piano. Are you interested in buying it?" No mention of the cockroach that would be included free of charge. As soon as I gave my name, the store manager said he'd send someone right over. When the truck drivers appeared to take the piano, I realized the manager had confused the name Sorkin with Serkin; he thought the piano belonged to Rudolf Serkin, the Austrian-born Russian Jew pianist who became an American citizen in 1939 and went on to become one of the greatest musicians of the twentieth century. My family had listened to most of his concerts and played records of his Beethoven and Viennese interpretations for years, not only because of his heritage, but because of his brilliance.

Clearly, I hadn't taken enough time to think about my decision. The movers had the piano out of my apartment and into their waiting truck before I could consult with anyone having a wiser solution. And to my utter dismay, that contemptible cockroach crawled out of the piano to reside in my apartment. For some reason, I had kept the 400 piano rolls and stored them at my parents' home. Mother sold them a few years later. This behavior, on my part, is one more example of how I had a tendency to take action without thinking things through.

I have never forgotten my experience working at the Broadway Department Store. I considered it more fun than work. Sort of like playing dolls, only the manikins were more like the movie star guests I'd seen come and go from the Sorkin house during all my childhood and teen years. Usually, I selected clothing and accessories from throughout the store, but on occasion, I created a design of my own and hired a seamstress to cut and sew the garment. It gave me untold pleasure to see it on display and know it was one of a kind. Sometimes I would do something crazy, like use bras for hats with artfully draped fabric to imitate a new Parisian creation. Since the store's display windows faced Wilshire Boulevard, there was always considerable pedestrian traffic. More traffic meant more people stopped to look.

Unexpectedly, I was offered a position as buyer and manager of the boutique department at the Boy's Market in Encino for substantially more money. Since the other perk was that I would be my very own boss, it was an offer I couldn't refuse. Although it helped that my dear friend Gerry was married to Al Goldstein, one of the brothers who owned the store, I still had to prove myself worthy of the position. I welcomed the challenge. The very first week of my employment, I became a retail clerk union member.

Second husband, Charles Crystal 1966

Charles and I missed seeing each other every day at work and decided to marry. Since it would be my second time down the aisle, I wasn't interested in a wedding extravaganza. Since Charles didn't have immediate family who would miss the formality, I was easily convinced we should tell no on, be compulsive, and elope to San Diego. Although we were both brought up in the Jewish faith, we checked around for the nearest church. We found a small inconspicuous one and didn't bother to check out the denomination. It didn't matter to us, as long as the minister would honor our marriage license, pronounce us husband and wife, and sign the document making our union legal.

I dressed in a simple pink suit and hat and Charles looked impressive in his blue suit. Since we needed two witnesses, the church secretary and handyman served as our bridesmaid and groomsman. Our marriage ceremony was over in less than ten minutes.

Under the glow of love and hopes for the future, we shared our first family dinner at a modest-sized restaurant and spent the night in an equally modest-sized San Diego hotel. The next morning, we returned to my apartment. This was our honeymoon, a far cry from the newsworthy dinner-dance following my first marriage and the month-long cruise replete with fancy wining and dining and lolling on the beaches of Hawaii.

Charles spoke increasingly about working with his brother and becoming a real estate tycoon, but that's as far as it went. He continued his work at the Broadway, and I continued to commute back and forth to Encino. I looked forward to sharing supper over a discussion of the challenges we'd faced in our jobs each day. Weekends, we'd take walks on the beach or go grocery shopping together.

Over time, it seemed that Charles became unusually moody, sometimes to the point of not talking when he got home or speaking in one-word sentences. When the weekend arrived, he was too tired to do anything. "You go," he'd say. "I don't need the hassle of all those crazy people mauling through the oranges." Either that or he'd blow up over minor things; throw a shoe across the room or something more frightening. I had never seen this side of him. If I questioned him about the cause of his stress, he clammed up or leave the apartment, slamming the door behind him.

I chose to keep a blind eye to these mood swings, telling myself he just missed our former routine at the Broadway and, perhaps, his ego was suffering a bit from his having to set up house in my apartment. Then he'd come home with his arms laden with packages. "Look what I bought, Carol! I've always wanted one of these gadgets. The store had a sale today. Look at this gorgeous neck scarf. It matches your favorite color lipstick." On occasions like this, his buying spree was unrestrained. I loved seeing him so excited and upbeat and joyfully exclaimed over each purchase. Of course it put a definite strain on our budget.

One day, Charles would be unusually talkative, bragging about the superiority of his work ethic at the store compared to his peers. A few days later, he'd be irritable to the point of finding fault with everyone and with everything I did. Or he'd slump on the couch looking and feeling like he'd just been fired. "I'm worthless," he'd mutter. "Totally, completely worthless."

"Why don't we go for a ride along the coast and have supper at that Asian chow mein café. We love it. It'll give us both a chance to relax. It's been a busy month."

"That sounds good to me. Might be just the thing I need to get out of this funk. But maybe we shouldn't. We can't afford to spend a single extra penny. Can we?"

"Make up your mind, Charles," I'd say, impatient with his indecisiveness.

My own disposition was changing as well. The days seemed longer and I hated having to battle the traffic home from Encino. I found it increasingly difficult to stay awake after preparing our supper and could barely rouse myself when the alarm went off in the morning. "I don't know what's wrong with me," I said one evening, snuggling up to Charles on the couch. "I feel different. I can't explain it, but something's not right. I'm going to make an appointment with the family doctor I've seen for many years. He knows me."

"How much will it cost?"

"That's it? You're concerned about the cost and not about me?"

"I'm concerned about you and the cost. I'm sorry you're not feeling well, but these Beverly Hill's doctors charge a fortune. You might not mind living on peanuts, but I do!"

The next morning, during my coffee break at work, I made the appointment with the doctor I had known and trusted since I was a child. Fortunately, his office assistant said she could squeeze me into his schedule the next morning. After answering a series of questions about my symptoms, enduring a physical exam and urinating in a cup, I waited for what seemed like hours in one of the examining rooms imagining the worst.

The doctor returned with a manila folder and perched on a stool not far from where I was sitting. "Maybe we should wait until you can return with your husband to discuss this, Carol."

My heart accelerated and I caught my bottom lip between my teeth to quiet my sense of panic. Did I need surgery? Did I have diabetes from my twenty years of sugar binging? Something worse. Incurable? "No, no, that isn't necessary. Charles is manager of his department at the Broadway and probably can't get off during weekday hours."

"All right." He pushed his glasses further up on his nose and peered at me through the lenses that seemed to enlarge the size of his eyeballs. "From what you told me during the exam and from these lab results, I can quite confidently say there's nothing out of the ordinary wrong with you, Carol. What you have is a common condition in young women your age. You're pregnant."

"Pregnant? I'm going to have a . . . baby?"

"That's what the lab tests show. It also explains why you're so tired all the time, even in the morning after a full night of rest, and why you fall asleep after supper. It's because your body produces extra blood during pregnancy, and this causes your heart to beat faster and harder than usual. You're only six weeks along, Carol, but an embryo has already formed in your uterus and all its major internal organs have started to develop. Fatigue is natural right now. It will lessen as your body adjusts. You'll continue to experience breast tenderness, frequent urination, maybe a little heartburn over the next month or so. You may experience considerable nausea, especially in the morning, and even vomit. For some women, these conditions will worsen, before they get better. Get yourself a box of soda crackers and eat a few before you sit up in the morning. They'll sop up some of the gastric juices in your stomach after so many hours without eating."

Soda crackers? All I could think about was what Charles would say about the expansion of our family so soon after our marriage. We were still newlyweds. How could we afford a baby? We'd need a diaper service. Could I continue to work without a nanny like Mother had for me? How could I deal with vomiting when I had such a long drive to Encino? I hated being sick! I had never paid attention to the pregnancy issues in my contract with the store. Would I be fired?

The doctor was still speaking and I tried to focus on what he was telling me, pushing aside my petty concerns and rejoicing in the miracle that was growing in my uterus.

On the way home from the doctor's office, I stopped at the grocery store for the ingredients to make one of Charles' favorite meals. Oh, my goodness, I was pregnant! I thought of what Mother would say. And Sandra. Everyone in my family. Would Daddy enjoy having a grandson or granddaughter?

Charles was both happy and worried. "Can we do this, Carol? We can barely support ourselves. Is this apartment big enough for us and a child? Is it safe? Maybe we should move. We could get a bigger place if we lived in a less expensive neighborhood." He leaped up from the table to rummage through the cupboards. "Where's that good bottle of wine we were saving for a special evening? We need to celebrate."

"I don't think I should drink anything alcoholic while I'm pregnant, Charles. Come and finish your dinner. I made your favorite meal for the occasion."

"It's cold now."

I remember having breakfast in a café with Dupsey that weekend. "For some reason, I think I'm having twins," I said. "I know it's crazy, but I feel it. It's like a special message has been sent to me. It won't get out of my head."

"You're right, Carol. That's crazy. Twins tend to run in families. I've never heard you mention that a single relative in your family was a twin."

"I'll have to check with Mother. Anyway, I'll know in a couple months. That's when the doctor will be able to hear their heartbeats. Wouldn't that be fun? Mother will be on the phone with everyone she knows, spreading the news. Twins!"

Dupsey covered her face with her hands. "What am I going to do with you? Think baby. Not babies. Until you know for sure, be happy about the one child you're about to bring into this world. What does your imagination tell you about the gender? Will it be a boy or a girl?"

I laughed. Dupsey always made me feel good. It felt wonderful sharing such happy news with one of my dearest friends. I hadn't told a single soul at work yet. I decided to wait until my skirts and dresses were too snug to wear without revealing my condition.

In the sixties, women still wore modest tops and dresses that hid their shape. You couldn't pay them enough to flaunt the size of their extended belly on the cover of some magazine in a revealing, too-small knit shirt or, heaven forbid, bare-naked. Lucy Ricardo was our role model as was Jacqueline Kennedy. Nude pregnant photos became popular in Hollywood in 1991 when Demi Moore posed naked on the cover of Vanity Fair. Mariah Carey, Heidi Klum, Brittney Spears and Jessica Simpson have appeared in little but a necklace since then, and today's young women seem to find this okay, without first understanding that these 'stars' wouldn't be doing this if they weren't receiving at least a million dollars for the notoriety.

My pregnancy placed an even greater burden on Charles. One day he came home with news I hadn't expected. "Well, I finally did it. I told my boss I'd have to cut my hours at the Broadway and work part-time. They'll have to do without my expertise. I expected to be promoted by now, and I can't wait around for the brass to make up their minds. I'm going to use the free time to pursue my dream job."

Fortunately, I was still working and earning a decent salary. And out of the blue, I received a call from Century City Hotel asking if I could create twelve impressionist paintings for their lobby and suites. That was right up my artist alley. The extra money would come in handy.

By now, my stretch with queasy was over and my appetite became ravenous. I started to eat for the baby and me, trying extra hard not to indulge recklessly in all the sugar-filled treats that Charles still brought home from his days of trying to get a foot in the doorway of real estate.

The Boy's Market cafeteria was set up with several food stations. I couldn't wait for my lunch break. I would hurry to be one of the first employees in line, then I worked my way around the buffet filling my plate with a little of everything. I sampled beef bourguignon, pasta primavera, tuna casserole and even Jell-O salads. It was an eater's paradise.

It wasn't that I was starving. I started my eating marathon at 4:30 in the morning sharing a bowl of Kellogg's Froot Loops with the birds. The cereal didn't appear on the market shelves until around 1962, but the O-shapes in red, orange and yellow appealed to my artistic palette. They had become one of my weird cravings. Not dill pickles. I don't think there was an hour I didn't eat something.

This was the most fun I ever had gaining weight and no one mentioned the rapid size of my belly. There was no more pretending I was simply packing on the pounds. I had to meet with my boss and ask about the company's procedure regarding an employee in my condition. There was no such provision called a 'maternity leave' in the sixties. "You'll need to take a leave of absence without pay, Carol. It's in your contract. If you don't return within two-three months, it's highly likely your position will be given to someone else. You have an excellent record with us, however, so I'm sure we can find comparable employment for you."

How could any job be comparable to the one I had? I was my own boss. I could be creative and work with fashion and fabrics and meet with inspiring buyers and wholesale distributors. I didn't have long to worry about it. Standing on my feet all day and walking from floor to floor, in addition to the roundtrip to work every day, caused a symptom I hadn't expected. I started to spot blood. In a state of panic, I called my doctor who said I should immediately come to see him. I was about eighteen weeks pregnant. Was I going to lose the baby?

Two hours later, I had my answer. The doctor removed the stethoscope from my protruding tummy. "I think it would be best for you to take that leave of absence from your job, Carol." He peered directly at me and then smiled. "Don't worry. You're not going to lose your pregnancy. You're going to have twins."

"Twins? Twins? I knew it! I told a friend that two months ago." I started to cry.

"There's nothing to worry about, Carol. Their heartbeats sounded nice and strong. You'll have to take it easy, that's all. Not overdo."

"Can you tell if I'm having two boys or two girls or one of each?"

He laughed and shook his head. "No, I'm not God. We don't have a procedure for determining that. We'll both have to be surprised on delivery day."

To say that Charles was shocked was putting it mildly. The news both delighted him and increased his sense of panic. What got the most reaction, however, involved my next revelation. "The doctor said I needed to immediately take a leave of absence from work."

"What!" He paced the floor. "Of course you have to do whatever the doctor says. We don't want to lose those babies, but what will we do for income? I'll have to work fulltime at the Broadway again. If they'll let me. We'll manage. I'll figure it out."

I will never forget one particular evening. I was resting on the bed when Charles returned at the end of the work day, "What did you do today?" I asked. Without warning, he came at me with his fist aimed right my stomach. I cringed and put up my arms to protect myself. At that instant my nose started to bleed. Nothing had made contact with it. It was simply a spontaneous episode. Charles was as frightened as I was when my hand oozed with bright red blood and droplets created crimson pools on the white sheet. He rushed to the bathroom for the Kleenex box. "Make it stop! I don't know what got into me."

The nosebleed had saved me from potential harm to our babies.

This is how we lived and loved during that first year of our marriage. There were other incidents that involved my husband's flash of temper. Several occurred while he was driving with me beside him. He would drive pell-mell down the street and then slam on the brakes to keep from hitting the vehicle in front of us or to stop at a red traffic light. My protruding stomach would come within inches of the dashboard. Cars weren't equipped with seatbelts until the mid-eighties. Weekend visits to my parents' home or to the coast kept my nerves on edge.

"Slow down, Charles! This isn't a racetrack. I want to reach our destination in one piece."

"Get over it, Carol. This is the way I've always driven. Stop your nitpicking or you can take the bus next time. I'll chalk up your incessant whininess to raging hormones, but keep in mind that this pregnancy thing is just as hard on me as it is on you. I do have a few good traits or you wouldn't have married me. And you're not perfect, by the way. If our positions were reversed, you'd have blown a gasket by now."

"You're right, Charles. I understand where you're coming from. I've always been sensitive to criticism, so I should know better. I've been a people pleaser from the time I was a toddler. If I didn't get the attention I needed, I'd pout or cry to get it. If I didn't please Daddy, he'd shout and leave the house. Then I'd run to Mother for comfort, and she'd feed me cookies or whatever she was baking at the time. I'm afraid my need for emotional stroking developed into a strong sense of insecurity, especially about my weight. I was an emotional eater. Still am. Food feeds my lack of self-confidence. You know that. And now that I have two babies growing inside me, it seems that any confidence I've gained since meeting you is being shoved aside. I don't feel worthy."

I reached over to stroke his hand on the steering wheel. "One of the things I love most about you is that you don't criticize me for the way I look, Charles. Sorry if I've been a grouch lately. But, I still wish you wouldn't drive so fast!"

Although I had shared some of my feelings with Charles while we were dating, I withheld anything that might shine the light on my major flaws. I didn't know how to be happy with myself. My aversion to criticism got me into the wrong first marriage, sent me in the wrong direction for gainful employment, turned me away from my passion for painting and toward working at the Broadway. True, I could incorporate my artistic leanings into my job, but I still had to please a boss enough to keep it. Then I met Charles, the first one to accept me as I was. Or so I thought.

No matter how many epiphanies I had about my own needs and why I reacted or overreacted to daily occurrences the way I did, it seemed I didn't have the ability to say or do things in a way that would respond fittingly to what Charles needed. I had always thought he was very self-assured, but maybe he wasn't. Maybe he was as insecure as I was. Men were expected to be the breadwinners. When we married, we both had great jobs with steady income. Now his wife was jobless and expecting twins, and we were counting pennies to meet our expenses.

Despite daily trials, I became increasingly excited as I felt the babies move in my belly. Mother called daily. Sandra called several times a week. Aunt Helen called and even Daddy and my uncles. Children were a gift of creation and the anticipation of adding two precious souls to our family had everyone counting the hours. I was blessed with a large and loving family.

Another blessing was the generosity of my parents, because as the birth of the twins approached, they felt Charles and I had to move from my apartment into larger quarters. This wasn't possible on Charles' reduced Broadway salary. We found a lovely place with two bedrooms on Exposition Boulevard, and my parents made the down payment and paid for the move itself.

The movers arranged the furniture and unpacked our belongings. Charles and I were alone for only a few minutes when I went into labor. "It's too early!" I exclaimed. Charles called my doctor for advice and five minutes later we were headed for the hospital. This time, I didn't care if he drove too fast. I couldn't get to our destination fast enough. Sharp pains seemed to increase with each passing minute. So did my fear. A million 'what ifs' raced through my mind.

Our twin girls were born the next day, February 24, 1967, arriving eight weeks too early. They were so tiny they had to live. One twin weighed three pounds and the other a half pound more, smaller than the baby dolls Sandra and I played with as children. To me, they were beautiful, and I couldn't bear the thought of possibly losing them. I blamed myself. And then I blamed Charles.

I stayed in the hospital for five days, which is a luxury today. Neither Charles nor I had anticipated leaving the hospital without our babies. Being a new mother you dream of leaving the hospital with a baby, flowers, smiles and love. We had another serious confrontation, and once again I ended up in tears. No babies in my arms and Charles drove me to the unemployment office to pick up my check. Life is rarely as we envision it when we're young and inexperienced; our hopes and expectations are what someone termed 'pie in the sky.' My life was so wonderful in one way and so utterly miserable in the other. I was a mother, and I weighed over two-hundred pounds and still looked pregnant with another set of twins.

Lisa and Jennifer, as we had named our daughters, grew in both weight and health over the next month. I made trips to the hospital to spend as much time with them as I was allowed so they would learn my voice and feel my love through the glass of their beds. In the meantime, I set up a nursery for them at home, with the help of both friends and family members. Mother was concerned about how I could provide for them on my own. "They'll need continuous care, dear. They'll wake up at the same time and want to be fed. If they're anything like you and your siblings, they'll wail throughout the diaper changes until they get their milk. It can be nerve-wracking."

One of my sister's friends employed several Mexican immigrants, and she introduced me to Anita, who became an indispensable member of our household. She spoke only Spanish, but somehow we were able to communicate through gestures and one-word phrases in both our languages. Family members were only too eager to assist with the girls' feeding and bathing and for walks around the block in their two-seater stroller, which was also a gift.

In the meantime, Charles had found new employment with the Boy's Market on Pico Boulevard near the house. We both breathed a sigh of relief with the addition of his regular paycheck. But it wasn't long before his irrational outbursts became even more disturbing. He would twist my arms and blow up for nothing, his face close to mine and contorted with rage. I wore long-sleeved blouses to cover my black-and-blue arms. Anita tried to tell my mother on several occasion, but they couldn't communicate in a meaningful way. I certainly wasn't going to tell her about my husband. I was too ashamed to admit I had, once again, chosen the wrong person to marry. I wasn't ready for any more lectures.

It seemed like the discord in our home would never end. I was worried about the effect such audible altercations would have on the girls. My silence and internal suffering resulted in abdominal ulcers. I dined on jars of baby food while feeding the girls, as it was easy to digest.

Our apartment was on the second floor and located near the freeway. It made daily life even more difficult, because Anita and I had to tote the girls down the stairs to the waiting stroller for every walk. Then Charles left my car on the street one night, and it was totaled by a driver exiting the highway too fast. There were no convenient grocery stores close by, and I had to wait until I could use his for evening or weekend shopping.

Lisa and Jennifer

Mother hated the climb to the second story as much as I did. She took her concern home and soon my generous parents found us a small house in the slums of Beverly Hills for about $34,000. It was literally two houses from the Los Angeles city limits, but it was in Beverly Hills. It required a bulldozer to clear out the backyard, but it was a house with a yard and became a bona fide home. The girls enjoyed many naps in their stroller outdoors while I relaxed in a lawn chair nearby.

Our neighbor was Mark Copage, the little boy from the television show *Julia*. Our houses were so close to each other, I could hear him rehearse his lines. Sandra Berkova, the talented violinist, lived two doors away and provided complimentary concerts. At least their sounds were pleasant on the ears. They had to listen to the crying of two babies and to the tirades of their father. Charles would fly off the handle at unexpected times. It seemed that he barely stepped into the house after work when the first eruption occurred. It took coordination for Anita and me to get the girls to eat and nap at the same time, and with escalating regularity, they would be jarred awake by a slammed door or raised voice. Unknown to us both was what is more commonly diagnosed today as 'bipolar personality disorder.' When the girls were eighteen months old, I filed for a trial separation.

13

DURING THE NEXT couple months, I experienced frightening episodes of sporadic and inexplicable hemorrhaging. I attributed it to the daily stress that was somehow affecting my hormonal system and dealt with it myself, without sharing the incidents with anyone. Especially not with Charles.

One Sunday, I took the girls next door to visit my neighbor, Esther Rubin. We were seated at her dining room table when I felt a gush like someone had turned on a faucet. Totally unnerved and embarrassed, I made a mad rush for her bathroom, hoping I wasn't leaving a bloody trail behind me. Again, I didn't share the cause of my abrupt departure from the table.

When the episodes happened with increasing regularity over the next three weeks, I knew I had to take action. One thing was certain. I wasn't pregnant and in the throes of a miscarriage. Fretting over my dilemma one more weekend, I finally reached for the Yellow Pages to look up the number for our family doctor, Dr. Vinetz, who was a wonderful and compassionate man. I trusted his opinion.

"What you're describing isn't normal, Carol," he said, after listening to the enumeration of my symptoms. "We'd better take a look and see what's going on."

The very next day, I was on his examining table with his sweet assistant Fanny holding my hand. Dr. Vinetz poked around for what seemed like an eon and then inserted a stainless-steel speculum. "Does this hurt? Do you feel pressure when I do this? How about here?"

Finally he stepped away from the table, pulled off his vinyl gloves, and seated himself on a stool next to me. "I'm not at all happy with what I was able to see with the speculum, Carol. You have a mass of considerable size in your uterus. Because of the frequency and extent of the hemorrhages you described, it should come out. It's a fibroid tumor that's feeding on your estrogen and growing larger. Sometimes, such tumors recede by themselves when a woman's hormones return to normal after giving birth. In some women, however, they seem to thrive. We don't want it to break off from the stem and cause a rupture." He paused and pursed his lips, as though waiting for an outburst from me. "You should know ahead of time, Carol. If we get in there and see that removal of the tumor will damage the lining of your uterus, we may need to take it out at the same time."

He rose and patted my arm. "I'll set you up for surgery on Monday morning at Cedar Sinai Hospital."

I can still recall the feeling in the pit of my stomach. The words mass and tumor, to me, meant cancer. I was only thirty-five years old, and if my uterus were removed, I'd never have another child. I'd never have a son. I mentally counted on my fingers. Only five days to go...

"Whatever the outcome, we'll be there for you and the girls, Carol," my parents said, offering their solace and support. Both my sister and Dupsey listened to my tearful tale in shock, and then shored up my sagging spirits with encouragement. "You absolutely cannot allow yourself to think the worst!"

I didn't call Charles. Not yet. I wasn't ready for his input.

That evening, after the twins were asleep, I thumbed through my copy of the Mary Baker Eddy blue prayer book. If there was ever a definitive time to believe in God and a Hereafter, it was now. It was also time to put my affairs in order. In a few days, I would be in the hospital for major—perhaps life-altering—surgery.

I read and prayed and sat on my bed crying. At that moment, not being around to love and raise my two beautiful daughters was beyond my comprehension. If I had cancer and was given a death sentence, would Charles be able to raise them on his own? Would he permit my family members to help him and to maintain a close relationship with them? Would the girls forget me over time?

No! I will not accept this diagnosis! I thought. Although I hadn't attended church for a number of years, a deep inner faith still lived within me. I started to read.

"…Health is not a condition of Matter, but of Mind; nor can material senses bear reliable testimony on the subject of health. The Science of Mind-healing shows it to be impossible for aught but Mind to testify truly or to exhibit the real status of man." (Science and Health by Mary Baker Eddy, pg. 120)

"Health is not a condition of Matter, but of Mind." I repeated this phrase over and over again. One by one, I recalled all of the wonderful convictions that had sustained me over the years, and I knew I was in God's hands.

My answer came to me. *Seek other opinions.*

The next morning I watched the clock and as soon as I thought medical offices would be open, I called the obstetrician/gynecologist who had delivered my twins. Miracle number one: Dr. Krohne was in town and able to see me that very morning. I thumbed through the Yellow Pages again and was able to make another emergency appointment that afternoon with a second gynecologist.

Then I called Mother. "I know you've probably got a list of things to do today, but could you come over here right now and stay with the girls until late afternoon. I need your car. Please don't ask questions until later. This is an emergency."

By the end of the day, I had been examined and probed by two specialists who knew only that I had been experiencing repeated bouts of spontaneous hemorrhaging; I made no mention of the mass felt by Dr. Vinetz, or that he had scheduled me for surgery. Both physicians came to the same conclusion. They could not feel anything… My uterus was in normal condition. Normal? No mass? No fibroid tumor? No need for surgery? How could this be?

Now I had a dilemma. Whom should I believe? All three doctors were experienced professionals.

By the time I had parked in my driveway and trudged up the walkway, my mother had the front door open. "Dr. Vinetz's office receptionist called an hour ago, Carol. He wants to see you one more time for a final assessment in preparation before Monday's surgery. Tomorrow morning at 9:00."

That evening, I again did my reading and praying. I couldn't make up my mind. All night, I tossed and turned and wrestled with the blanket. Twice I rose to pad into the girls' bedroom to examine their sweet faces as they slept.

The next morning, when the doctor's nurse coaxed me into the awkward position for the dreaded examination, I squeezed my eyelids shut to block out the sight of both bare feet in the reprehensible stirrups. I didn't open them until Dr. Vinetz touched my shoulder.

"Carol?" He was smiling. "This time, I didn't feel or see even a hint of the oversized fibroid tumor that would indicate surgery is required. I can cancel Monday's procedure." He shook his head. "I don't have a medical explanation for this abrupt change in such a short time period. Guess we'll have to chalk it up to a miracle."

Once I had redressed, I hugged Dr. Vinetz with unshed tears clouding my eyes. It took forever to reach the sanctuary of my little home, but immediately after the front door closed behind me, I gathered Lisa and Jennifer into my arms for a tight hug, hating to let go of them. Mother had cared for her grand-daughters for a second day and went to my small kitchen to make us some tea, fearing the worst. I followed her, holding the chubby hands of each of precious daughter. We would all celebrate with cookies!

"It's a *miracle*, Mother. Dr. Vinetz said it himself. I've been granted a miracle. There's no sign of a mass in my uterus. No surgery. It's been cancelled."

Not only was the fibroid gone, but I never experienced another spontaneous bleeding in my lifetime. *Not ever.*

It wasn't until after I had put the girls to bed for the night that I compared the high I was feeling at that very moment with the low of the evening less than two weeks before. I remembered thinking, that first night, of the barely used padded hangers in the clothes closet and wondering what I should do with them.

This miraculous healing was such a magnificent demonstration to me of what faith can do that I felt compelled to continue on the path of discovery. I realized that God had not forsaken me. He was waiting to be asked for His blessing. I thanked Him then and I thank Him now.

Even with the weight of this health problem lifted from my shoulders, I felt burdened by the heaviness of another issue. Spousal separations don't really work. Not when children are involved. Charles wanted to visit with his daughters daily, and I wanted them to grow up knowing their father. I didn't have a right to keep them apart. But most of his visits took place in our small home, because he had rented an even smaller apartment near our house. He didn't have room for another set of cribs and couldn't afford to buy them anyway.

At the time, both girls were young toddlers who delighted in their walking skills, although they rarely walked. They became adept, fleet-footed runners who dashed from room to room while laughing with delight. Not only that, they became climbers, seeming to challenge each other as to who was the most daring. Up onto the couch. Down to the floor and up onto a chair. Down to the floor and into the kitchen to climb onto other chairs and peek at each other over the tabletop. Their new skill kept me running as well, nervous about falls and injuries. They had reached the age of preferring mobility and struggled against confinement in my lap, their highchairs, and even in their two-seated stroller.

The girls were also increasing their vocabularies and using a few two-word sentences, like "Mo app-uh!" but the words I heard most often were "Mine!" "Up!" "No!" Although they were both adorable and kept me entertained by their cute attempts to copy my speech, I was fully aware that my role as their mother also involved teaching them acceptable behavior, like not grabbing a toy from the hands of their sister, not touching things that were not toys, and not hitting anyone for any reason.

Charles seemed to encourage misbehavior, or perhaps it seemed that way because he wanted them to believe his leniency meant he was the better parent. I tried hard to focus on his good side as I always had, but our so-called 'shared' life became increasingly miserable. I tried to remain a family for the sake of the girls, occasionally thinking that we could work things out, but any time spent with him was unbearable and downright frightening.

One evening, we were supposed to go out as a couple to see a movie, and he came to the house to pick me up. He arrived early to say goodnight to the girls and then flopped onto the couch to flip channels and watch a television show. "Are you about ready to leave, Charles?" I asked. With narrowed eyes and pinched lips, he threw me a look of fierce irritation and then hurled the remote control at me with all his strength. I dodged just in time and cringed as it hit the living room wall with a resounding smack, leaving a visible pock mark. Smothering my gasp of fear, so the girls and their sitter wouldn't hear me, I pointed at the door. "Leave. Now. The evening is over."

Every time Charles resorted to such violent impulses, I was glad we were separated and he wasn't living fulltime in the house. He was totally unlike the person I had come to love before marriage. How could I live with him when I never knew what would set him off? What if he lost control with the girls? They had heard his uncontrollable anger many times but not seen the physical abuse that kept me in long sleeves and up-to-the-neck blouses.

Still, I couldn't make a decision on what to do. Was the problem me? Did I provoke him? Were there some magic words I could use to halt or even prevent episodes?

Then came the occasion when Jenny wandered into the living room at the very moment Charles wrapped his hands around my neck in a chokehold, his face red with seething rage. Frightened by the looks on our faces, she wailed her protest. That did it. I would not have our daughters exposed to any more verbal explosions or physical abuse of their mother. I was raised in a calm environment, and Jenny was already suffering from the early signs of a panic disorder.

Gagging from the pressure of Charles' thumbs on my throat, I uttered a guttural order. "Stop!" It was enough to break through some invisible wall blocking his consciousness. He heard Jenny's cries and saw the terror in my eyes and backed away, covering his face with trembling hands.

"You're sick, Charles," I said in a voice that sounded amazingly calm under the circumstances. "You must see a doctor. You're a danger to yourself and to all of us. Go now, so I can comfort Jenny."

I started divorce proceedings that week.

14

A DIVORCE MEANT I was without a car. Mine had never been replaced. One day indelible in my memory, the girls required a prescription and the only way to get to the pharmacy was to haul them with me in their Radio Flyer red wagon.

I placed a bed pillow between them, propped them up back-to-back against it in the wagon bed, and pulled them slowly to the Rexall drugstore on Pico Boulevard while thinking wistfully of the gorgeous Lancia Aurelia I had driven while living in Rome. Those days were gone, but I wouldn't exchange my darlings for a dozen Aurelia's.

At the time, I was grateful to have the wagon, but on the way home, I determined to change our future lifestyle. It was too risky to think about returning to my art career, or lack of one. Any job I took had to bring in more money than I had to spend on salary for a mother-replacement.

The very next week, I read about a job possibility in the 'employment wanted' section of the newspaper. Marcia Lehr, who had become well-known in Hollywood circles as the premier wedding and party planner/designer, was looking for someone to help her with the hand-addressing of hundreds of invitation envelopes. The location of her shop immediately caught my attention. It was on Robertson Boulevard within biking distance from my house.

I felt the first rush of adrenaline since giving birth to the twins and picked up the phone. "Mother, another potential miracle just dropped into my lap. I saw a job description in the want-ads of today's paper and know it was written specifically for me. It sounds like something I could do at home when the girls are asleep." I read it to her and asked if she could watch the girls once again while I went by the shop for an interview.

Mother agreed wholeheartedly and, while waiting for her, I searched through my wardrobe for the most appropriate outfit. Not too dressy. Not too casual. Professional, but approachable.

Two hours later, I was seated next to Marcia as she showed me samples of addressed party and wedding invitations. "I'm impressed with your art background, Carol. I believe we could work together, but I don't want you to think this work is easy. You say you've never written in any form for calligraphy. It takes hours of practice to get it right, and I am very particular about quality. I demand perfection, because my clients expect it of me."

"I'm willing to learn."

"I can tell that you are, but 'willing to' and 'can' are worlds apart. Watch me. I usually write in Spencerian Script. It was developed by a young man in the mid-19th century—Platt Rogers Spencer. As you can see, it's very elegant and has many loops and flourishes." She reached for an envelope and a pen that she dipped into a pot of black ink.

For the next several minutes, I watched every movement of the pen as she addressed a sample envelope in a style of calligraphy. The capital letters swirled into works of art.

"May I take a few of your samples home with me?" I asked. "I have a good eye. I think I can mimic your writing with a little practice. I'll return first thing in the morning to show you my work. I couldn't ask you to hire me without first seeing if I have the talent required." I held back tears all the way home, both from elation over the prospect of becoming a wage-earner again and from pure anxiety over whether I could learn the difficult calligraphy technique in one night of practice. I wanted the position. I wanted to work with Marcia Lehr.

As soon as Lisa and Jenny closed their eyes for the night, I tiptoed from their bedroom and took a seat at my desk. Mrs. Lehr had given me a pen, two tips, a bottle of ink and a plentiful supply of paper in various sizes and weights. She had also provided a chart illustrating the capital and small letters and figures in the same script style for dates, house and phone numbers. I propped it up in front of me and started to write copies of each letter and then over and over again, until I was satisfied with the results. By that time, I had also consumed at least a dozen chocolate chip cookies.

In the morning, after dressing and feeding the girls, I stuffed my best Spencerian Script examples into a canvas bag along with the pen, tips and ink.

Marcia Lehr hired me. And as if that weren't enough, she kindly agreed to my working at home. I showed her photographs of the twins and gave her a shortened version of my marriage difficulties that had left me to raise them as a single mother. "Until I can afford to buy another car, I'll have to bike to work," I said.

"That's the preferred method of transportation in several countries of the world," she said. "You'll be riding in style."

Marcia was a godsend in more ways than I can count. Her generosity and friendship was bountiful, including a salary that soon allowed me to buy a used car. It was in good shape and I breathed a sigh of relief. Now I could get the girls, who Marcia called "Tootsie and Wootsie" to the pediatrician for checkups or illnesses, to the homes of their grandparents and aunties, and to parks for romping in the grass. Having a car at my disposal also meant I could make better use of my time for grocery shopping and other errands. Marcia also introduced me to Weight Watcher's; we attended weekly meetings together and discussed our ongoing battle with weight, after I confessed my cookie binge while learning the elaborate and graceful Spencerian Script.

Marcia was one of the most warm-hearted people I was ever privileged to know. She was the queen of all the Hollywood parties and forever a queen in my heart. She would be so proud of how her son and daughter have taken over the reins of her company and made the business an even bigger success today while maintaining her reputation for producing only the finest work. To this day, I remain in touch with her family.

Another wonderful event happened. After Anita had to return back to Mexico I heard about Japanese exchange students studying at the "Beverly Hills International School of Language". It was located near my house. That is how my beautiful Miyuki Tomita God-daughter arrived. She was like an older sister to the girls.

Charles continued to visit the girls, although he came less often now that we were divorced. It seemed that all he could deal with was the control of his erratic behavior. There was a part of me that always felt sorry for him; he was like a lost soul. For the rest of his life, he remained in the small apartment he had first leased upon our separation and worked as a night manager at the Toluca Market on Pico Boulevard. Sadly, he never became the real estate appraiser he had once aspired to be.

15

O N APRIL 8, 1973, the Maestro, my beloved father, suffered a massive heart attack and died. Picasso died on the same day. Both gifted artists in different fields. One known and respected and talked about by millions worldwide decades after his death. The other known by a few musicians, actors, film producers and lovers of jazz and dance tunes nationwide of his generation. But to members of his family and to band/orchestra music aficionados of the mid-1900's, his music lives on.

Daddy and I had spoken earlier that evening and ended our conversation with, "I'll talk to you tomorrow." Instead, I received a very early phone call from my brother Donald, who was living with my parents at the time.

"Sorry to greet you so early with bad news, Carol. Daddy died last night."

"Daddy . . . what? Just like that, he died?" I heard myself say the words, but a voice over the phone delivering such an unexpected message wasn't real. I had laughed and talked with him just before bedtime. He was getting ready for a cross-country trip. He hadn't said a word about not feeling well. I felt myself go numb and then cold. "Is this a joke, Donald?"

"I wouldn't joke about something like this, Carol." "Are you at the hospital? Is Mother with you? Should I come?" My heart was in my throat and it took all my strength to hold the phone receiver steady in my hand.

"We're at home. There was no reason for him to be taken to the hospital. Neither of us felt a pulse. I called the police. They came to ensure he died naturally. Mom had Dad taken to Hillside Memorial Park Mortuary. Right now, she's pretty much in shock."

"Does Sandra know?"

"Not yet. I called you first."

"I'll call her. Tell Mommy we're on the way."

I awoke Miyuki, and within the hour, I was with my siblings and mother in the living room. We hugged, momentarily speechless and anesthetized by our personal sorrow. But there was no time to grieve. Not yet. Not for those closest to the man called husband and father. There were relatives and close family friends to call, a decision to make about the rabbi and the day and time of the funeral and burial and a reception and who would cater it. And an obituary to write.

"Dad was at the piano when it happened," Donald said. "He was evidently making some changes to the order of his orchestrations for that Jean Flagler party in Washington, D.C., next week. I was up in my room when I heard Mom shouting for me. It was late. About 11:00 p.m. She thought she heard him cry out, and when she didn't hear his footsteps on the stairway, she went to investigate."

"He died in my arms." Mother's voice sounded far away and as forlorn as a mourning dove's soft, drawn-out calls that sound like perpetual laments. She had been unexpectedly bereft of her lifetime partner and it was heartbreaking to see her suffering. "I'll call one of Daddy's orchestra members and find out if he can contact Jean Flagler," I said, once my brain was functioning again. "She'll need to find another orchestra for her party." Remembering the funerals I'd attended throughout my life, my thoughts jumped from one topic to another in rapid succession. I mentally turned off the 'emotion' spigot. It was the only way I could remain standing and supportive.

Sandra had the same concerns. "Should the orchestra play at a reception, Mother? Is it proper? Or maybe just an ensemble of three or four for background music? Where should a reception be held? Here at the house or someplace bigger? Should it take place directly after the burial at Hillside or on another day so we'll have more time to plan something appropriate?"

The questions seemed to never end and both Sandra and I were at a loss for answers.

"We'll have it here, of course." Mommy grew in strength of will at the first pause. "This is your father's home. We'll welcome all who loved him directly after the burial. No set time. We'll keep the house open as long as necessary. Carol, call the caterer I've used so many times. They will know exactly what to do."

Fortunately, the staff at Hillside Memorial was accustomed to planning Jewish funerals that not only followed traditional beliefs but for those families that didn't. Since mine rarely went to Temple except for the Jewish holidays—at least while my grandfather was alive—I was surprised when Mommy said she wanted a rabbi to conduct the funeral service and graveside burial. I had always felt removed from Judaism, as my father's work was the Pasadena Society and he rarely discussed his ethnicity. In those days, few Jews did, especially in Hollywood, because of the anti-Jewish attitude that infused the war years.

Word of Daddy's death spread rapidly and his funeral service was attended by about four hundred people. Friends, neighbors, actors, producers, and dozens of musicians were there. Each had special and unique memories of Daddy's impact on their life. If I had been one of them and not a daughter, I would have lingered around to listen and learn things I didn't know about him. Instead, I clung to Mother and Sandra and moved about like a zombie wherever we were directed to go by the Hillside staff.

We were given instructions by the rabbi directly before the funeral service, so we knew what to expect and also at the following burial service. He recited a prayer that was a blessing reaffirming the value of life and faith held by Jews: Baruch attah Adonai eloheinu melech ha'olam, dayan haemet (Praised are You, Lord our God, sovereign of the universe, the true judge.). He pinned black ribbons to our garments—over my mother's heart and on the right side for my siblings and me and for Daddy's sister Lee (brothers Harry and Myron had already passed away)—and then cut the ribbon with a razor he pulled from his black suit pocket. He explained that this was a Jewish rite known as kriah; the torn ribbon symbolized our inner sorrow and mourning and the tearing of the fabric of our family. The ribbon has taken the place of tearing one's clothing.

The slow ride in the black limousine that closely followed behind the hearse holding Daddy's coffin seemed to last forever as it wended through the paved cemetery road. We were led by a Hillside assistant to a row of chairs placed at the graveside for the immediate family. I had attended other funerals and burials, of course, both Jewish and non-Jewish ones. This time, however, I was one of the principal mourners. Everything felt . . . different.

After Daddy's coffin had been lowered in the grave, the rabbi led us in reciting kaddish, a prayer that encourages mourners like us to confront our dear one's death and then look forward to our future without his presence. I didn't understand until weeks later that kaddish means 'holy' and is an action we take to praise God. The rite must be taken in public and in the presence of at least ten Jewish adults, called a minyan; we certainly met that qualification with so many family and friends from the Hollywood community present.

Directly after the interment, those present for the burial and another vast number of Daddy's business acquaintances, musicians and other friends joined the family at Mother's house. We had arranged for a caterer and there was food everywhere. Strangely, I could not eat a thing. While I remained in shock over the devastating loss of my father, people streamed through the house for the next few hours. The mood was somber, not at all like the joyful ambiance of most Sorkin events. I literally stopped eating for three days.

Since Daddy's passing, I continue to hear his music played over the sound systems in elevators, malls and on the radio. It's like he is saying, "Hello, Carol, I'm okay. Put on a happy face and enjoy your day." I have never tired of watching reruns of movies produced in Hollywood between the Forties and Sixties, when the background music was provided by his orchestra or his participation in one as a musician who could play several instruments. Of all the instruments he played, however, the saxophone remains my favorite.

16

OVER THE NEXT several weeks, time seemed to race ahead faster than I could live it. I wanted to 'be there' for Mother, who was feeling frazzled over the mountains of decisions to make and all the paperwork that comes with the death of someone like Daddy. The purpose and order of her days had changed in a finger snap. In the weeks and months after his funeral, she also mourned the loss of parties and receptions for his musician friends and clients. Although she received invitations from many, she felt uncomfortable attending without her usual escort. She was now the "widow of Barney Sorkin" rather than the "wife of Barney Sorkin" and just beginning to learn who she was as an individual at a time when women were still known as the matriarchs of their family unit—the glue that held them together. She had lived through the war and the Great Depression and the deaths of several family members, but this was different.

I was mourning, too, and it was difficult to keep a stiff upper lip as I tried to bring comfort and a new sense of order to both her life and mine. By the end of the first couple months, I felt like a failure. How could I be a comforter when I needed comforting myself?

I turned to my customary soul soother: sugary treats like chocolates, do-nuts, cake, pie, ice cream, pudding. The form didn't matter as long as it was sweet. Of course the adding of another one or more thousand calories each day took its toll on me. It wasn't long before I was digging in the back of my closet for clothing I'd saved in a larger size during another time of binging.

I was still working long hours with my calligraphy assignments, and the girls demanded more and more attention as beginning grade-schoolers who embraced each new experience with enthusiasm and wanted to talk and talk about them for hours on end.

Marcia Lehr saw what was happening to me. I had long ago put aside everything I'd learned about portion control in Weight Watchers while attending meetings with her. I blamed it on cooking to satisfy the children. On not planning a menu for the week ahead. On Daddy's death. On my mother's need for longer talks on the telephone and increased visits. Or that I couldn't think straight and had difficulty squeezing in enough time to sleep.

Marcia told me about Dr. Joseph Murphy, who had written the Power of Your Subconscious Mind and many other books. "Dr. Murphy often speaks at the Ebell Theatre on Wilshire Boulevard," she said. "Why don't you look into attending one of his lectures? It wouldn't hurt, and he might say something that speaks directly to you and strengthens your resolve."

By now, I was feeling like a boat without a rudder or even oars to slowly row myself to any definitive destination. I was adrift in a turbulent sea of anxiety and apprehension about future uncertainties. The title of Dr. Murphy's book intrigued me. What did I have to lose?

After the first lecture, I was hooked. I started to attend his lectures, which always attracted large audiences. After one of them, I swallowed my fears and hurried toward the stage to join several others who were praising his presentation. I saw that he was, in reality, a small-boned man about my height. On stage, he appeared much taller. I also understood why his presence seemed so godlike in the spotlight; he had a full head of pure white hair.

Finally, it was my turn. "Do you ever schedule personal appointments with individuals like me?" I asked, my voice sounding more like one of my daughter's, high and diminutive.

Perhaps he saw the desperation in my eyes. He was more than agreeable. "I don't have a private practice of any kind, if that's what you're asking, Carol, but I would be happy to meet with you in your home or mine." When he gave his address, I learned it was just a few blocks from my house.

A week later, as soon as I had delivered the girls into Miyuki's hands, I walked to Dr. Murphy's house and rang the doorbell, eager to exchange thoughts with this gifted person. "Come in, come in, Carol. We'll sit in my living room. It's more comfortable than my office. May I get you something to drink? Water or a soda?"

"Nothing, thank you." I glanced at all the framed photographs of him with well-known people and articles from various journals and newspapers. In his own niche, he was a celebrity.

"What can I do for you, Carol? You seemed troubled when last we spoke."

The words tumbled out of my mouth so fast, I almost forgot to breathe. I told him about my chronic insecurity and battle with the feelings of worthlessness and unworthiness that resulted in out-of-control eating and weight gain. "Sometimes I can actually feel the angst growing like black mold in my body that's thriving on the warmth and darkness inside. I want to stop it. To scrub it away once and for all."

"I hear you, Carol. First, you should know that yours is not an uncommon problem." He rubbed the end-of-day whiskers on his cheeks. "So, this is not a recent struggle?"

"Unfortunately, I've had it since childhood. I was given chocolates and cookies, instead of hugs and praise, because my parents were busy from dawn to midnight every day of the year. I find myself repeating the pattern. I, too, work from dawn to late at night—out of necessity as a single mother of twins—and I resort to giving cookies to my daughters rather than hugs and my attention." I hesitated. "Actually, two major events in the past year have fueled my current struggle—divorce from the twin's father and the death of my own father."

"Hmm, I see. Well, both are traumatic experiences. Your life as you've known it has drastically changed. Two of your confidants are no longer available to you. Often, such painful incidents drive people away from eating. They starve themselves and suffer a rapid loss of weight. But, on the other hand, it's not uncommon for others to turn to food. That seems to be your choice."

I nodded. "Eating makes me feel better. For the moment anyway. I have a special affinity for sweets of all kinds." I quietly poured out my heart to this man and practically begged him to help me. He was renowned for his wisdom. If anyone could free me forever from my food addiction and compulsive behavior, he could. I finally stopped talking and waited to receive the healing words than would end my problem and bring about future bliss.

Dr. Murphy was quiet for what seemed like an eon. "When you get home, Carol, I want you to look into your dresser mirror and repeat, 'I am a child of God. I am a child of God.' Do this several times a day and think deeply about what it means."

That's it? Six words? That was going to heal me? That was the best advice the famous Dr. Joseph Murphy could give me? I tried not to show my disappointment. Where were all the words of deep wisdom? Where were the practical, beneficial and specific rules that I could immediately put into use toward becoming a stronger and happier person? I wanted a plan. Ten steps. Easy to follow instructions. Suggestions of what to read.

All the way home, I groused about the pitiful piece of advice I had been given. It would never work. With each step I took, I felt more depressed and deflated. My anticipation had been so high. I had placed this man on a high pedestal where someone with such a great mind deserved to be. I had thanked my lucky stars for the glorious opportunity to visit with him one-on-one and receive personal advice that came from years of experience working with people like me.

I tried the ritual. Religiously. I peered into a mirror every time I passed one and recited the phrase. Before I went to bed, I gazed into the dresser mirror sobbing, "I am of child of God. I am of child of God."

Each week, I gained another two pounds.

The face in the mirror reflected my feelings of despair and failure. My life consisted of work, sleep, laundry, cooking, grocery shopping and house cleaning. I rose at four o'clock some mornings to finish work assignments so that I could deliver them to Marcia after taking the girls to school. This, after addressing envelopes until 11:00 p.m., because I could no longer focus on the script. My life was not only affecting the girls' behavior, it was affecting mine. I developed an increasing impatience; just about everything annoyed me, from the beeping of a car horn to the chirping of a bird.

This was my life in the mid-seventies. I was approaching my forties.

"Of course," I reasoned on good days, "I'm not the only woman in this position. Every major city has hundreds to thousands just like me." But a woman suffering from emotional or physical wounds can't see further than her front door. She knows she is absolutely the only woman in the world suffering her fate.

Determined to do something about my condition, I became a "meetings" junkie in the next few months. I attended local gatherings of Over-Eater's Anonymous, Alcoholics Anonymous and Weight Watchers (again!). I was not an alcoholic, but I found the truthful sharing of daily temptations and falling by the wayside—only to rise up for another effort to succeed—powerful. Each organization had the same basic tenet: that to truly succeed in changing our addiction, we needed the fellowship of others going through the same struggles, specifically one partner who would be available at all times to talk us through difficult moments. And we needed to take one day at a time. One hour at a time, if necessary.

At the end of each AA meeting, we would recite the Serenity Prayer. "God grant me the Serenity to accept the things I cannot change, Courage to change the things I can, and the Wisdom to know the difference."

Unfortunately, reciting a prayer does not guarantee you can put it to work in your life. I alternated between extremes in behavior, fasting for a few days and then gradually adding a meal, until I was eating three meals a day with no in between snacks but stuffing as much as I could into those three meals. They always ended with a desert. Feast or famine. No sensible portion control.

My compulsion to eat for personal and momentary contentment continued. As did my guilt and misery.

One of the most painful memories I recall was rising from bed at one o'clock in the morning and driving to an all-night convenience store for a box of ice-cream bars. I left the girls sleeping alone in the house and never gave a thought to my not being there in the event they should wake up and call out for me. Fortunately, I made it home safely before that could happen. I gobbled down the entire box of bars and finally returned to my bed still feeling hollow and forlorn.

Food from the grocery store does not satisfy the soul. The soul needs spiritual food.

My behavior showed a total lack of self-control that brought nothing but dejection. I hated myself. I adored the girls and knew I was a good mother. How could someone so blessed be so destructive in her personal life?

I came up with a new set of reasons. Ones I used with great success to elicit understanding, rather than criticism, from friends and family who fretted silently and with carefully constructed verbal suggestions. For instance, I needed to be healthy and strong to handle household chores; if I were thin; I wouldn't have the needed stamina and would be more prone to catching viral illnesses. Or, I subconsciously used my size as a shield against any potential suitors; a plump body kept men at arm's distance. After all, most men, especially in Beverly Hills, preferred thin. Anyway, I wasn't ready for another relationship. My past ones had ended in failure.

At one particular Over-eater's meeting, I was invited to a prayer group that met in Westwood, California. It was there that I met a wonderful woman who was instrumental in my eventual healing. Janet Levy. She had shared Catherine Ponder's resounding affirmation: "I have unshakeable faith in the perfect outcome of every situation in my life, for God is in absolute control." I loved this confirmation of faith and have used and shared it often over the years. It became a declaration of my own unshakeable faith and trust in God.

We ended the meeting with the Serenity Prayer, as in those of AA. Then Janet gave us each a Miracle Card with the words I desire an image on the front. The card was blank on the back. This small white paper card held some sort of metaphysical healing, because it became my passport to a new beginning. I was intrigued and gave a lot of thought to my desires. I settled on three: peace of mind, a slimmer body that suited my height and bone structure, and a magnificent, love-filled marriage. At the time, each seemed far beyond my reach.

Another woman at the prayer meeting mentioned attending a study group at the Science of Mind church located on La Cienega, very close to my home. I had walked past or driven by it many times and not given it a second look, as the architecture was quite unpretentious. I was surprised and pleased when I walked through the entrance and caught my first glimpse of the stunning, stained-glass windows. Each one was like a kaleidoscope that continuously transmitted patterns of muted colors on the interior of the church. Needless to say, they spoke to my artistic nature and instantly produced a feeling of serenity.

The study groups were in the evening, and after hiring the neighbor girl across the street to stay with my daughters during my absence. Miyuki had to return back to Japan they no longer needed fulltime now that they were in school, I started to attend one that met once a week.

At first, all I heard were words, lots of words that were often difficult to comprehend. It was comforting to me, however, to sit and relax. Nothing was required of me.

It wasn't long before I felt my life changing in every realm.

There were about fifteen regular attendees in my particular group. a tapestry of people who were as eager as I was to hear the speakers, Patricia and Alex Turnbull, a charming couple who had been in the field of religious science for years and had once worked with Ernest Holmes, the founder of the church. Patricia was a petite, soft-spoken woman with meticulously manicured hair and nails; Alex was a distinguished-looking gentleman who always dressed in a suit and tie. As I got to know them better, I would sometimes fantasize about what it would be like to enjoy such a marriage. One of mutual respect and support. One where my husband would be a kind and loving man.

The Turnbulls would read from the Science of Mind textbook and answer our questions. We would all take notes. No one was ridiculed, judged, or made to feel less important than the other despite our vast differences. We were told that the Science of Mind "is not a special revelation of any individual; it is, rather, the culmination of all revelations." I didn't understand this at all. Nothing made sense to me, but just sitting and listening was comforting. At least for the time I spent there I wasn't eating!

Then Patricia continued to read. *"We take the Good wherever we find it, making it our own in so far as we understand it. The realization that Good is Universal, and that as much Good as any individual is able to incorporate in his life is his to use, is what constitutes the Science of Mind and Spirit."*

She had my full attention now.

"We have discussed the nature of The Thing as being Universal Energy, Mind, Intelligence, Spirit—finding conscious and individualized centers of expression through us—and that man's intelligence is this Universal Mind, functioning at the level of man's concept of It. This is the essence of the whole teaching."

I continued to attend the class once a week. As I became more comfortable, I allowed myself to look about the room while I listened. Other attendees were also checking out how attentive others were; it seemed that several of us were having trouble grasping the concepts.

I had already purchased a 1938 edition of *Science of Mind* by Ernest Holmes and read more of it at every opportunity. I read on Page 166 that *"...this thing which is causing him to suffer now is not a law, has no right to be, is no longer effective through him, cannot suggest anything to him,"* and that when a practitioner declares and removes any obstruction and states that the person is now all right, he/she is free from that condition. It can never return.

Slowly, I learned to accept myself regardless of what I looked like, the mistakes I had made in the past, and even that, up to now, I had a compulsion to use food as a comforter. No one was more surprised than I was when I realized I could rebuild my feelings of self-worth.

This was 1977, four years after Daddy's passing. I had found something upon which to create a new me. I signed up for classes to become a Science of Mind practitioner.

One evening, I prepared a dish using ground veal I had purchased at Ralph's Market. I was about to enjoy my dinner with the girls and, without warning, bit down on a small piece of bone. Somehow, I had chewed with such force I broke a tooth. My mouth was bleeding, and I reached for my napkin to prevent blood from dripping onto my blouse. The girls watched me with wide-eyed interest. I assured them I was all right. Then, all I could think of was that I didn't have an extra dime in my account to spend at the dentist. At least, it wasn't how I chose to spend whatever I had in the account.

The bottom line is that the dentist pulled the broken tooth. There was no such thing as porcelain overlays in those days. I was so upset by my appearance that, of course, I turned to extra food for solace.

Later that week, on Friday evening after dinner, I drove the girls to Baskin Robbins on Canon Drive, in Beverly Hills. While waiting for the girls to select their favorite flavor for a one-scoop cone, I instructed the employee behind the counter to fill the largest ice cream tub with "a scoop of all 31 flavors." I watched with wildly beating heart as Mint Chocolate, Jamoca Almond Fudge, Butter Pecan and Strawberry Ripple were ladled into the tub, followed by all the other flavors.

The filled container was so heavy; I could barely carry it into the house... I must have checked my watch a dozen times while getting the girls ready for bed. As soon as I closed their bedroom door, I headed back to the kitchen. Selecting a tablespoon from the silverware drawer, I removed the massive carton from the freezer, and standing at the kitchen counter, I began to conquer the entire caloric contents. I savored every flavor and noted the difference in texture. Nuts, fruits, chocolate, caramel, peanut butter, toffee and on and on. I was on a mission of self-destruction; I thought I was living out my longtime fantasy. I didn't have to make a flavor choice, and I could have as much as I wanted now, no one was watching or judging me. But, surprisingly, after I had scraped the last spoonful from the tub, I still felt empty.

That really scared me. Why was I not stuffed? And then it came to me. There never was going to be enough ice cream to fill my emotional hole. Ice cream-or any type of sugar, food, alcohol, drugs- none of it could fill an emotional hole. Oh my God, I was overwhelmed by the sense of emptiness I felt. I had hit rock bottom. I was miserable, unhappy and in pain. Again I realized there was never going to be enough ice cream to satisfy my craving for sugar-filled comfort. I had glibly recited in AA meetings and Weight Watchers that I was addicted to food. Now I fully understood that I was not addicted to food. I was addicted to trying to fill an emotional hole. The seriousness of my insatiable craving. It was controlling my life as effectively as alcohol or destructive drugs.

At that moment, a vision of my grandfather's teeth soaking in a glass of water at his bedside passed through my mind. If I continued to live as I was, the day would come when my own teeth would occupy such a tumbler while I slept. Probably sooner, rather than later. If the loss of one tooth could humiliate me, being toothless would keep me in my bed, never to see the light of day.

One day in March of 1977, I listened more intently to the words of the practitioner at the Science of Mind Institute. I don't remember the specific day. Perhaps I should, because of the impact and significance it represented in my life. *"When a practitioner declares and removes any obstruction and states that the person is now all right, he is free from that condition. It can never return."*

My mind raced through the possibilities. For the rest of my life, I would be free from the urges that had such power over my self-control. This was a tall order, but in a grand design of the Universe and with God in, thru, and around me, I felt I could do it. It would involve an unflinching and steadfast faith, but it would bring a freedom to enjoy my life once again, perhaps for the first time ever. I would be emancipated, liberated, unhampered, and released of my unimpeded need for comfort through sweet calories.

I desperately wanted this.

I often used prayer, especially on the occasions when my need for Divine intervention and power literally drove me to my knees, always remembering that my faith during previous times of seemingly impossible resolution had brought unforgettable miracles.

Once again, I embarked on a journey to repair my fractured existence. As I had, when attending Overeaters Anonymous and Alcoholics Anonymous meetings, I heard many others declare an ability to beat their addiction one day at a time until it grew to years. "Just for Today" was always the motto or mantra. My new plan was to abstain from any sugar in any form for one day. Twenty-four hours. Just 1,440 minutes. My mind accepted ten minutes at a time easier than thinking of the whole day. I could do it. With God's help.

There is a wonderful quote by Elizabeth Kubler-Ross, Swiss-American psychiatrist and author of On Death and Dying (c1969), which expresses her theory about the five stages of grief that made greater sense to me at this time:

"It is only when we truly know and understand that we have a limited time on Earth and that we have no way of knowing when our time is up that we will begin to live each day to the fullest, as if it were the only one we had."

I had to develop a plan, one that was simple and I could follow.

My Plan... Step 1 – faith
  Step 2 – wisdom and self-awareness
  Step 3 - preparation (the development of A blueprint)
  Step 4 – execution of the blueprint

I went to bed that evening with the full realization that there would never ever be enough food to fill the emptiness I felt, regardless of the support and love of my dear family members and precious daughters.

Step 1-faith

I prayed to God that night to give me strength and courage as I embarked on this new journey. I had been blessed throughout my lifetime with God's miracles and this time I was desperate.

Step 2- wisdom and self-awareness

It was not going to be history repeating itself. I would give it my all. Failure to me was not acceptable. I was ready.

Upon awakening the next morning, Saturday, I ate a sensible breakfast. Believe me, after all my Weight Watchers classes and recipes, I knew sensible up the kazoo. I got all my utensils ready: my teaspoons, measuring cup and a food scale. I set a kitchen timer for every 30-60 minutes just to make it through that first day. Just make it for 1440 minutes. My relationship with timing goes way back to my childhood years of piano lessons as I listened to the metronome tick the proper tempo of the music. At the time, it had been an annoying sound to me, as my fingers tried to find the right keys. Now, I listened intently with one ear, so I could return to the kitchen every time the timer beckoned me for a resetting. Each ding would mean I had accomplished one hour of my goal.

But I knew setting a timer wouldn't be enough. If I did nothing but think about how many minutes remained before the resetting was required, I would continually think of the treats that the timer was supposed to warn me against! I had to get involved in other things. I took a walk with the girls, played songs for them on the piano, read them stories, and helped them reorganize all their dolls and other toys. After all, our brain can only think of one thing at a time, if we're focused on that one thing.

The hard part was after I said goodnight to the girls. The house seemed to echo with my breathing. I straightened pillows on the couch, rearranged objects on tabletops, and cranked up the television set to become engrossed in *The Bionic Woman* starring Lindsay Wagner. She made every hard task seem easy to conquer. I needed to acquire some of her superwoman capabilities.

That night, I headed for bed without consuming a single sugar product. Once I had brushed my teeth, my focus turned to keeping them clean. I read a chapter of my Science of Mind book. Sunday morning, I woke up feeling ecstatic. I had achieved my goal—twenty-four hours without a single milligram of sugar. I went to the mirror in my bedroom and stared into it. Although I looked the same, there was a new spark in my eyes. I fell onto my knees and sobbed "I am a child of God." At that moment, I felt a real connection to the Divine Power of the universe.

Step 3- preparation of the blueprint

I savored my triumphant moment, but quickly reminded myself that my success would be short lived unless I performed in the same way for another twenty-four hours. One day more. I couldn't think in terms of a lifetime. A lifetime was a long road, and it would doubtlessly be filled with many detours. I had been on it so many times I knew where the pit stops were most likely to occur.

At the moment of this writing, I can say that I have walked on my new path for thirty-nine years without consuming real sugars. The temptation was always there, but I kept to my pattern of resisting that moment and then through that day, often through breath-stopping moments of weakness. Always, I have reminded myself that I could have all of the sugar-based treats I wanted tomorrow, but for today, I would abstain.

Step 4 – execution of the blueprint

It took a great deal of mental muscle-building to sustain me. Whenever I would state emphatically, "I do not accept this!" regardless of the circumstances, something both internally and externally happened at the same time to make me pause and think. "What made my resolve successful this time? What did I do differently?" As I dissected such experiences, the one overriding message was always, "There will never be enough ice-cream to fill me up, so why bother? Think about the result of giving in."

This made a significant impact on me; each time I was successful in choosing not to give in to a needless consuming of empty calories, regardless of what was happening in my life at the time, I could celebrate a mini-victory for that minute, hour, or day. And each time I  experienced these successes, my self-confidence grew. I would use visualization and see myself, dancing, living a happy life. Poise under pressure, as it were. I was no longer the woman who would open a cookie box and eat the contents to the last crumb while still in the car on the way home from a store. I was even brave enough to speak up against the urges of my mother to "try just one bite, Carol. Surely one bite won't hurt you."

"No, Mommy. No more cookies or cake or pie or any of your other delicious desserts. You know I can't take just one bite. I am finally learning that each 'one bite' means I cannot stop until I've eaten a slice or a whole pie. Help me be who I want to be."

It sounds so easy, but it's not. Even today, I have moments that present a war of wills, but the way in which I deal with them is different. I would envision how I would feel an hour later, I was building a mental muscle and it felt great.

Important steps have been not testing myself, not bringing temptations into the house. Distract myself with other actions, sewing, dancing, walking, and new adventures. Keeping a journal became a major tool.

I looked forward to my Science of Mind study groups and understood, with increasing clarity, that words have power to influence, to persuade, to comfort and to lead us down the wrong pathway. It is necessary to think before acting or reacting. I learned that I had to pray for a specific demonstration without outlining how it would come to me.

With an artist's mind and curiosity, I noticed anew that every piece of furniture, every car brand and style, every bit of clothing, the buildings and houses in my neighborhood and city had a blueprint. Even down to the smallest nut and bolt. I would need a blueprint, too—a Carol Design for living a new and happier life.

When I wrote on the blank side of my Miracle Card that I wished for a slim body that suited by height and bone structure, I honestly thought it was a pipedream. I made it my primary goal, because the size of my body was tied to my addiction. Food. The more I ate the more weight I gained. My size contributed to my insecurity and unhappiness. When I was unhappy, I ate to neutralize my pain.

During the process of studying how to control my craving for sweets, I learned that my mind-set was influenced by the superficial Hollywood attitude towards weight. Fairly or unfairly judging the worth of someone by this personal criteria was part of daily conversation. This is not what Science of Mind or Christianity teaches, however. Since I was a child of God, I had assurance that I was acceptable at any weight, no matter how many pounds registered on my bathroom scale. God looks on the inward heart, not on our outward appearances. For me, though, how I looked on the outside had a negative effect on my health and my self-confidence. My choice of sweet food as the "cure-all" for all perceived problems crippled my ability to be my best. Coming to that understanding took time.

A lot of time.

I wasn't ready for too much logic yet and certainly not for a choice between growth of my spiritual life or reduction of my size and shape. I was living my Blueprint Design for the New Me by cutting out pictures from magazines of bathing beauties and gluing a photo of my face over theirs. In this way, I could visualize what I might look like when Hollywood thin. I plastered the door of my refrigerator with these pictures, hoping this approach would assist in my determination to stay focused on my goal.

This was uncharted territory. Even while gazing at these photos, I instructed myself to resist subtle sabotage, lest they discourage me enough to believe my goal was hopeless. It would be difficult to unlearn the firmly ingrained hand-to-mouth habit that went with watching television or reading a book. A jar of peanuts on my lap was part of relaxing.

I stopped buying jars of peanuts. If they weren't in the house, I couldn't eat them. It was an intriguing process to purposefully change old habits, and I was fascinated by how my decision-making was influenced by my mind.

As my weight diminished pound by pound and those fashion jeans were easier to don, I became a full believer in the process. I prayed and studied and faithfully attended my Science of Mind classes, eager to become a licensed practitioner. I also reread the Miracle Card I had tucked under my lingerie in a dresser drawer. Truthfully, I read it every day.

As my scale and clothing showed progress on my first wish, and as I experienced an ever-increasing peace of mind, I decided I was ready to meet my soul mate. With eager anticipation of such a momentous event, I attended potluck dinners and other social functions for singles with regularity.

And all the while I sat at the dining room table addressing envelopes in fancy calligraphy; I listened to Science of Mind tapes. The words subconscious, omnipresent, subjective and causation were not in my everyday vocabulary. The more I understood them, especially in context, the more readily they became part of my everyday vocabulary.

17

A S MY STUDIES progressed, so did my self-confidence. I was finally able to put the pieces of my former marriages to rest and achieve the peace of mind I had yearned for. It was amazing. After tiptoeing into belief in a Power I couldn't see or touch, I strode with assurance into an unshakable faith that the perfect outcome for any number of difficult life situations was possible. My trust in this Power was profound at the time. I felt like a Gold Medal winner.

And I still do.

For the first time, I felt consciously connected to a loving Being who made my wellbeing a priority. I marveled at the generation of comfort, serenity and contentment this knowledge brought. The more specific my prayers became, the more amazed I was at the extraordinary results and healings.

It is difficult to describe, but I can only image that my feelings were not unlike those of a bungee jumper plummeting through space while being securely protected by a tether anchored in an immoveable and omnipresent rock. One that is far older and more reliable than even the Rock of Gibraltar, which is stated to be 200 million years old and has withstood the trauma of storms, the battering from roiling seas, centuries as a fortified battlement, and a changing populace from the Phoenicians to the British.

Where once I had been preoccupied and brought to a standstill by problems, my studies revealed they were simply exaggerated molehills based upon my heightened vulnerability, which, of course, resulted in a weakened sense of power. Through my intensive studies in Science of Mind, I could accept each problem as a summons to prayer.

Yes, there were difficult days when I pestered Mother or Sandra with elaborations of my woes. Far too many to count.

This time, though, I had a plan on paper in my handwriting. I could own it, read it daily, and be reminded of who I was and who I wanted to become and why. I arose each morning mindful of my many little successes, instead of the failure of the day before.

This time, the failures only disheartened me temporarily. The road would be long and fraught with setbacks, but if I wanted a happier and more fulfilling life, I had to change what I had been doing unmindfully for years. I continued my studies with the goal of becoming a licensed Science of Mind practitioner. The extra meetings and late-night studying became part of my daily routine, outside of being the best mother I could possibly be. The girls were changing, too. Their lives included music and dance lessons and visits to the homes of friends. I loved every new thing they experienced and remembered the good things about my life at their age. I also remembered my disappointments, loneliness, and yearning to feel more loved by my busy parents.

My interest in resuming a social life outside the potluck dinners and 'singles only' socials grew, but now the idea of seriously dating again at my age and as a mother of two young girls seemed illogical and too difficult to handle.

Another crisis in confidence. Another reason to find solace and direction through prayer. A firm believer in possibilities, I gave this last 'wish' on my Miracle Card considerable reflection. I would rather remain without a husband than to leap into another dating situation with some man who couldn't see beyond my outward appearance. My svelte body might serve to catch his attention, but it was for me to enjoy—a visible demonstration of my ability to forgo sugar-filled food in favor of something spiritually satisfying.

I wrote a long list of the qualities I valued in a for-the-rest-of-my-life husband and step-father of my daughters. God wanted me to have a wonderful life. Marriage to Mr. Right was surely a significant part of it.

Mr. Right would love and cherish and respect me, as I would him. It would take time for us to find each other. If God so willed, it would be lovely if our introduction grew into an enchanting evening and burgeoning love affair like Deborah Kerr and Cary Grant had *in An Affair to Remember.*

Okay, I was still an idealist. Along with my lengthy list of spousal requirements, the 'wonderful life' I envisioned was more like a contrived Hollywood romance that invariably brought me to tears by the time The End scrolled across the screen. Or, like the romance described in lyrics of myriad tender love songs, especially those Daddy's orchestra played; lyrics that were indelible in my mind and sealed in my soul as tightly as plastic wrap around a bowl. Songs like "Isn't It Romantic?" by Rogers and Hart. "If dreams are made of imagination, I'm not afraid of my own creation." Although I wanted to resist waltzing into my next love affair with eyes closed, I still longed for the emotional entanglement Hart described as "music in the night, a dream that can be heard."

God would provide. I believed that. Patience, though, was not one of my virtues. It was something I needed to pray about acquiring! Somewhere, the man of my dreams was waiting to be discovered. A man with a marvelous sense of humor, who was kind and affectionate, intelligent, even-tempered, honest and forthright, considerate, and genteel. A man who oozed integrity, who enjoyed his chosen vocation and was successful in it.

A man who was humble and generous enough to accept another woman's children into his home and be supportive in their upbringing.

Oh, and a man who wasn't hesitant to admit to failings and faults and was sincere about wanting to correct or change them as much as humanly possible. You know, character flaws, like being arrogant or a perfectionist or being temperamental enough to use physical force to command obedience and unearned respect from his wife. Memories of that kind of spouse still lingered and hurt.

My 'future spouse list' remained on the bedroom dresser where I could glance at it often. I was on a new pathway to a forever-after contentment and willing to place my trust in God to erase all lingering doubts and fears I had about such a future. Yes, I was wise enough to understand I was human and all human beings stumble. We all say and do things under stress or exhaustion or frustration that we later wish we could take back. Things go wrong when we're too busy to deal with them. Our car won't start. The kitchen drain is clogged and the sink is overflowing. A child wakes up with a fever and we have to juggle a work deadline with a doctor appointment. At times like these, we forget to pray for patience and calm.

Despite my temporary fallback to old behavior on such occasions, I grew much closer to achieving an unshakable faith in God.

Notice I said 'closer.' That means snack food and anything with sugar still tempted me when stressful situations overwhelmed me. Remember. My workplace was the dining room table, not some cubbyhole in a distant office building. Food was readily assessable. Although I did the grocery shopping, those eye-catching packages of chips, tiny cheese crackers, time-saving convenience foods, like instant potatoes and Hamburger Helper, would find their way into my basket. Even a package of the girls' favorite cookies. Who was I kidding! I used to reward myself, after addressing a full box of envelopes for a charity dinner, with "just one cookie." Well, two cookies.

My daughters had no interest in monitoring my eating patterns. Ditto for the dogs. It was up to me to uphold my plan. That meant I had to become more innovative in meal preparation, because I was dealing with a shrewd recipient who knew how to manipulate the system. Me.

I became a regular reader of magazines devoted to recipes, like Gourmet, Bon Appetite, Weight Watchers and the Pleasures of Cooking, scouring them for recipes that could be adjusted to lessen or eliminate the sugar ingredient. And I bought a food processor, a "Cuisinart" a fairly new kitchen gadget in the 1970s, to prepare vegetables in artistic ways that stimulated the eyes of the beholders.

As I made daily attempts to focus on health and resistance to sugar, my already sweet daughters accepted most of my kitchen creativeness. There were the so-called french fries of oven-roasted parsnips that we called Twigs, because they tasted like what we imagined a slender tree branch would taste. There was my famous coconut ice cream made from dried-out sauerkraut and coconut extract, which joined the 'never make again' list, as did the 'mushroom chips,' made with unflavored gelatin and curry, and the asparagus pudding with chocolate extract.

Day after day, I explored untraveled avenues to strengthen my resolve.

The studio of Richard Simmons was nearby, but I limited my exercise to walking the dogs around the block. On such walks, I would pass a women's clothing shop and could rarely refrain from stopping to gaze at the featured dresses and pantsuits on the super-thin models in the windows. I knew, without entering the store, that nothing on the store's racks would fit me.

One day, I felt ready to go beyond window-shopping and left the dogs at home. As soon as I opened the door, I headed directly for a rack of colorful dresses I had spied during my former forays, purposefully avoiding the gazes of the employees. I took my time and examined each dress in detail. Fashions changed with the season and to ensure women bought new wardrobes with frequency. The current styles featured princess-line waists, knee-skimming skirt lengths, cowl necks and neck scarves, all similar to the Halston designs I'd seen worn by the three actresses on "Charlie's Angels" during my weeks of self-confinement.

One dress, in particular, caught my eye. It was exactly like one recently worn by Elizabeth Taylor in gorgeous eye-popping red. She was short. So was I. The dress emphasized her tiny waist and ample bust line, before flowing over her hips in soft-fabric flair. How I wanted that dress!

I moved on to a rack of peasant-style blouses with flowing sleeves, and three-piece pantsuits, some with bell-bottom trousers, which was a design disaster for short women who weren't genetically inclined to be reed thin. The wide pant bottoms just emphasized the 'you know what.'

Finally, despite my fear of being questioned by a salesclerk, I chose a pair of jeans. They came in three sizes: small, medium and large. I surreptitiously held the size small jeans in front of me, decided they would likely fit only one side me, draped them over my left arm anyway and headed for the checkout counter. They would be an incentive to persevere. Even though I wore size large pants, usually from the Lane Bryant store, I doggedly resisted any inner voice that told me to save my money.

The too-small, super-tight, skinny-leg jeans—all the rage after the disco years of bell-bottomed ones—hung in my closet for quite some time, but I never forgot they were there.

After several weeks of strict portion control and no in-between meal snacking, I removed the jeans from their hanger and tried them on with high hopes. I had seen enough photographs in the newspapers to know that the process often involved a crew to administer the Heimlich maneuver. I called my in-house troops to assist me as I lay prone on the bed to flatten my stomach. The girls struggled in turn to zip them up, once they had grunted with me yanking them over my hips. Finally I was able to rise to my feet. Once perpendicular to the floor, however, I couldn't move or breathe.

Fashionable attire should not immobilize the wearer.

"Mommy, you look like Frankenstein!"

The girls rolled on the floor, thoroughly enjoying their clever comparison. I was afraid to even smile for fear I'd bust a gut or rip a seam. Nevertheless, I found comfort in knowing both legs were encased in the jeans and the zipper had reached the waistband button. That meant I was continuing to progress on the fulfillment of my first wish.

Believe it or not, those size-small jeans eventually slipped on with ease. I rejoiced in this monumental proof that faith can, indeed, move mountains. At last, I could get rid of all my large and extra-large clothing. What a great feeling to be comfortable in my own skin.

Me. After I learned to substitute positivity for food.

Due to a tight budget, I was unable to take bona fide vacations. They were a past luxury my meager salary (by Beverly Hills standards) would no longer support. Every extra week I worked meant I could remain self-supporting. I was okay with that. Every visit with nearby family members was like taking a mini-vacation.

Then, unexpectedly, I was given the opportunity to accept a three-week writing assignment that allowed me to take a two-day break plus the weekend. Four days in all.

It was August of 1977.

After discussing the possibility of a short trip with my mother, we drove to San Diego with plans to stay at the San Diego Hilton. I was as thrilled as my daughters were, especially when Sandra, brother–in-law Charles, and niece Jacqueline decided to join us. It was so much fun to be together, and the laughing and talking was nonstop. It seemed that every fifteen minutes, the radio DJ played "I Just Want To Be Your Everything," Andy Gibb's popular song that had just come out in July and zoomed to the top of the charts. I wasn't surprised. He had become a heartthrob worldwide, and was even more handsome than his older brother, who had already earned musical fame as the Beach Boys.

As nothing more than a hobby and a way to put my feelings on paper, I had been writing lyrics for potential songs sometime in the future—ones I could at least play at home on the piano for myself, if nothing else. Remembering this, Sandra said, "There's a marvelous singer performing in the Cargo Lounge, Carol. Moki Graham. You should hear her. Why don't we go there tonight before dinner? Charles would enjoy her, too, and Mother can watch the girls for us."

"Sounds perfect," I said, eager to do something pleasurable that was totally adult. "I'll meet you there at 7:00 after I've fed the girls and gotten them ready for bed."

At the stroke of seven, I stood at the entrance of the Cargo Lounge waiting for Sandra and Charles and wondered if I should go ahead and secure us a table. Dressed in a white suit, I tried to hold the evening newspaper without transferring the black ink to my skirt. I had folded it to reveal a listing of thoroughbred horses participating in races at the Del Mar Racetrack for our visit the next day. I had loved the track's history ever since learning about the horse Sea biscuit who won by a nose in the much talked about race in 1938. We had all watched Seattle Slew become only the 10th thoroughbred in history to win the Triple Crown in May and June, including the Kentucky Derby, the Preakness and the Belmont. Since Mother and I were both lovers of hats, we were totally captivated by those worn by the women attending the Derby.

I groaned to myself when I saw that the tips of a couple fingers already contained ink smudges. Gazing through the dimly lit lounge, to see if Sandra and Charles were already seated, I noticed a man at the bar openly smiling at me. Feeling self-conscious, I strolled past him and seated myself at the only empty table, much too near the bar.

In less than a minute, he approached me. "Would you like to dance?"

"No, thank you . . . but, would you like to sit down? I'm waiting for my sister to arrive with her husband."

I have no idea what prompted me to say that and was honestly surprised when the gentleman accepted my invitation. Taken aback, but instantly intrigued, I checked him out while pushing the newspaper to the other side of the table and casually opening my evening bag for a tissue to clean my finger of newsprint. The ensemble of piano, bass and saxophone was playing a seductive love song in the far corner of the room, making the lounge seem like an archetypal Parisian nightlife experience.

What I noticed first about the stranger was that he had a beautiful smile and a velvet voice. His beige, lightweight suit, appropriate for late summer, was beautifully set off by a wide-width tie—customary in the 1970s—with swirls of aqua blue, pale orange, navy and grey. Trying to appear nonchalant, I glanced down at the tip of the tie. I could faintly see the CM logo and knew it was a Countess Mara design. I had learned all about the still famous Italian menswear fashion label during my summer in Rome. Not only had I found the CM designs to my liking artistically, I had purchased ties to send home to Daddy and Uncle Moe.

To me, the tie spoke of this unknown gentleman's good taste. I knew that Frank Sinatra often wore the label and had even ordered special ones custom made for himself. Unbidden, Mother's words also came to mind. On several occasions, when we bought Father's Day ties for Daddy, she had stated with alacrity that a man's personal quality could be equated to the quality of his silk tie. I think it had more to do with personal taste and favorite colors. I have known several wonderful men over the years with perfectly dreadful taste in ties.

"Before we launch into a discussion of your beautiful eyes, let me introduce myself," the man said. "I am Ion Hunter. Richard Ion Hunter. I live in Beverly Hills, Michigan, and I'm in San Diego for a business conference. My eyes grew bigger. "Beverly Hills, Michigan? I'm from Beverly Hills, California. I never knew another Beverly Hills existed. I'm Carol Sorkin Crystal, by the way. Divorced. Mother of young twin daughters. Here for a very brief vacation. Just through the weekend."

My perusal of the Michigan man continued as we chatted with amazing ease, laughing about the irony of meeting someone from the same city name. I tried not to become too interested in him, knowing it was merely a conversation in a bar, but I found him charming and inquisitive, with an authoritative presence quite different from other men I'd met in California.

When Sandra didn't show up, I accepted a second invitation to dance. It had been months since I'd enjoyed myself on the dance floor and I couldn't help remembering Daddy as the music swirled around us. Ion and I danced, laughed, and talked for three hours, finally ordering something to eat from the limited bar menu. Too soon the once filled lounge had emptied. Ion walked me to my room and we made plans to meet the following night.

On Thursday, after spending the morning with the girls and the afternoon at the races, Sandra, Charles and I went to the famous Hotel Coronado for dinner. It was another not-to-be-missed experience for anyone visiting the area, and I had always looked forward to an occasion to revisit it. We had to first cross the long San Diego Bay Bridge, because the hotel was literally located on an island, built in the 1880s right on the beach to take full advantage of the sun, surf, and vista. Immensely popular from the day it first opened, the Hotel Del Coronado became the location for several books and movies; the one that fueled my interest the most was the 1959 movie Some Like It Hot starring Marilyn Monroe, Jack Lemmon and Tony Curtis.

The hotel, which is still the second largest wooden structure in the United States, had just been designated a National Historic Landmark (1977), and as we planned our quick jaunt to San Diego, we had unanimously agreed it would be on our must-do list. After all, it had been the playground of Hollywood stars and host of royalty. Both Mother and Daddy had spoken of it often, because its activities invariably made the newspaper gossip columns. Now, as I write this, I can add that sixteen of our presidents have also enjoyed short stays in the Coronado's finest suites, beginning with President Harrison and including Barack Obama.

The hotel's Crown Room was crowded, as usual, and the service painfully slow as formally dressed waiters provided service to its 250 tables. Normally, I would have welcomed a leisure evening of wining, dining and ogling in such a luxurious setting. The exquisite crystal chandeliers—designed in the shape of crowns by the *Wizard of Oz* author L. Frank Baum—sparkled from the 33-foot high dome and made the vast expanse of gorgeous dark cherry and mahogany woodwork and columns gleam under their dimmed illumination. Floor-to-ceiling windows allowed us a breathtaking view of the property under the setting sun.

Despite all this splendor, my mind was somewhere else.

I made no mention of my plans to meet Ion Hunter back at our hotel for a nightcap. After all, he was a bar pickup, and I didn't know enough about him to share anything meaningful. All I knew was that I had thoroughly enjoyed my evening with him and looked forward to one more hour in his company. Every ten or fifteen minutes after we'd finished our entrees, I surreptitiously stole glances at my watch while brushing my right hand over its face. Both Sandra and Charles wanted coffee and dessert, a reason to linger and soak up the atmosphere. Normally, I would have shared their enjoyment.

Just as I was about to ask when we would be leaving, Charles flagged down our waiter and paid the bill.

We arrived back at the Hilton so late, I accepted the very real possibility that Ion had headed back to his room, which was probably the best decision anyway. I was succumbing to the return of timidity and my old pattern of feeling ugly and unworthy of his time.

But there he was, seated at a table in the courtyard, where the smog-free night air allowed the viewing of a dark sky prodigious of stars and the pleasure of citrus and night-blooming jasmine aromas. And, he was peering at the entrance I would be most likely to use. I waved and excused myself quickly to avoid dragging a curious Sandra and Charles to his table with me. Introductions weren't necessary. Ion was a vacation weekend diversion. Thankfully, Sandra understood that.

Again, Ion and I fell into a comfortable conversation sharing our interests We had a way of relating in a way that brought easy laughter, and it felt so good. Time passed while we sipped slowly on our drinks and watched one table after the other fill with hotel guests and then empty as they strolled off to their rooms.

Ion told me he was in San Diego with his adopted daughter from a previous marriage, and that he was a labor attorney who settled union strikes. I told him I was an artist and a calligrapher, but mostly a single mother of grade-school twins. I provided a brief commentary on why their father and I were divorced.

I was leaving for home the next morning, Friday, and Ion was returning to Michigan on Sunday. We exchanged phone numbers and, once again, he walked me back to my room. My family was already asleep, and as we had the evening before, we said our goodbye in the hallway. But this time, he kissed me. Granted, I had been kissed more times than I can remember upon this writing, but this first kiss from Ion was the most magical, heartfelt, soulful kiss I had ever experienced. I remember it with clarity. It was like being awakened by Prince Charming after ingesting a bite of the poisoned apple (Snow White) and falling into a deep sleep.

Mother was at the wheel of her huge Lincoln sedan, and I was busy daydreaming as I peered out the side window. A couple of wrong turns later, we realized we were lost. "And hungry!" the girls added, from the back seat. We had left San Diego later than expected, because there is no such thing as a 'quick trip' to their famous zoo, which had been on the girls' can't-miss list.

I saw the sign saying we were in Newport Beach and Mommy saw one for the Fashion Island Mall. She turned into the massive parking lot and parked—or as we always said, "docked"—her car. Giving in to the girls' preference, we ate at the Jolly Roger restaurant where they were given paper pirate hats. After a brief stop at the indoor koi pond, we headed back to the car. No shopping excursion. Neither Mother nor I had the energy.

Not paying attention to where I was walking while keeping an eye on the girls, I stepped clumsily off the curb and stumbled. That's when I noticed a card-sized brown envelope on the pavement; someone had obviously dropped it while also in a hurry. There was no name or address written on it, so I carefully lifted the bag and pulled out a card. After reading and then rereading it, I immediately felt that it was a gift to me from God. I read it again.

The most wonderful things of all things in life, I believe, is the discovery of another human being with whom one's relationship has a glowing depth, beauty and joy as the years increase. This inner progressiveness of love between two human beings is a most marvelous thing; it cannot be found by looking for it or by passionately wishing for it. It is a sort of Divine accident. - Sir Hugh Walpole

At the time, I had no idea who the author of these inspiring words was. I only recently learned that Sir Hugh Seymour Walpole was a well-known English author of many works of fiction during the early 1900s (1884-1941). It was during my research that I also learned we shared a passion for art. He willed fourteen works from his collection to the nation of Great Britain. I recognized the names of all but a couple artists and was impressed that Walpole had the insight to invest in works by Gauguin, Cezanne, Renoir, Édouard Manet and even Picasso. One of the names that caught my eye was Maurice Utrillo, a French painter who specialized in cityscapes, many of which I had seen reproduced on postcards sold in gift shops and airport newsstands while studying art in Rome.

Over the ensuing years, I have wished many times I could have met and thanked the original owner of the card, because Walpole's words became unforgettable and progressively more meaningful.

Once I was back in my familiar surroundings and busy with my customary routine, I still found myself reflecting on what had transpired in San Diego. Everything was the same, as far as cleaning, cooking, working, studying my Science of the Mind lessons and spending the last days of summer vacation with the girls before they returned to school were concerned. But I was different.

Without giving any thoughts to what might happen next, I determined to call Ion and tell him how extraordinary and marvelous his kiss was and how it made me feel. Even the thought of being so brazen was foreign to me, despite growing up in the world of film, where female stars often depicted unabashed behavior (especially those called coquettes). What would this man think? What would he say? Would he hang up and die laughing?

Ion answered the phone and I briefly explained my reason for calling him. He asked for my phone number, although we had already exchanged them in San Diego. "I'll call you later." Obviously, he wasn't in a place where he was free to converse. I hung up not knowing if such a call would ever take place. And why should it? I had sounded like a character on Loony Tunes. He had said he was no longer married, but wasn't looking for anyone else in his life.

Why would a sane man with options galore become involved with a woman halfway across the continent that had two young daughters and three dogs?

My daily routine continued. I was a single mother who just happened to work at home, which was still quite uncommon, especially in Beverly Hills. When I wasn't addressing envelopes in carefully executed calligraphy, I washed clothes, shopped for groceries and other needs, cooked meals, and walked the dogs. I spent as much quality time with the girls as I could when they weren't in school. I jumped every time the phone rang.

Ion didn't call.

Nevertheless, I envisioned a beautiful and happy married life. But these visions were sometimes clouded with questions. Was I worthy of an authentic reciprocal relationship? Had the broken pieces of my former marriages really been put to rest or would they continue to haunt me? Could I nurture my wounded ego with the further help of the unfaltering inner Power that had already fed and filled my once empty soul and taught me that contentment is a personal choice?

Yes, yes and yes.

Husband or not, I would have boundless joy and share it with the girls and everyone we knew and deeply loved. Still . . . who was I to question the wisdom of God who had taught me that wishes are just that, without prayer, faith, positivity and constructive actions. Our wishes can and do come true in time, if they aren't detrimental to others or ourselves. True love cannot be found through wishes alone. So, I prayed and kept hope alive.

Sandra, right; Mother Babe, center; me, left

18

I WAS NO longer a silly teenager or even a young working woman with unrealistic concepts of what marriage meant or involved. In just a few short years, I had already experienced what screenwriters create for the primary character of their next film. One crisis after the other until she hits the bottom, learns why she continually makes wrong choices, changes her lifetime of harmful habits, finds inner peace, and envisions a future for herself and her children that will enhance the contentment she has already found.

Putting into practice everything Science of Mind was teaching me about turning negatives into positives, I added specific images to my visualizations of the future, finding motivation through the lyrics of familiar love songs, the stories of forever-love in movies and books, and the pictures torn from magazines that depicted happy couples and families.

At first on a whim and then in earnest, I purchased several special issues of magazines devoted to nothing but weddings. I scrutinized each page, on work-free evenings, and dog-eared those that contributed to my Carol Designed Blueprint for the Future. I even took Mother to Bullocks Department Store in Century City, California, and combed the racks for a periwinkle blue chiffon dress, the color and style I envisioned wearing in my next and last wedding. If such a gown had miraculously appeared, I would have purchased it without a second thought. After all, a bride needed a wedding dress.

"I don't understand, Carol, dear," Mother said, clearly bewildered. "When are your nuptials taking place? I thought Ion was no longer in your life. You have been dating other gentlemen. Recently, you have been packing your belongings, and today you are shopping for a wedding gown. Is there something you want to tell me? Is this another hasty–? You aren't pre–?"

"No, no. Nothing like *that,* Mother. It's hard to explain without sounding completely batty. I see visions of myself as a bride one last time. Soon. I want to be ready."

For the time being, she accepted this cryptic reply.

I remained focused and waited.

Some days were far more challenging than others. I calmed my misgivings by listening to music or taped Science of Mind lessons. Thankfully, eating remained my source of bodily fuel only and not solace.

Long-distance phone calls were expensive. Very few people made them except on special occasions or for business purposes. Chatting was kept to a minimum or the monthly phone bill would skyrocket. Most people keep in touch through letter writing, a lost art in these days of digital messaging.

Nevertheless, Ion finally did call and we began corresponding weekly by phone, finding our former ability to converse on diverse subjects and even to laugh again. On one such call, he mentioned an upcoming business conference at La Costa Resort and Spa, located halfway between Los Angeles and San Diego, and invited me to join him. Without skipping a beat, I accepted. Even if it meant I'd need to work all night for a week to finish work assignments, I would not miss the opportunity to see Ion again.

I knew about La Costa through friends, but had never visited there. It was, even in 1977, a luxury resort. "Ion's invitation was a surprise, Mother, but not unexpected. I won't say anything more until I return." Mother agreed to watch over the girls and the dogs and did her best to pump me for more information.

Three days in advance, I packed a suitable wardrobe, my tape recorder, and a couple special candles. Yes, I was and still am a romantic.

As I drove to La Costa, I prayed and made an acronym of the word HOPE—Holding Optimistic Persevering Energy.

Once again, Ion and I met in a courtyard and practically ran to each other for an embrace and kiss that I hoped would never end. Ion escorted me to our room and then left for a conference, which allowed me ample time to unpack and relax after my drive.

There I was, alone in the bedroom of a suite reserved for Ion and me, trying to quiet the wild thumping in my chest and keep from performing a jig of joy. With trembling fingers, I lit the oversized votive candle in a clear glass holder, turned on the tape recorder, and inserted the tape of Barbara Streisand and Barry Gibbs songs I had carefully selected. While humming each melody, I changed from my slack outfit to a beautiful black silk gown that draped over the curves of my much slimmer body. I felt sexy and glamorous . . . *and* as nervous as I had been at my daughters' first dance recital.

As I peered at my image in the huge bathroom mirror, I was thrilled over the result of my hard work and thanked God again for providing the unceasing assistance needed to fulfill the first wish on my list of three.

But, what was I doing at La Costa? I was literally going to share a room with a man who was not the original Ion. We had both changed. All I knew was that I liked how I felt while with him and was positive he was the groom in my visions of the future.

I smiled then. I knew something else. I knew his real name.

During one of our phone chats, he had hesitated. "Carol . . . I have to tell you something."

I had literally stopped breathing. What was he about to tell me? That he wasn't divorced after all? That he wanted to end our phone-friendship before it went any further? He had already married someone else and just wanted to keep me on the sideline as a California date? I had gripped the phone receiver with white-knuckled fingers.

"Carol, my name isn't I-on. It's E-on. Robert Ian Hunter."

"*E*-on? But, you let me call you *I*-on for months now!" Frankly I was delighted to hear his correct name. Ian with an E sounded perfect. Considering how we had met and where, I wasn't surprised I hadn't correctly heard his introduction over the loud bar music. And, really, what a gentleman to allow our friendship to blossom before revealing such an important thing as the correct pronunciation of his name.

I knew the evening would be unforgettable, and it was.

Ian was sweet and gentle and, once again, completely captured my heart. Yes, I had been a married woman two times and was the mother of twins. But in all those years I had not experienced genuine *love*-making. It was far more beautiful and electrifying than anything I had ever fantasized about.

"I've been thinking about it, Carol. I want you to fly out to Michigan in late October and spend a few days checking out my Beverly Hills. You may not like it."

I drew a large black X on the kitchen wall calendar at the end of each day, becoming increasing excited as I saw the equally large O encircling Trip Day.

Ian met me at Metro Airport in Detroit and we drove to his Beverly Hills, a village suburb established in 1958. "It's only about four square miles," he said. "Your Beverly Hills is almost six square miles, not much bigger."

"I had envisioned your village being similar to Dearborn's Greenfield Village." I said eager to impress him with my homework on Michigan. "Maybe we can visit it while I'm here, unless you have made other plans, of course. I can't say I'm a history buff, but the European cities have preserved most of theirs, rather than demolishing buildings to create skyscrapers. I know that Greenfield was created by Henry Ford, who was a strong believer of the need to preserve America's history, especially anything having to do with technology."

"I'll take you there. Technology was Ford's specialty, as far as the car industry is concerned, but he was impressed with what others were doing at that time to improve lives. His friend Thomas Edison helped him, and in gratitude, Ford named his museum after him. You know about Edison. The man who didn't create the light bulb, but made it infinitely better than it was and then created the whole electric system to keep many bulbs burning at the same time, ultimately throughout the entire city."

I had read extensively about Greenfield and was eager to spend time there absorbing the sounds of manufacturing and bustling of people employed to wear costumes of the early decades, drive old automobiles or horse-drawn carriages and ride the streets on three-wheeled bicycles. But right now, I wanted to check out Ian's neighborhood. Everything was relatively new. His Beverly Hills history, like mine, could be counted in decades, not centuries.

A couple stop signs later, Ian turned up the short driveway to a rather non-descript cottage. "I've lived here with my cat Whitey ever since my divorce." From the time my feet first touched the sidewalk leading to the front door, I was alert for visible signs that would offer me reassurance that the decision to make the trip was part of a Divine plan and not a more typical whim on my part.

Again, we spent a glorious evening and night together, sharing more about our growing-up years, our hobbies and talents, his work and my off-and-on-again interest in painting. I already knew that Ian worked as the executive director of the National Automobile Transporters Labor Division. In other words, he was responsible for settling strikes between the employers and the Teamsters. I knew about the Screen Actors Guild, another American labor union that represented film and television principal and background performers, but knowing about and understanding the work of unions had never been my interest.

I awoke early the next morning and set out on a walk around the neighborhood while Ian was busy on the phone with work-related matters. The first thing I saw was an adorable black Scottie walking his master, not the other way around. "What's your dog's name?" I asked.

"Barney."

"That's my father's name!" A coincidence or a sign? After a very brief conversation, I continued my walk, smiling to myself.

I kept smiling the whole ten days I spent in Michigan. Ian did his best to show me what everyday life in his Beverly Hills was like. I expected it to be different from my home environs, and it was. Infinitely.

As I came to know him better, I found him very methodical and cautious, the exact opposite of one who made impulsive judgments, as I often did. He was decidedly one of the most centered and well-balanced men I had ever known. Even more reasons to love him.

We had dinner on Saturday evening at the London Chop House. While sipping an after-dinner drink, Ian hesitantly proposed. Proposed *marriage*. I was leaving the next morning and perhaps he felt pressurized by the confidence I had exhibited regarding our undeniable love connection. Whatever compelled him to speak the words on his heart; I was thrilled and immediately accepted. We gazed into each other's eyes and held hands, but that wasn't enough to express the depth of our feelings. We left the restaurant and practically ran to the car to share a few kisses. We were both in blissful love, our eyes blinded to anything but how we felt at that moment, knowing we could now talk about forever after.

At least we thought so. He grew quieter on the journey back to his house... As I have said, he was not an impulsive man. What could possibly be more impulsive than proposing to a woman after knowing her for only fifteen days and whose grade-school daughters you've never met?

Upon arriving back home in California, a few days went by before I heard from Ian again. He said, "he needed more time"! Ours was very possibly the shortest engagement in history. It lasted only hours.

I forced myself to step back and take stock of what I allowed to happen— yes, maybe even encouraged to happen. It wasn't too late. The circumstances required rationalization. For Ian's sake. Here was a good man placed in an uncomfortable position. I had basically implied 'it's now or never.'

I was horrified and genuinely disappointed with my behavior. It in no way demonstrated what my Lessons in prayer had taught me. I had been manipulative and inflexible. The kind of energy emanating from me had in no way revealed the changes I had experienced over the past few months while studying to become a Science of Mind practitioner. How could I remain engaged to a man when I wasn't fully mindful of what *unconditional* love meant? Such love did not come with a checklist of must-haves and must-dos.

Neither of us knew what our future would hold. By Thanksgiving time, however, we were both of a mind to meet each other's children to test the waters again. In every spare minute outside my other obligations, I studied and prayed and sought input from other practitioners.

In December, Ian flew to Los Angeles with his daughter. We had worried needlessly. We all met with high hopes and found ourselves thoroughly enjoying our time together as a make-believe family. I had invited Mother, Sandra and Charles for cocktails that first evening. They would not have forgiven me if I hadn't given them the opportunity to meet the man with whom I was so smitten. Cocktail hours had time limits, so I didn't have to give up an entire evening with Ian. It's one thing to talk on the phone daily, despite the ghastly cost of long distance calls in those days, but quite another thing to be together in the same room again. We had been stealing long looks at each other ever since he arrived, but the main purpose of the visit was to introduce our children to each other and to us. He already knew I was very close to members of my large family of relatives.

I must mention that the University of Michigan, Ian's alma mater, was playing in the Rose Bowl on New Year's Day, and I learned that he was a fervent fan of the sport and his favorite team. There would be no discussion about where we would be during those hours. Ian came with tickets in his pocket.

On one of the days before that red-banner day, we trekked to Magic Mountain with our girls. A goat ate our map. It was frustrating and funny. Maybe, I thought, it was a sign that we were in uncharted territory, both literally and figuratively, and needed to watch our steps and not assume we knew the way into the future.

We celebrated New Year's Eve with dinner at a famous Beverly Hills restaurant and both Ian and his daughter were thrilled to recognize a few movie stars. Believe it or not, Los Angeles didn't hold public fireworks displays until very recently (December 31, 2013), so the girls didn't miss them when we headed for home.

Like millions of other Americans who couldn't celebrate the passage of one year to the next to the next viewing a live fireworks display, I had grown up listening to the radio broadcast of Guy Lombardo and his band, The Royal Canadians, with Mother and other members of my family. It was always performed from the ballroom of the New York Waldorf-Astoria Hotel and always ended with the poignant and unforgettable "Auld Lang Syne." Daddy, of course, was absent from this family tradition, as he was performing with his band at a club or private party. Guy Lombardo was a favorite of his, perhaps because he played the saxophone, as did Lombardo's brother Carmen in his band.

When television became affordable and popular in most American homes, CBS featured Lombardo and his band every New Year's Eve between 1956 to

1976. Now, as Ian and I cuddled together on the couch in my small living room, we watched the television screen display dazzling sprays of light and vibrant colors erupting in the night sky with explosions of sounds to the accompaniment of the "1812 Overture." We remembered with wistfulness the remarkable band leader who had just died in November. I have learned, since that first New Year's Eve with Ian, that Lombardo's annual performance was not only a tradition in my home, but it had achieved status as the longest running annual radio special program—fifty years—obviously an American tradition.

When the clock stuck midnight, Ian and I celebrated the incoming New Year with our own fireworks; the stars were perfectly aligned now, and we decided that life for us would be extraordinary, if we chose to make it so.

The next morning, we drove with the girls to Pasadena for the Rose Bowl Parade and then on to the Rose Bowl Game. It was a joy to be together and to observe the ease with which our daughters adapted to our potentially permanent union. Michigan, unfortunately, did not win the game despite our very vocal cheering section. That was the only regret in Ian's entire visit. Otherwise, it had been perfect.

Once again I was happy and at peace. Even the girls recognized the change in my demeanor. I quizzed them, eager to hear their honest opinions about our holiday company. They had fun. They liked Ian and his daughter. And, yes, they would look forward to spending more time with them.

The girls returned to school and I returned to my calligraphy work. The phone did not ring. No calls from Detroit. Not one.

I worried and became frustrated. Had Ian returned safely? Was he ill? Had he been in an accident? Or . . . was he breathing a sigh of relief that his visit to my Beverly Hills was over? Was he rebelling against any pressure to make a lifetime commitment to me?

My misery grew like mold on cheese. The situation had become all too real him. I was, indeed, the mother of two very young girls. Twins. He had spent his hours on the plane evaluating what that involved and how it would affect his personal and business life. Great sex and enjoyable dinners with me in dimly lit restaurants didn't equate with coming home to a cluster of kids playing with a dozen Barbie dolls in the living room or baking miniature cakes in their Easy Bake oven with clutter all over the kitchen counters.

How could I ever recover from such a purposeful rejection by someone I already deeply loved? Why could our relationship feel so utterly right for me and not for him? Ian had decided to end our romance before it led to additional fatherhood. His decision not to pick up the phone and speak with me was the best way to handle it.

For him.

Well, it would be another testing time for me. Would I go back to my destructive behavior and find comfort in a tub of ice cream? No. I had learned how to handle my insecurities and to find comfort through the inner Power of prayer and meditation.

I would continue to pray; only *this* time I would listen quietly for the reply. God answered prayers, but in His own time and way, not mine. And if I were being honest, what if what I was so sure I wanted wasn't meant to be for an important reason?

The tears started anyway and would not stop. Yes, at the frightful thought of scrubbing Ian from my life, my unshakeable faith faltered. It was still in its infancy, and I was still struggling with the concept of selflessness. Like a child who wanted a cookie when supper was only minutes away, I still wanted something representing "sweet love" to provide comfort and be by my side always. Comfort *my* way. Not from God. Not from my faith. From a man.

From Ian.

The thought of never seeing or hearing from Ian again continued to test my relationship with God. I cried. A lot. I had a private pity party every night as yet another day and then another passed by without the only call I wanted.

Then I heard that quiet voice speaking to me from deep within. No knee-jerk reactions were appropriate. It was not up to me to make a decision for someone else. Ian could make his own decisions. He wasn't responsible for gifting me with happiness. Abraham Lincoln had once said, "Folks are usually about as happy as they make their minds up to be." Just as I had worked to change my diet, forgo sugar-laden food and treats and lose the weight that had troubled me for so many years, I must finally come to another understanding.

Happiness comes from within. Through the right prayer requests, maybe I could become happier with myself and with my life exactly as it was.

Only then. Maybe. *Definitely.* I would be ready to share my happiness with someone as wonderful as Ian Hunter.

Frankly, I had no clear idea of what a typical work day entailed for him. No doubt a lot of multitasking. Conferences. Scheduled and unscheduled meetings. Incoming and outgoing phone calls all day long. The man had a thousand things on his mind and had spent a week away from his responsibilities.

The hours and then days passed, minute by minute. I propped a framed copy of the Catherine Ponder affirmation on my work desk: *I have unshakeable faith in the Perfect Outcome of every situation in my life, for God is in Absolute Control.*

I read this over and over again. The tears still came, and I'd quickly wipe them away for fear I'd ruin another already addressed envelope in the fancy calligraphy. What was Ian's problem? Did he honestly think it was okay to treat me like this? It was so out of character for him.

Wait a second. Was he waiting to hear from me? Was this his way of testing me to see how I reacted to *his* sudden abandonment? Wasn't that essentially what I had done to him after his proposal? I had waited until he took the step and spoke the words. Only then did I seriously question whether or not my quick acceptance was right for my girls. If we married, we'd have to move to Michigan, away from everything and everyone familiar to them. Maybe that wasn't fair. Maybe this. Maybe that. Maybe we should think beyond the moment.

Poor Ian.

I knew what I had to do.

The next morning, I was awake by four o'clock. It was way too early to call Ian's office to inquire about his whereabouts, even though Michigan time was three hours later than California time. Then I remembered his talking about an upcoming schedule that had him traveling to Ohio for a conference with union officials. Which city? *Think, Carol.* I used my mystic mind and called a few hotels where I thought he might be staying, finally hearing a welcome yes to my inquiry. A Robert Ian Hunter was registered as a guest. The hotel clerk buzzed his room. By now, it was approximately 7:30 a.m. in Ohio.

Ian answered immediately.

"I release you!" I said.

"What? Carol? Is this you? How did you know . . . ? Never mind. Listen, I can't talk right now. I'm preparing for an important case this morning. Less than an hour from now. I'll call you back later. I can't give you a definite time."

"Calling back isn't necessary. Goodbye, Ian. Have a good day."

It was done. I would consciously move on with my life and continue to seek inner peace and joyful fulfillment. How could I expect to guide others to the same end as a Practitioner if I didn't trust that God was in control of every situation in my own life? It would be difficult to let go of my conviction that Ian was my Prince Charming. I was, after all, a human being with a full range of feelings and flaws. In time, however, I would.

In time, Ian might cultivate a deeper sense of trust and some inner happiness, too. Perhaps he was still in mourning over the failure of his former marriage and still adjusting to living alone in his quiet house with his quiet cat. He would remain in my prayers. Hopefully, we could at least be phone friends.

Ian did continue to call me throughout the year, at odd times, often when he had liquid courage or knew I was sleeping. At such times, he said he wanted to see me again. He missed being with me. My reply was always, "No, Ian. I will not subject myself or my daughters to any more of this nonsense."

Intuitively, I knew Ian was not a man who would play with my emotions while dating other women. I came to recognize that he was truly overwhelmed by the enormity of a commitment to me; one that involved school-age children, homework, PTA meetings, dance and music lessons, children's illnesses. He had been there and done that. And for heaven's sake, I had three dogs! He was a cat person.

I was not oblivious to his concerns, but I would move on with my life. I joined Great Expectations and started to date other men. This time, I didn't let an instant physical attraction interfere with the importance of first developing a friendship. Through my continued studies to become a Science of Mind Practitioner, I learned that through a deeper connection with God, our inner Power, we come to recognize and shun the once unhealthy patterns that take us down the wrong roads. The more often we put into practice our new model, the more often we'll trust our instincts. Now, I had personal experience in how well this worked. I still hadn't returned to my old eating habits.

I could put the process into words now. If we bake enough bread, we'll know the ingredients and the steps necessary to produce a perfect loaf without needing the recipe book. But invariably, if we don't refresh our memory by reviewing the written steps, we'll produce bread that doesn't rise because we forgot to add the yeast. When we drive to and from work five days a week month after month, we'll know how to interpret the numbers on the dashboard dials without referring to the driver's manual. But invariably, we'll daydream and forget to check the oil or gas gauge and end up stalled on the highway shoulder. Driving without a dilemma-waiting-to-happen requires our purposeful attentiveness.

Again, I resumed my dating life, but it wasn't as pleasurable as I had hoped. Invitations were sporadic and diverse. It wasn't difficult to meet 'available' men. They were everywhere—at the grocery or hardware store, a department store in the kids' clothing section, in a Walmart parking lot or a lovely park. I nearly always had the girls with me and many times a couple of their friends. When a man noticed I wasn't wearing a wedding ring and initiated a conversation, I would let him assume all four of the girls were mine if I wasn't in the mood or even remotely interested. I found myself doing silly things, but enjoyed being as carefree as the girls were.

It had taken considerable study for me to feel comfortable sharing my Science of Mind lessons with family and friends. The one fundamental that convinced them I'd found something beneficial to change my life in a recognizable and good way was the same one I practice to this day—faith requires action. A thoughtful action. One that produces a significantly positive result.

"Each time we repeat it," I explained, "the consequential success becomes a memory that contributes to our peace of mind. When the same or a similar incident recurs (like my being too quickly enamored by a man and then emotionally invested in him), we will automatically repeat this successful action without hesitation or confusion. It becomes second nature. We don't question it, even when it doesn't make sense at the time. Look at me. You're all eating pie ala mode and I'm enjoying my creation icy lemon sherbet. No sugar."

I continued my studies to become a Practitioner. When I was ready to take the exam, at the Science of Mind Church headquarters. It was both oral and written. With great joy, I received the news that I had passed both and achieved one of the most important goals I'd ever set. I hadn't given up despite all my trials and tribulations. I was now a Licensed Practitioner. Hallelujah!

Mother and the girls attended my graduation exercises at the Founder's Church in Los Angeles. It was in 1978, a red-banner year. As of the writing of this memoir, I have been a Practitioner for over thirty years and earned my Emeritus Award.

Mother, the girls and me at my graduation ceremony.

As a Licensed Science of Mind Practitioner, the first Requisite I needed to embody was its tenet to have "a full sense of sacredness of trust and confidence in the patient." I could never "…betray this trust no more than a priest, lawyer or physician who cares for the patient"

The Practitioner's business is

"…to uncover God in every man. God is not sick, poor or unhappy. God is never afraid, confused and never out of his place. The premise upon which all mental work is based perfect God, perfect man, perfect being. These are the tools of thought with which a practitioner works. The work is IN HIS OWN MIND. Never anywhere else. Always in his own thought and never tries to get away from the mind within. We are practicing scientifically when the mind refuses to see the apparent condition and turns to the Absolute. One must believe that to be a successful practitioner, his word is the law of that whereunto it is spoken. To not think that the disease as being connected to him or any part of him. To realize that man is born of Spirit and not of matter. He sees his patient as a living embodiment of Perfection.

"The more completely the practitioner is convinced of the power of his own word, the more power his word will have. THERE MUST BE A RECOGNITION THAT THIS POWER OF THE WORD, OPERATING AS THE TRUTH AND REALITY OF BEING, CAN DO ALL THINGS. Therefore, the person whose consciousness is the clearest, who has the most complete faith, will be the best healer." (From The Science of Mind Book by Ernest Holmes, c1938, Dodd, Mead & Company.)

Boy, oh boy, what a titanic responsibility for anyone to take on. I would need to remain anchored in a sacred trust and conviction and become a comforting and guiding force to help other wounded and suffering humans. I knew, from experience, how the transformative the kindness, understanding and healing words of a Practitioner can be when life's trials seem too difficult to overcome. I was both honored and eager to reciprocate. I took the oath and obligation with unconditional love.

Weeks passed.

I didn't allow the elapse in time to discourage me, especially since I knew my acclaimed change in dealing with life's up and downs was being viewed with interest by those who knew me. If I moped around and couldn't enjoy life to the fullest, my faith was ill placed.

One Saturday morning at breakfast, I rested my arms on the table and peered at each daughter, thinking about my approach to gaining their cooperation. "Would you like to go shopping with me today to buy some packing boxes?"

Jippy shrugged and pulled her mouth to one side.

"What are they?" Chippy went for more information.

"They're special boxes that come in all sizes to hold lamps or dishes, pots and pans, toys and clothes. Whatever we want to keep if we move to a new house."

"Are we moving?" Jippy was more interested now.

"Not right away, but I think we should be ready. Then when the time comes, we won't have so much work to do. If the boxes are here, we can pack a few at a time." I know it sounds crazy because we had nowhere to go! It was an act of pure faith and demonstration.

"Sure, I'll go." Chippy pushed away from the table. "You coming, Jippy?"

I had already decided the best approach was to drive to a moving van company and purchase a load of boxes. They would come in bundles and be easy to haul into the house and pile up in a corner of some room. Since the girls had never moved from the house where they took residence on the day their father and I brought them home from the hospital, they had no concept of what packing up and moving to a new home was like. The day was an adventure and, by now, they were both accustomed to following instructions, even when they seemed zany.

In no time at all that first weekend, we had filled several boxes, which we stacked in one corner of the living room. In the ensuing couple months, I held a garage sale and sold some furniture pieces and other items I didn't need any more. The funniest comment was, "I would like to buy your wrought iron head-board." Sorry, it's not for sale it was my gate. One customer bought my beautiful teak coffee table that still showed the girls' teething marks on the corners.

"No problem," he said. "I'll just sand them away and match the stain." He had his cute young daughter with him and we chatted together about raising girls. Before he left, he asked me out for "a family date." When they came to pick us up, I decided, with motherly concern, that the child needed a bath before we could go anywhere!

Over the next eighteen months, Ian tried communicating every month or so, on the phone. Each time, hearing his voice, that velvet voice stirred my never dormant desire for a permanent relationship with him.

19

IT WAS THE first week of June of 1979, and every day illustrated those described in a travel brochure as 'perfect' Southern California weather. I didn't begrudge our dogs' eagerness to their daily walk around the block and usually took my time, in order to fully enjoy the pristine landscaping of my neighbors' yards and color-coded gardens in rows or sections of complementary hues.

On one of these walks, I reached the final fifty yards or so from the house and heard my girls shouting for my attention. "Mommy. *Mom.* Hurry! Ian is on the phone waiting for you!"

"Let him wait," I said, shouting back the first reply that came to mind. I didn't increase my pace one whit. When I reached the yard, I stooped to pat and play with the dogs, keeping to our customary routine. My daughters watched me from the steps. Finally, I strolled into the house, stopping to drop a kiss onto the foreheads of my messengers.

"Hello, Ian," I said. "I was out walking the dogs. Did I keep you waiting long?"

"No problem. Listen, Carol, I'm coming to California to see you."

"Why? I guess alright Whatever you want. Do you have a date in mind?"

"I thought Thursday, June 14th, if that's all right with you."

"That's fine. Let me know which airline and flight and I'll pick you up. Where will you be staying?"

"I'll make reservations at the Beverly Hillcrest Hotel. It's not far from your place."

The next day, Mother offered her advice. "Carol, give the poor man a chance."

This time, I was determined to allow my training and faith in God to provide the lead. I needed all the help I could get after so many miserable years of being ripped apart and psychologically dismantled by the men in my life. Armed with my restored self-respect, however, I felt more than ready to weather whatever challenges another reunion with Ian would bring.

The morning of the 14th arrived, and I started the day with prayer. I continued to pray as I readied myself for the trip to airport, again asking for Divine guidance that would prevail over every hour Ian and I spent together. "And please," I implored, "give me a sign that this get-together is meant to be."

In the next instant, I heard, "Because. Be Wise. Become."

Ian arrived with a garment bag containing his dress clothing and one suitcase for everything else. He looked like a man on a mission. We chatted about his plane trip, the weather, our daughters, and everything else that wasn't personal. Since it was close to the supper hours, it seemed ridiculous for me to simply drop Ian off and drive home.

"I thought we could have a drink together and then have dinner in the hotel," he said. "Unless you'd prefer going somewhere else."

"That's fine," I said, taking my hint from him. We would take it slowly this time and not get carried away. Talk and more talk was necessary. Of course, it was equally important to see if our former attraction for each other (and our passion!) still remained. "I'll wait in the lobby until you check in and take your things to the room."

We had an amazingly relaxed and enjoyable evening talking about President Carter, the Bee Gees and Donna Summer's newest hits that played every hour on the radio, and even about which movies we intended to see during the summer.

"High on my list is *Moonraker* with Roger Moore as James Bond. I've been a fan of every 007 film since Sean Connery played Bond in *Thunderball,* back in 1965," Ian said. "What about you?"

"Probably *Escape from Alcatraz* starring Clint Eastwood," I said. "I've been to San Francisco so many times over the years; it feels like a requirement to see the film."

And so the evening went, as we tiptoed into the waters polluted by time, distance, evasion, and uncertainty.

After spending Friday together as a family, beginning with breakfast, we chose the acclaimed Benihana Restaurant for dinner to celebrate Ian's 39th birthday. It was new to the city and had received rave reviews. What fun we had. Ian and I enjoyed every bite of the tender Kobi steak and even the chicken, giant shrimp and assorted vegetables prepared right in front of us on a teppanyaki steel grill. Our highly trained Japanese chef royally entertained us with his intricate knife work, theatrics, and magical tricks that completely delighted the girls as we perched on stools to dine at a narrow counter that separated us from him. Laughter punctuated our dialogue and I didn't want the evening to end.

The girls had been fond of Ian since their first introduction, and with every hour they spent together, their bond appeared to grow. He was far more attentive to each of them and to me than on previous occasions and seemed genuinely interested in our activities, including the daily dog walks. He even asked me, "Do the girls need braces before they get much older?" What kind of question was that?

We spent all day Saturday taking in some of the tourist sights, again with the girls. Ian had asked, on our trip from the airport to his hotel, that we drive to Malibu on Saturday evening and have dinner at some restaurant where we could watch the setting sun reflected on the waters of the world's largest ocean. Just the two of us. His plan was to leave Los Angeles on Sunday afternoon and fly directly to Washington, D.C. for a meeting with union lobbyists. *Here we go again.*

I had no idea what was going on in Ian's mind. He had seen plenty of sunsets over the waters of the three Great Lakes, whose shorelines formed the rims of Michigan. Perhaps, he was finally . . . . No! I would not go there with my thoughts. I had been disappointed too many times, and that's putting it mildly.

I called Ellen Lehr, Marcia's daughter, who planned all the great parties in Los Angeles and asked for suggestions.

"I can think of only one restaurant that meets your requirements, Carol," she said. "Paradise Cove. You know the area. It's still a privately-owned property in Malibu, but it has that restaurant built by the original owner, the Sandcastle. It's right on the beach, not on the cliff overlooking it. You will have an expansive view of the famous pier, the equally renowned beach, and the ocean while you dine. If it's a clear night, you'll be able to gaze at every minute of the quite spectacular sunset. But, Carol, I would strongly advise you to call the Sandcastle today and reserve a window seating."

"Paradise Cove. Of course. I've known about that area for a couple decades, Ellen, but never visited it in person. I feel like I've been there dozens of times, though. *Gidget* and those other bikini and surfing movies of the 1960s were filmed there. Sandra Dee. James Daren, Frankie Avalon. Right?"

"The one and only. And if your guest is a fan of the *Rockford Files* television series, he may find the history of the cove even more to his liking. The trailer home used by the detective, played by James Garner, still resides in the Sandcastle's parking lot."

The Sandcastle. I couldn't remember Mother, Sandra or any of my friends speak of the place. Fishing and surfing had never been our forte. But Paradise Cove was the backdrop for the Beach Boys album cover of *Surfin' Safari*. That I could remember.

Even after I made the restaurant reservation, I couldn't get the name of the place out of my mind. Sandcastle. Of course! A *Charlie's Angels* episode early in 1978 was called "The Sandcastle Mysteries." The Angels were relaxing at Kris's seaside home when they learned a strangler in the community was burying his victims in the sand and one of them was a friend of Kris. Charlie Townsend, their never-seen boss, gave them permission to conduct their own investigation when the local police were stymied. The filming took place on the beach right in front of the Sandcastle Restaurant and the Paradise Cove Pier. I loved movie history then and still do.

After spending the majority of two days with Ian, either alone or with the girls, I looked forward to my last evening with him, even if much of it would be spent in the car. He dropped the girls and me off at the house, after another day of fun, and then headed back to his hotel to clean up and change clothes.

I needed to do the same. As soon as I unlocked the entrance door, the girls dashed to their room with the dogs sprinting after them. The mailbox by the door was full and I gathered up the contents to take to the kitchen.

As I tossed the mail onto a counter, I noticed a letter topping the usual weekend advertisement fliers. That's odd, I thought, recognizing the handwriting. Ian hasn't said anything about writing me a letter. After scanning the first paragraph, I went to sit at the table. My legs felt too weak to hold me upright. I started over and read more slowly.

June 10th, 1979
Dear Carol

I will soon transverse more than two thousand miles to renew a relationship, memories of which defy logical explanation. I will submit myself, once more, to the presence of a woman so complex and so joyous that she, in a few months and so long ago, vastly altered and gloriously transfixed my self-perception. I write, of course, of you.

Thoughts cascade through my mind as I approach Thursday. I ponder the impact of my return upon your mind and anticipate the excitement and joy which will pervade mine when at last I see you. My visit will be painfully brief, but I sense that, notwithstanding its brevity, it will be momentous. To once again share with you your presence is an event to which I impatiently look forward.

When I arrive I want to maximize the time with you and do not want to explore the geographical highlights of LA. Rather, I wish to enter your mind so that we might reverse the circumstances which created the void which has marred the last eighteen months.

As I will explain when I arrive, I expect that within the next few month's developments involving my professional activity may occur that will delay any judgment of a more personal nature. Commitments, therefore, to more sensual and profound interests will be compelled to wait the emerging destiny of my working life.

I trust that Jennifer and Lisa are fine as well as the canine members of the Crystal family. In conclusion, I look forward to seeing all, but in particular I desire to see you. There is much to say and feel when I arrive. I will, thus, delay any further dialogue until that splendid moment.

With deepest love,
Ian

It was a beautiful letter. A complex letter. Full of nuance that was hard to define. It was too late to take back the hours we had spent exploring Los Angeles with the girls. He hadn't shown irritation with me, though. In fact, I was impressed at how well he got along with Jenny and Lisa and seemed to welcome their affection. The rest of the letter was confusing. In one sentence, he seemed eager to put the past eighteen months behind us, and in the next, he was warning me that his business would still keep him busy half a country away and our future didn't look any rosier.

No, he used the word *delay*. That wasn't the same as *end*.

I didn't mention receiving or reading the letter when Ian picked me up an hour later. I didn't want to discuss it during the long drive on the Pacific Coast Highway unless he asked about it.

Ian and I reached Malibu and searched for the private road that would take us to Paradise Cove. Thanks to Daylight Saving Time and a predicted sunset of 8:30 p.m., we had plenty of time to peruse the full expanse of the beach and the 820-foot pier constructed in 1945. As soon as we caught our first glimpse of the pier, we started a one-upmanship game to test our memories of specific movies and TV episodes featuring it as a location site.

The Sandcastle didn't fit the image I had created in my mind. It was definitely on the sand—the beach extended from the water's edge to just below the row of windows that faced west and measured at least fifty feet. But the Cape Cod exterior, including a steeply pitched roof, low profile and white clapboard siding, seemed impracticable, considering its location.

"The style is entirely suitable for this location, if you consider the reason for the builder's choice, Carol." Ian walked around the car to open my door and help me out. "The Cape Cods of New England were designed to hold up in stormy weather and clapboard is layered one over the other to prevent the entry of water."

When Ian opened the entrance door, we were greeted to the blaring sound of the Village People's *YMCA,* which had reached the top of the Pop Chart earlier in the year. It was Saturday evening, disco music was still the rage of the decade, and the casual beach atmosphere pulled in guests who thrived on the upbeat tempo. And *volume.* We had to lean towards the hostess to hear what she was saying to us. Somehow, we were able to place our drink orders. At the same time, we turned to peer out the window.

Ian reached across the table for my hand. We sat there, without trying to talk above the music. Donna Summer's *Last Dance*. Was it an omen?

When the waiter came for our dinner choices, Ian asked him if it would be possible to turn the direction of the bar lights so that they wouldn't reflect in the window and inhibit our view. I will never forget his dinner choice for us. Sand dabs. I had honestly never heard of them and couldn't image Mother asking for them at the seafood counter of our local grocery store.

We were told that sand dabs were traditionally served only in restaurants and were a California seafood specialty. Ian was enthusiastic about trying anything that couldn't be caught on a fishhook in one of the Great Lakes. Despite the name *sand dab*, which did nothing for my vivid imagination, we both found this small flatfish delicate in flavor and very moist. It was served pan-dressed and grilled.

All the while we ate our dinner; we kept our eyes on the fiery red star called the Sun as it slowly dropped behind the distant horizon. Maybe it was because I was seeing it with Ian, but I concluded it was the most glorious sunset I had ever seen. At first, the sun at twilight created a magical streak of glittering gold light that reached directly towards us across the water. Then the continually changing colors of the sky, from vivid crimson to every shade of pink, washed the water in the same shimmering colors. Too soon, the last sliver of the sun disappeared as the earth rotated. The show was over.

The moment was Zen-like in its intensity. Drama personified. *Perhaps, if I paint my version of this moment, I'll tone down the colors ever so slightly*, I thought.

Ian tightened his grip on my hand and gazed lovingly at me with his penetrating gray-blue eyes. Practically shouting over the music's volume, he said, "Will you marry me?"

It was like someone had snapped off the music and dimmed the lights at the same time. I couldn't hear or see anything but Ian. This was the moment I had waited for, prayed about, believed would happen. "Convince me," I said, in an equally loud voice, never pulling my eyes from his. *"Why* should I marry you?"

Was I crazy? What kind of answer was that to such an earnest proposal? I reached for my glass of water and sipped daintily from the rim, just enough to wet my lips and prevent another regrettable word from slipping through them.

Ian didn't hesitate. He told me everything I wanted to hear, but this time, his words were rooted in clarity and purpose. I listened and sipped the water and felt my pulse increase and my heart thump harder. A good time later, Ian said, "I want you to become my wife because it's the wise thing to do, Carol."

Because. Be wise. Become. This was the moment I had prayed for. Believed would happen. My prayer for a sign to signify that Ian was, indeed, my soul-mate. Because- of love, be wise, become -Carol Hunter. It made perfect sense. This wonderful man was willing to accept me as I was, with two daughters and three dogs and a large extended family that would likely inject itself into our lives in ways he could never imagine. I was a different, new and better me. Because of our deep love and increased wisdom, I could become Mrs. Hunter.

"Yes, yes, *yes.* I would be so *happy* to marry you, Ian." We were still talking over the disco music and had to laugh like teenagers experiencing their first summer love. I was Gidget and Ian was my Moondoggy.

Ian and I had waited for so long to make this decision; we didn't want to spend any more time away from other. We made plans to marry in July so the girls that Lisa and Jennifer would have a month to acclimate themselves in their new environment before returning to school right after Labor Day in September.

"One month? How can you possibly we do that? Surely you're joking." Mother looked at me with a pure sense of panic reflected in her eyes.

"We can do anything we decide to do," I said. "You're an experienced par-ty giver and attendee. You know what's necessary and what isn't. It'll be fun."

I still had in mind finding a periwinkle blue chiffon dress. This was one task I couldn't relegate to anyone else, because I didn't know my current size.

When Sunday arrived, I piled Lisa and Jennifer into the car and headed, once again, to Bullocks in Century City. The three of us went directly to the bridal department to search through the dress racks. Not a single one in periwinkle blue. I selected three styles in different shades of pink and took them into the dressing room, mainly to see which size fit me best.

"Nope, these won't work," I said. "They're better suited as a prom dress." The three of us trooped back to the racks with the dresses.

"Mom, look! A blue dress. Is it periwinkle?"

"It's soft and billowy, just like you said. Is it the right size?"

I was as excited as the girls. There it was. The dress in my dreams, a perfect shade of periwinkle blue and made of exquisite chiffon, with a soft floral design and handkerchief hem. I was in total disbelief. How had we missed it on our first perusal of every dress in the department? "Where did this dress come from?" I asked the salesclerk who also appeared out of nowhere.

"A customer retuned it while you were in the dressing room," she said. "She had purchased it for her daughter and it didn't fit."

Another miracle. "I'll take it," I said, holding it against my body and peering into a full-length mirror nearby.

This demonstration of faith took approximately *ten minutes*. I emphasize this time element for finding my wedding dress, because it took *three years* for the demonstration of my faith to ensure Ian was my true soulmate and would become my forever husband. By the way, I have worn my periwinkle blue dress for every wedding anniversary, and as I write this book (2016), the dress will be thirty-seven years old. Incidentally, since the waist was elasticized, it didn't require much alteration to fit me. The dress is still spectacular!

Only one bakery could create the wedding cake I pictured in my mind. Although it had been several years since I'd been a customer, I knew their desserts were noteworthy. I selected an all-white, melt-in-your-mouth, iced two-layer cake with a surprise chocolate mousse filling. The exterior was covered in white flowers of several varieties and sizes, including roses, calla lilies, stephanotis and jasmine.

Mother took care of the luncheon menu and decor, as it was an early afternoon ceremony that would take place in our Sorkin family home. I planned to slowly wend my way down the staircase and onward to the far end of the living room where our loving family and dear friends would be watching and commenting on my look of utter joy.

Ian flew from Michigan to Los Angeles on Wednesday to enjoy the pre-wedding festivities taking place before our Saturday ceremony. Auntie Martha was so sure our marriage would never take place; she refused to buy a new dress until Friday. Ian's mother, Vera, and niece, Kathy arrived on Thursday, as well as Ian's best man, Colonel Dick Meacham. This was the first time I had the pleasure of meeting Dick and found him a tall and elegant gentleman who would grace our ceremony with his very presence. His wife, Leila, could not attend, but they have become our cherished family throughout the past many years.

We made good use of everyone closest to us. Our daughters could hardly wait to dress up in their flower girl dresses and practiced walking in a slow and measured step several times. Sandra served as my matron of honor and Jacqueline my bridesmaid. Charles escorted Mother. Donald took Daddy's place and escorted me from the bottom of the staircase to meet my groom. Dick, his best man, and my cousin, Judge Jess Whitehill, who would officiate, stood waiting and watching our procession. Ian was dressed in a dark blue suit with the blue-and-silver-patterned tie we had selected to coordinate with my dress. Very handsome. Very irresistible.

Like any bride, I was glowing with the deep love that threatened to overflow with a rare burst of tears to express the depth of my happiness. I felt beautiful in the periwinkle blue dress of my dreams and my upswept hairstyle decorated with white jasmine flowers. In my year-long wedding research (when I was strengthening my faith in God) I learned that star-shaped jasmine is worn by brides worldwide and considered a symbol of love and romance. In the Philippines, some couples exchanged necklaces of jasmine instead of rings, believing they meant "I promise you." And in some Asian countries, brides believed the flowers' fragrance infiltrates the soul and opens it with a euphoric response that communicates trust and an affirmation of commitment to the groom. Yes, while white roses have special meaning, too, and are used by most brides as a symbol of their (supposed) innocence and purity, but jasmine spoke of everything my *heart* wanted to convey.

As soon as I was an arm's length from Ian, he took my hand in his and never let go. While Bob Walters, Daddy's longtime orchestra pianist, played the Paul Williams and Roger Nichols song, "We've Only Just Begun," (recorded by The Carpenters in 1970 and played many times by Daddy's orchestra at the formal parties of Hollywood elite) we gazed into each other's eyes. *"So much of life ahead; We'll find a place where there's room to grow."* My cousin asked the traditional questions, we gave our resounding I Do's, and Jess pronounced us "man and wife."

Our mothers, who were seated on chairs next to the couch and surrounded by Uncle Moe and Helen, Uncle Jack, Auntie Martha in her new dress, and other family members and dear friends, smiled at each other. As Ian and I kissed, they applauded and rushed to hug me and shake Ian's hand and offer their congratulations and best wishes. I voiced my silent gratitude to God for this demonstration of what a deep faith can provide.

When everyone had enjoyed the champagne and hors d'oeuvres, which were substantial enough to amount to a full meal, it was time for the cake-cutting ritual. I gazed at the stunning beauty of each flower variety appearing as realistic as the fresh flowers on the tablescape. It was picture perfect. Ian and I posed with our hands on the silver cake knife handle and smiled at the cameras. I received his approval of the cake's magnificence, although I must say he was far less interested in its appearance than he was in eating his measured slice. The customary bride and groom figures topped the cake and I already had plans for preserving them.

Auntie Helen, Uncle Moe and Mother at our wedding

I knew the cutting of the first slice of our wedding cake, with both our hands on the knife, was symbolic of the beginning of our new life as partners who depended upon each other for strength, and that the feeding of a small piece of this first slice to each other was thought to bring good luck and fortune. I also knew that our faith in the strength of Divine power was the most important source of all.

The eyes of all our guests were on us once again. Ian and I cut into the cake and then a second time. I placed the knife on a tray provided for this moment, picked up the cake server and used it to slide the sliver of our wedding cake onto a plate. The heavenly aromas of vanilla and chocolate swept over us. Pure ambrosia for the gods, appealing and mouthwatering, I handed

Ian a paper napkin, with our names and the date printed on one corner in silver, and kept another for my own use. Then we each took up one of the small squares of the cake slice to feed to each other. We posed again with our mouths open to receive the cake. Ian knew in advance to ensure nary a crumb would touch even my lips. I lifted my napkin to dab at my lips and surreptitiously deposited the cake into it.

That's right. I never tasted a single bite of my magnificent wedding cake. And, no, this wasn't carrying a good thing too far. Would you ask an alcoholic to take just one sip of his or her wedding champagne? Sugar was my alcohol. I was a sugar addict and I had come too far to indulge on even such a momentous occasion. I thought of my daughters and the example I was setting for them. I thought of Ian and the woman he had fallen in love with. I thought of all those with whom I had shared how Science of Mind was providing me with the incentive to seek Divine assistance and to deepen my faith in possibilities. Resisting the strong urge to taste what I had spent so much time selecting for the enjoyment of our guests gave me a lifetime example to call forth on other one-of-a-kind occasions.

Over the years, Ian and I have traveled extensively. In Vienna, I turned down its renowned Sasher Torte; in France, I turned down everything from éclairs to mousse and crème brûlée; and in Munchin, Germany, the famous *kaiserschmarrn,* a delectable caramelized pancake with run-soaked raisins. I never felt deprived, because there were many other gastronomical specialties to taste, including savory spinach and ricotta croissants, which have no sugar.

Mother, bless her, was a wonderful cook. From the time I was a young teen and beginning to care about how I looked and felt, she would say, "Just taste it, Carol." And I would, over and over again. Each time, I would kick myself for having so little self-discipline. Each time, when Mother held out a spoonful of the dessert of the day, I would think I was stronger, more in control. I could resist. But I would give in and give Mother the response she needed for her efforts. Then I would be right back where I started. It didn't matter how many months of success I had achieved or how much self-satisfaction I had with my ability to say no, without feeling regret or guilt. Subconsciously, I wanted to give in. To test the boundaries.

I remember struggling for nine months and reaching my goal . . . the loss of forty pounds. Then, I tried one teaspoon of regular Jell-O. ONE. The consequence? I regained all forty pounds and a couple more for good measure. One little bite always led to a second and a third, and before long, I wasn't tasting. I was devouring. That serving and many more after it.

Millions of people worldwide have the predilection for some substance that triggers an addition detrimental to their health and too often to their ability to form and maintain close relationship with family members or friends. Their primary 'love' is the sugar, nicotine, alcohol, prescription or illegal drug, or even sex; each has the ability to create comfort or to block out painful thoughts.

With Divine help, the same hand that picks it up can be the one to put it down. When we come to know ourselves and our weakness and seek help through prayer, it is possible to resist temptation and to avoid putting our self in situations that will set us up for failure. It takes time and practice and patience. The building of a mental muscle, as it were, can and will support and guide us until we succeed.

My mental muscle helped me plan what I would do with my piece of wedding cake, after the ceremonial 'feeding' by Ian, with as much care as I had selected the cake's recipe and icing flower embellishment. I knew it would be difficult, but this time, I would not give in to my curiosity about the texture or taste. I was on a sugar-free pathway that I designed. I would continue to follow it, regardless of the challenge.

Ian and I spent our honeymoon at the Mission Bay Hilton Hotel in San Diego and marveled several times at our quite extraordinary chance meeting in its bar. We laughed over the vehicle he had rented for the occasion. Ian, who represented the Car Haulers Industry, somehow ended up with a clunker without a horn.

Our children had attached colorful streamers to the back bumper and a sign on the trunk lid that read Wedding of the Century. And it was. Other passing drivers tooted their horns at us all the way to the hotel and on the streets of San Diego. We didn't need a horn to blare our response that we were madly in love. They could see it on our faces as they peered through our open windows.

Ian and me on our honeymoon

20

W<small>E FLEW TO</small> Michigan two days later with three dogs and three daughters, as Ian's adopted daughter Holley had decided to move to Michigan with us. Ian's cat Whitey didn't join us until our boxes from California were delivered. Our new home was a lovely Tudor in Beverly Hills —the one with a different ZIP Code.

Jenny and Lisa were excited about having an older sister and found plenty to talk about during the flight and as they explored every nook and cranny of their new house. The next morning, however, both greeted Ian and me with elephant tears. "They want to go home," Holley said.

"You *are* home, my darlings." I held out my arms to them. "This is new for me, too. But when I was about your age, I moved with my family all the way across the country from New York to California. I learned to love it there, and I will love Michigan, too. So will you. I promise. Let's pretend we're on a great adventure. We can compare how many new things we've learned by suppertime. Look at the trees and flowers, the shape of windows and number of doors to the outside. Do the neighbors have dogs like ours? Or children your age?"

By now, the tears were gone and the new game had started.

Both Ian and I realized we would have challenges in abundance in the upcoming weeks, but we were still in the blooming stage of love, and at least for the time being, the chaos around us seemed manageable. Even though my dogs chased his cat relentlessly, and we were instant parents of three children and had to build relationships of trust to unify as a family, we remained amazingly centered and unruffled.

With my Miracle Card wishes completely fulfilled, I reveled in the inner peace and joy that comes through faith and prayer and a positive attitude. Ian and I were close and able to touch and embrace each other at will, knowing that any future goodbyes would be for mere hours or a couple days, not months. I was confident our daughters would form new friendships and come to love long winters with snow. And my dogs? They would be happy as long as I continued to feed and play with them.

I wanted to celebrate.

With ice cream.

That's right. Ice cream. The temptation is always just a thought away.

I jotted two more things on my to-do list and starred both. First, find a nearby Science of Mind church and then find the packing box that held my study material and tapes. I wanted to be ready for any unexpected bumps, twists and turns and daily renewal of inspiration is necessary.

I didn't walk around with my head in the clouds waiting for a divine revelation. And I wasn't invulnerable to days where I was impatient, fussy, grumpy, moody, selfish, truculent, tactless . . . well, you get the picture. I was and am human.

And temptation to soothe my weary body and soul? Not a day went by, especially when the girls were home for three meals a day and wanted snacks while studying, and I was doing the shopping and cooking without appreciation of my efforts, when I didn't yearn for at least half a tub of ice cream. Mothers want to please their children.

The temptations came with every social engagement. I was enticed by the alluring aromas and visual appeal of new entrees and desserts served at the frequent dinners, luncheons, buffets, and cocktail parties that were a part of our Michigan-based world. I wasn't exempt from wanting to taste each one. Or to please my host. Or to avoid appearing rude or unthankful or picky or difficult to please. Or to relieve stress. Addictions are not only mind-tricks to cover loneliness and regrets over all our past indiscretions, but also for our fears of future judgment, ridicule, rejection or failure. In other words, all the 'what ifs.'

I enlisted a few new friends to act as my professional testers. They enjoyed and enthused over the tantalizing dishes prepared by our hosts or chefs and then described the flavors to me bite by bite. Silly and entertaining as it was, this system of tricking my mind worked. Even today, I can fully savor elaborate preparations without actually eating them. I have cravings galore, but I approach them differently. I visualize myself in the dentist chair having implant surgery, or I hold a few anise or fennel seeds in my mouth as distraction.

Over time, I learned that a craving only lasts for a few minutes and distraction works to dispel it—even if the distraction means marching through the house while lustily singing a few rounds of Disney's *Zip-a-Dee-Doo-Dah* or the much-loved children's song *Mairzy Doats,* which has been passed down through families since 1943.

I also remind myself that temptation is no respecter of persons, regardless of income, importance, race, beliefs, or sexual orientation. Without a strict resolve and support system to end a destructive habit (even if it's only one person), a gambler is rarely able to resist one more opportunity to win a fortune, a drug addict remains alert to where and when the next 'fix' will take place, and a Casanova (Don Juan, philanderer) is ready for a new conquest with the rising of each day's sun. A sugar addict, like me, is one taste away from a galloping indulgence.

These days, all of us are bombarded with temptations of a new kind via television ads—must-have digital products with magical capabilities that allow us to make our voices heard worldwide in seconds. Smartphones and iPads. Too many of us, our family, friends and business associates become addicted to texting and snapping instant photos of ourselves or others to send into a system that will make them available to viewers worldwide (even potential employers) *forever.*

It's not only children and teenagers who find it humorous and safe to hide behind diatribes against peers, parents or anyone with a different opinion. Adults do, too. Most ignore the fact that their ugly behavior and inappropriate language will be available to anyone with knowledge of how to search for and find anything associated with their name. Such investigations may become the reason why a college or university turns them down for entrance as a student, or why they are unemployable in the future, or why they don't receive the promotion they expected.

Addictions of any kind are harmful.

Addictions are created by us; we fool ourselves into thinking we're in control of them. We're not.

Addictions require a change in our mental chatter. We don't *need* french fries or ice cream or alcohol or illegal drugs or cigarettes or just one more hour playing Angry Birds on our smart phone to get through the day or the pain we're trying to forget. We *need* to learn *why* we think we need them and exactly what we think will happen if we don't imbibe.

Addictions require our admission that we have one and that the consequences are seriously affecting our work and social lives, our relationships, and most of all our health.

Addictions require action of another kind that brings satisfaction and occupies our mind; for instance, a sport, a morning walk with a neighbor, bird watching, a hobby (knitting afghans for the elderly; scrapbooking; sorting family photographs), a sport (e.g., golf, tennis, racquetball, swimming, darts, horseshoes) or volunteering at any of the many local organizations that serve the needy (e.g., Meals on Wheels, Wounded Warriors, Red Cross, Animal Welfare League, Humane Society, food banks, women's cancer centers).

What worked for me was to learn about the power of faith and prayer, and to practice the tenets taught by the Science of Mind Church. They have brought me abundant enjoyment of life and thankfulness for even the smallest of blessings. You may find similar strength and convictions from the belief systems of other churches.

Before I married Ian and moved to Michigan, I had finally matured more fully as a woman and embraced the many roles this involves: daughter, sister, wife, mother, friend, and colleague, even niece and aunt. However, it took much longer to realize that a Hollywood pedigree, inherited wealth, or a lifetime collection of things wasn't as important as my relationships with the people in my life. My ZIP Code address wasn't as significant as my understanding that "home is where the heart is." Pliny the Elder, a Roman author and philosopher in the first century, is credited with saying this, and although his often-quoted adage rings with truth, like most of us I had to leave the nest, where I was the most comfortable, in order to reach my dreams.

One online dictionary interprets *home* as "the abiding place of the affections." What a wonderful legacy to leave to our family. I still want my daughters and granddaughters to believe that. Home is not a house or an apartment or even a room, but a place where our love dwells. A place where there is heartfelt concern, compassion and support.

Of course, many from my mother's generation stated unequivocally that the kitchen is the heart of the home. Heaven, help me! Mama's cookies were the start of my addiction. Cookies were the quickest way to stop my whining and need for immediate attention.

With the passage of time, I became increasingly aware that my conscious thinking could bring about certain outcomes, especially when they came as specific answers to prayers. In a similar way, I could subconsciously get my sixth sense to kick in at unanticipated times; I'd either perceive events that would take place or certain particulars about them.

My faith had become such an integral part of my being that I was more responsive to messages regarding people, places or things that were unknown to me—those not previously experienced or gained through use of the usual five senses (see, hear, taste, smell, touch. Such messages were a blessed gift and I embraced them all.

Otherwise unexplainable events seemed to occur with regularity during my life. At first, I thought they were a fluke or coincidence or that I simply had a stronger intuition than other people. Over time, I interpreted them as demonstrations of God's answers to my prayers or warnings of things to come.

For instance, Ian and I had come to the conclusion that our Beverly Hills home was feeling cramped and no longer suited our needs. Our daughters were growing like weeds, required larger closets for wardrobes that suited four distinct seasons, and more storage space for their accumulation of everything girls find necessary. The kitchen and bathrooms were dated and dysfunctional. We started the search for a larger home.

Nothing our realtor showed us seemed right for one reason or another. Closets too small. Not enough bathrooms or bedrooms. Not enough outdoor storage space. Inadequate backdoor entry space for winter boots, coats and hats caked with snow. We drove block after block on our own, snatching whatever time we had outside of Ian's work schedule. Surely something special would capture our attention.

Quite unexpectedly, we found the perfect house on White Oaks Trail in Birmingham, not more than a ten-minute drive from our first home and in the same school district.

Mrs. Crusoe took us a tour and through friendly chitchat on several subjects we learned her sister lived in Pasadena, California, which is about twenty miles from where I grew up and until I became Mrs. Hunter. My interest grew. Her sister, Romaine, wrote poetry and sent them on Christmas parchments that she had given as gifts.

I was flabbergasted. Literally. It was one of those jaw-dropping moments. "Romaine Lynch? I'm the calligrapher Romaine used!" My voice cracked from excitement. "For several years, I inked her poems on the Christmas gift parchments using my dining room table for a desk! I knew she sent them to friends throughout the country, but never expected to meet a relative of hers in Michigan. It's a small world."

Some would call this irony—a quirk of fate. I called it a Divine demonstration that comes after prayers of faith and the patience to wait for it and recognize it upon fulfillment.

We loved the house. It had everything we needed. We signed the purchase, sold our current home, packed up our belongings and arranged for the short-distance move. Mrs. Crusoe welcomed us at the door and escorted me to one of the now empty rooms. Empty except for one thing. There, on one of the walls, she had mounted one of Romaine Lynch's Christmas parchments.

Ian and I flew to California a few times a year to visit Mother and the rest of the family. Mother would entertain as many relatives as possible during this time, if busy schedules didn't collide with the dates.

Uncle Moe had taken to Ian from their first introduction before we married and looked forward to our visits if he happened to be in Los Angeles. That Ian was the director of the Car Haulers Union and continually involved with the Teamsters influenced his interest, I'm sure.

Ian's star rose even higher with Uncle Moe when he shared with him our encounter with a fascinating stranger we'd met while staying at La Costa. We were having a pre-dinner drink at the hotel bar and stuck up a conversation with James Hoffa—son of the infamous Jimmy Hoffa—who was in Beverly Hills on business. Ian recognized him immediately; I had no idea who he was until we were introduced.

After some time passed, I had voiced a strong feeling that wouldn't let go of me. I call it an ESP moment. "You're going to be president of the Teamsters Union one day, James."

He had looked at me and laughed. "No way!"

Uncle Moe laughed at the tale. "That's a good one."

At the time, James was a labor attorney in Detroit and represented Teamster members in workers compensation cases and various other personal legal matters, as well as those for joint councils and local unions and served in this capacity for twenty-five years. As I write this memoir, James Hoffa is serving his third term as General President of the International Brotherhood of Teamsters, (1999-2015 and counting). Although skeptics of ESP abound, I choose to believe I have this scientifically unexplained gift and my out-of-the-blue pronouncement was validated after the passage of many years.

Another time at La Costa, Ian and I were already in the elevator when an impeccably suited gentleman on the next floor joined us. He looked directly at me and said, "How are you related to Moe Morton?"

"By blood," Ian said.

The elevator stopped on another floor and other people entered the elevator. Nothing more was said, but this brief encounter and very personal question by a total stranger bothered me. When I saw Uncle Moe, I queried him. "Who do you think this man was and how do you think he connected me with you?" I asked.

He merely shrugged and said, "Beats me, Carol. I wouldn't worry about it. You'll probably never see him again."

A short time later, I learned the man was "Allen Dorfman, a multi-millionaire Chicago financier who owned Amalgamated Insurance Agencies Inc. and who earned the majority of his money as Jimmy Hoffa's appointed kingpin to run the Teamster's pension funds and be his link to organized crime. Under Dorfman's control and influences, the funds grew from $1 billion to almost $7 billion and were used to finance most of the central Las Vegas strip, including the Stardust Casino. The casino's purported ownership, by nine mob bosses from four states, was concealed from prying eyes, especially the IRS and the FBI, because they were skimming millions from the earnings and secreting the money out of the country for investments beyond the reach of the government.

Clearly, Uncle Moe knew Dorfman. I had overheard snippets of conversations about Mother's brother for years as a young girl, but never really understood the subject matter and didn't ask questions. Over time, I came to learn he was involved in the Vegas business of the mob and, of course, my first two husbands had questions. Like Uncle Moe, I would just shrug. He protected me from knowing the details of his real life outside our family gatherings. One straight answer would lead to more questions from me. Since he and Auntie Helen had no children of their own, my love and acceptance were important to both of them. They didn't want to jeopardize our relationship. Neither did I.

Ian and I weren't surprised to read in the January 21, 1983, newspapers that Dorfman had been killed the night before by eight bullets to his head while walking in the parking lot of a famous Lincolnwood Hyatt (known as the Purple Hotel because of the color of its bricks). Lincolnwood is a suburb and about ten miles north of downtown Chicago. Sixty years old, Dorfman faced up to fifty-five years in prison after his upcoming sentencing on February 10th; he had been convicted for labor racketeering and attempting to bribe a U.S. senator from Nevada, along with the Teamsters' president and a couple other mob cohorts.

The next day, Ian and I learned the FBI had collected evidence, through their wiretapping of Dorfman's office. He was still advising mob bosses, *after* his conviction, on how to deal with their funds in a hurry and how to work around the wiretapping of competing mobsters' offices. Ironically, he was oblivious of the wiring under the very chair on which he sat and relayed the names of his contacts.

The FBI believed Dorfman was killed by out-of-town assassins hired by these crime syndicate bosses who, even after three decades of alliance, decided his lengthy prison sentence would strip him of usefulness. Since he has nothing to lose, he'd likely divulge information about their ties with him.

Reading these details about someone Ian and I had stood shoulder-to-shoulder with in an elevator returned all the details about his appearance and mannerisms. I could still his voice in my ears.

On another one of our California visits, Ian was invited to have lunch with Uncle Moe and his close friend, Sidney Korshak, at their favorite Beverly Hills restaurant, Jimmy's. Ian had found the conversation lively and thoroughly enjoyable. Uncle Moe was a confident and charismatic man, albeit close-mouthed whenever subject matter became too personal. He was fun and supportive and loved our family.

It wasn't until Uncle Moe died that I realized the extent of his Chicago and Las Vegas mob connections. He had been the brains behind and/builder of Acapulco Towers, a seven-floor condominium-type hotel located in the hills above Acapulco Beach, completely hidden from anyone's curiosity when frequenting or vacationing in the area. Major mob bosses and their gangster partners-in-crime from several countries stayed there whenever they wanted to conduct business in private or needed a safe hangout when 'on the lamb' from pursuers in the States. For a couple months in the tourist season, these wealthy underground men, who knew how to lead double lives and 'beat the rap,' would invite their friends in high places, including those in the movie industry, to vacation at Acapulco Towers for relaxation and socializing by the pool.

Moe was a central figure in such arrangements as manager of the facility, because he and Helen had a home in Acapulco and knew everyone from the president of Mexico to the plumbers, electricians and cab drivers hired to work for him and keep their mouths shut.

Uncle Jack had other connections to the Vegas monsters. He took their under-the-table casino winnings and either made off-shore investments for them or placed sizeable bets at the race track and then sheltered the even larger payouts from IRS agents. When his activities as a bookie were discovered at the Del Mar track, he was permanently barred from every racetrack in California.

I had always struggled to fit these pieces of their lifetime puzzle together, because they were so far removed from my personal life, but they started to make sense the more Ian and I learned. Memories returned of the visits and conversations at our house with their father—my grandfather, who lived with us until he died and who usually, cranked up the radio news volume just enough to garble their words. All the illegal and dangerous dealings both uncles got into made me rethink how and why they had gotten into such a lifestyle.

First, I could no longer deny my role in perpetuating the family secrets. Just as I had denied having an addiction to sugar long into my young adulthood and blindly allowed the consequences to become an enabler of my poor lifestyle choices, I had denied learning the truth about my dear uncles.

And they had, no doubt, become addicted to power and money and the extravagant existence they provided. Both had been womanizers until they married, and neither had children. Jack's wife died young, and he never remarried. Their peers and employers were either professional gangsters or crooked cops, politicians, business people in every industry, and anyone else who was willing to pay generous fees in exchange for nondisclosure. Their father, my grandfather Benjamin Mitnick, had supported his family as a bootlegger during the Prohibition. In this case, 'like father, like son' was their reality. Life was tough as an immigrant during the Great Depression, WWII, being Jews in the United States when millions were being tortured, starved and murdered by the Nazis in every European country. That doesn't excuse a disregard of our country's laws.

Once again, I learned that admitting the awful truths about the people in our life doesn't have to destroy or diminish the positive roles they played in it. We all role-play, to a certain extent. We smile when we are sad. We agree rather than disagree, especially if remaining silent avoids an argument. We tell 'little white lies,' if being truthful is hurtful to another person we care about. That being said, we must not whitewash self-destructive behavior and choices that cause harm to another. Our maturity can reach the point of forgiveness, but that doesn't mean we should forget or condone the deeds.

It took me a long time to name anything positive about my two failed marriages. Unknown to me, the relationship I had with my first husband was based on a lie; he wasn't what he claimed to be. But I *allowed* him to change my outward appearance with the 'right' clothes. It was *my choice* to fall in love with him and take marriage vows. When his lie was exposed, I *allowed* myself to wallow in self-pity and return to my addiction for comfort. The positives? He encouraged me to take pride in my artistic talents and use them profitably in the retail business. The ensuing success I experienced at The Broadway provided the work ethic and experience that benefited me in later employment that supported my second husband, our daughters and me.

I had walked into that relationship with eyes wide open, too. I believed our companionship and my being needed by someone would replace the psychological relief my brain got with a sugar fix, much like that experienced by a cocaine, Valium or martini addict. I had no personal knowledge of the symptoms that predicted his potential for physical and verbal spouse abuse. Again, truth resulted in my self-esteem taking another nose dive. The positive? My wonderful twin daughters.

The strength of my Science of Mind belief system and prayer life was tested time and again, but never more poignantly than when I was driven to my knees over a daughter's affliction.

Soon after we moved to Michigan, Jennifer experienced an increasing number of panic attacks that had started in her preschool years. Ian and I were fortunate to find highly skilled medical help to help both her and us learn why they occurred and how to go about keeping them at bay. Her doctor taught her several coping skills that worked well enough to lessen the frequency and extent of the attacks. There were months when everything would go well, and then something would trigger another attack.

Despite this disorder, Jenny experienced many achievements throughout her junior and senior high school years and enjoyed a wide variety of subjects. When we met with her school counselor to discuss college options, he said, "I'm afraid that, despite her above average grades, Jennifer is simply not college material."

Our jaws dropped. Such a negative statement coming from a counselor was enough to railroad the efforts of any student, let alone someone with Jenny's panic disorder. He obviously didn't understand the power of words or that such blatant negativity can doom a young adult to mediocrity forever. I dug in my heels and talked with my disconcerted daughter about the power of positive thinking. She was "The Little Engine That Could."

In late August, Jennifer and Lisa packed up and headed to Michigan State University in East Lansing, located about an hour's drive from our home. This was the first time they would live away from the family, and both were eager to begin their new life.

We decorated their large dorm room with new bedding, lamps and framed photographs of the family, the dogs and the cat. During this process, we met the two freshman girls in the adjacent room. After hugs and kisses, Ian and I finally left them and headed for home, already feeling like empty-nesters.

Everything was great for about twelve hours. Then the phone calls started. Jennifer was clearly exhibiting homesick symptoms and the vocabulary of fear that signaled an oncoming panic attack. She was anxious about attending her first class, having lunch with strangers, having to make new friends. Everything required a decision. Maybe she'd make a mistake. Maybe the professors would think she was dumb. Maybe no one would like her. Maybe she'd be late to a class because she couldn't find the right building.

I offered encouragement, and we discussed several of the coping skills she had used successfully in the past.

The phone calls continued for about a week. "Mom, I can't sleep. I can't focus on the lectures or take notes on them. I can't eat and fee ill. I'm shaking so hard, I don't want anyone to see me. I hate this. Lisa is having a ball. Why can't I be like her?"

I spoke with Lisa for her assessment. "Mom, she can't get out of bed today. I'm worried."

"I'm coming to get her, Lisa. Help pack up her things and remain calm. Everything will be fine. Panic disorder is curable, honey. She simply needs time to focus on nothing else for a while. Without schoolwork and extracurricular activities crowding her mind, she can do this."

I returned to the campus and brought Jenny home. My heart ached for her. She was so depressed. Her dream of being a college student and sharing experiences as a young adult with her sister had gone up in smoke. I prayed for the ability to do and say the right things. College was not going to happen for her *for the moment.* It would. In time.

Jennifer remained home for about nine months, isolating herself upstairs in her room, drawing, reading, consoling herself and becoming increasingly more acrophobic. She couldn't drive a car, let alone sit in one. On several occasions, she literally opened the door while I was driving. This was unacceptable and dangerous, and I prayed in desperation for answers. She refused to see the doctors who had helped her during her high school years. She felt like a failure.

I knew the feeling. In fact, I struggled with it again. Her panic attacks were my fault. I had allowed myself to suffer years of verbal and physical abuse instead of ending it after the first attack. I had chosen to do nothing and think things would change with the dawning of a new day. My child had heard and witnessed this abuse and become emotionally scarred.

By now, I had years of experience in knowing that answers to prayer come with our deepening faith, but the right ones would *not* come in my time or Jenny's time, only in God's time.

Knowing I was being guided in our journey, I explored any and every avenue that opened up to us, leaving the house only long enough to make trip to a bookstore, the grocery store, and only the most important social occasions. I learned that, according to the National Institute of Mental Health, over forty million Americans suffer from some form of anxiety.

Then, the miracle happened.

Ian and I learned about Terrap, a group in Birmingham, Michigan, that offered classes for those suffering from various emotional problems—like OCD, phobias (e.g., fear of flying, fear of germs), panic disorder and acrophobia—to assist them in understanding their condition and to find personal and workable solutions. Jennifer, already eighteen, needed effective ways to deal with her debilitating condition in order to have a fulfilling life. Like my addiction, she would need to identify what triggered her anxiety before she could attempt to control it. This required her determination to replace the fears with optimistic thoughts and the time spent worrying with more productive activities that were distracting and rewarding. Mind over matter. Retraining the mind to respond to new cues. Dr. Larry Canto and his caring staff possessed a wealth of knowledge, patience, and genuine love for every participant in the therapy group and became her miracle.

Although Jenny still wrestled with irrational fears and the need to avoid any activity that might trigger one that didn't give her a means of 'escape' (i.e., if she didn't drive a car, she couldn't cause a car accident; or, if she didn't try to join a sorority, she couldn't be rejected by the members; or, if she didn't attend a class, the professor couldn't ask her opinion about the subject matter), Jenny decided she was ready to return to Michigan State the following fall.

Mustering all the courage and inner strength required to meet and successfully overcome each stressful situation that arose, and at long last supported by the right combination of medication and medical staff, Jennifer not only graduated with a BA degree, but went on her earn her PhD in clinical psychology.

Once again, my prayers, faith, and experience as a well-versed Science of Mind practitioner reminded me of the powerful gifts we all have to heal, restore and rebuild our lives.

When we're going through severe discomfort, pain, grief, loneliness, financial turmoil, illness, despair and any other life change, no matter how temporary, we want a solution. It took concerted effort and many setbacks, but in the process of gaining control over my thoughts, so I wouldn't revert to my out-of-control sugar addiction, I found that something as temporary as a pause before acting or responding verbally could improve my attitude toward the difficult situation.

For example, I suffered a serious rotator cuff injury that required surgery and my wearing a sling that immobilized my arm 24/7, with only short reprieves of two-minutes hourly during the daytime hours. It inhibited even passive movement without strict supervision. This continued for three months. I prayed for a demonstration of healing and read my Science of Mind materials for much need encouragement.

Month Two arrived and so did my impatience. I could deal with aches and pain, but not with inactivity. My walks around the neighborhood or tag-along trips to the grocery store with Ian provided distraction and a modicum of exercise, but I longed to do something productive on my own. There were days I wanted to scream to high heaven with my frustration or rip that sling off my body. Then I'd think of the millions who were in my same position somewhere in the world—or suffering from the pain of far worse situations—and stop my private pity party.

Still, what I wanted was some immediate form of physical gratification that could, in turn, calm my inner exasperation. Remember, physical activity can produce a similar 'high' that recovering addicts want when looking for instant comfort or peace of mind. That's one of the reasons so many people of all ages have taken up jogging in recent years. To get that high that comes with increasing the endorphins.

Strange as it may seem, the one thing that eased my annoyance with being so confined was to mop the kitchen floor with my one useable arm and hand. I admit it was taxing, but I tried, I didn't give up, and I was successful. I'm not saying the floor was spit-spot clean, but the 'before' and 'after' was visible to my eyes.

Finally, the torn tendons of the rotator cuff, which had to be reattached to the shoulder bone, healed enough for the second phase of my treatment—strength and agility rehabilitation. Unfortunately, after being immobile for so long I couldn't lift my arm more than a few inches. My muscles had atrophied. Slowly over the next few weeks, I was pulled, stretched, massaged, and exercised three times a week. My doctor shook his head over my endless voicing of the same questions. "Why is this process taking so long? Are you sure there isn't something else we can do? I'm healthy and agile and willing to try anything."

"Patience, Carol. It takes from twelve to sixteen weeks for the migration of cells to reach the surgical site and begin the remodeling phase to create scar tissue. That scar tissue has to be strong enough to withstand what's involved in the cuff's muscles reaching their maximal tensile strength. If you do too much too soon, you might end up extending the healing process by tearing the suture site. It's still fragile. I'll decide when you're ready to add something more to your routine. For now, perform only as much as I think you're ready to tackle. Your rehab therapists are working closely with me to have you on the right schedule."

His message was clear. No do-it-yourself therapy at home.

On the last day of rehabilitation, I was ecstatic.

The ordeal had been both a psychological and physical challenge. I had leaned heavily on Ian, my girls, friends, and my faith, but with their tireless encouragement and assistance I had reached the top of the mountain. Hallelujah!

By now, my hard-working and uncomplaining therapists had become friends. After four grueling months of therapy, we shared many hugs and smiles. In one last hurrah, I decided to show off and prove that their hard work on my behalf wasn't wasted. I could stretch my arm to its former dexterity.

A yardstick had been affixed to a wall in the therapy room for measurement of progress. On each visit, I gingerly walked my fingers up the wall and stretched my arm upward. Such a seemingly simple task, but more difficult when my muscles and tendons are less elastic than in my more youthful years. Over and over, I followed orders and inched my arm slowly and only slightly further up the yardstick, repeating the same simple routine each week. On this last day of rehabilitation, though, I challenged myself to make one more supreme effort and wow the onlookers.

"Look at me," I said, setting my fingers into motion like a spider creeping up the wall in no particular hurry to reach the prize. Then, acting on impulse and not a scrap of wisdom, I thrust my arm upward to touch the top of the yardstick.

Wahoo! *I did it.*

In that glorious moment of victory, I felt a snap and groaned aloud. *Oh, my God, what did I do?*

Clutching my throbbing shoulder, I turned to face the horrified group of women who had stopped applauding my success a mere second after hearing my cry of pain. Instantly, they determined what had happened and went into action. A couple of them immobilized my arm and placed me carefully on the closest gurney. Another one dashed to get ice packs and set them in place. Yet another called for the closest doctor while my surgeon was located.

It was my fault. I had created a totally unnecessary disaster and reduced months of healing and arm movement rehab to zip. Nada. I had envisioned a graduation day with a diploma and fond goodbyes. I'd get neither. No one else was to blame. Only me.

An urgent MRI confirmed our deductions. I had torn the repaired area of my rotator cuff. The truth was hard to take in. As addicts of anything we want to do, I slipped into denial mode and then the blame-game. This wasn't happening to me. It shouldn't have happened to me, not after all my praying. Maybe the procedure had been faulty. Maybe I should have worn a different sling model. Maybe—

"I have to reschedule you for surgery, Carol," my doctor said. "It would be best for you to be admitted to the hospital right now. If you want to go home and make plans, you'll have to wear a hard sling and be extra careful that you don't cause the tear to worsen. The condition of the repair site has been compromised, and we may not see the same results."

I spent all evening rehashing the stupidity of my action with Ian. "What should I do? I know I need the surgery again, but I'm dreading the long rehabilitation. Okay. I don't have a choice. Another surgery is necessary. This time, though, I think I'll do my therapy at home. I know the schedule and every movement by heart." I saw his frown. "You don't have to reprimand me, Ian. I get it. I can't take matters into my hands. My medical opinion has nothing to do with the carefully drawn blueprint for my treatment produced by the professionals. They told me repeatedly that slow and steady wins the race."

"Listen to yourself, Carol. What you just said sounds exactly like something you'd say as a Science of Mind practitioner. It's okay if people come to you for help and advice, because they trust you for your experience and knowledge, but you don't want to accept it from a medical expert with impeccable credentials in surgery."

That made me laugh. "You're right. Despite my many years of faith-answered demonstrations, I'm still a work in progress. God is the Supreme Healer, not me, and my orthopedic surgeon is an instrument to fulfill this demonstration of my faith. I took over and needed a lesson in humility. Humility and patience. Both are virtues worth every effort to acquire. Hopefully, I'll acquire a greater appreciation for the difficulties experienced by those who ask for my prayers and a demonstration of *their* faith."

After an uneasy night of little comfort or sleep, I sat in the den watching the Don Imus Show on TV while mulling over my predicament. Unexpectedly, he launched into a story about his own shoulder problem and raved about the skill of the New York City surgeon who returned it to normal. *Shoulder* surgeon. For some reason, I jotted down the doctor's name and spent the next several minutes on the phone, instructing the operator to locate and put me through to his office. It was Friday, and I couldn't wait out the weekend before taking action. Because my situation was pressing, I was able to set up an appointment for an immediate consultation. I was instructed to bring a copy of my MRI and have my medical insurance cards with me the following Tuesday.

"What were you thinking, Carol?" Ian said, later. "There's nothing wrong with the surgeon you have. There are very likely a dozen or more Imus-type patients who rave about *him* right here in Michigan. How are you going to manage the airport crowds and the long flights there and back? What if there's a delay? What if someone bumps into your arm while rushing down a corridor?"

I had in my head that the New York surgeon was going to perform an Imus miracle for me, too. Ignoring the rationality of Ian's questions, I checked airline schedules. I'd have to be at the Detroit airport very early to make a 6:30 a.m. flight, but that meant I'd arrive in New York about 8:30 and make it to my 10:00 appointment. My return flight would leave New York at 6:30 that evening, so a hotel reservation wasn't necessary.

Ian's arguments replayed in my mind over the next hour, and to make him happy, I let my fingers do the walking through the Yellow Pages and called the office of another orthopedic surgeon in Birmingham. After a quick explanation of my situation to his nurse, I plied her with several questions and learned he used a slightly different technique to repair a re-torn rotator cuff; but, regardless of the technique, I'd have to wear a sling for at least three months. That was standard protocol.

"His schedule is quite full," she said. "He won't be able to see you until next Wednesday. That's quite a long wait for you, but let's ink your name in for a 10:30 appointment. Come a little earlier than that to fill out all the paperwork."

Amazingly, on Monday morning, this Birmingham surgeon's office called me back. "Another patient has cancelled his appointment, Mrs. Hunter. The doctor can see you tomorrow morning at 9:30, if you'd like to move your appointment up a day."

"I'll be there." This was happening for a reason. I knew that, and I honestly dreaded the thought of such a major event taking place so far from family and friends. What would I do about the follow-up visits? Who would supervise my weekly progress and rehab? Ian would be pleased.

I consider this swift change in my far too hastily made plans an unearned blessing. I was sitting with other patients in the waiting room of the surgeon in Birmingham, Michigan, watching the CNN morning news show on a small elevated TV set in a far corner. Without warning, the voices of the news crew elevated as cameras focused on smoke pouring from the top floors of a World Trade Center Tower. A plane had evidently crashed into it.

Right in front of our eyes, we watched a second plane show up and fly purposefully into the second Tower. The words 'terrorist attack' caught the attention of everyone in the waiting room and those working behind the desks. We had barely caught our breaths, when the cameras switched to Washington, D.C. where another plane had crashed into the Pentagon. The anchors said every flight going into and out of New York was cancelled. Every minute after that was worse than the previous one. We were horrified. Fear caught in our throats we all looked at each other and I realized, without saying a word that I would have been on the freeway into the city, but for the grace of God.

Yes, it was September 11, 2001.

Ironically, Sandra and Charles were at the Los Angeles Airport waiting for their plane to arrive from Portland, Maine, via Boston. They would be passengers on the return flight. A loud and overly excited voice barked a message over the airport loudspeakers. "All flights arriving from New York or departing from LAX have been cancelled until further notice." Word spread like a lethal virus from person to person: terrorists had flown into New York's World Trade Center. America was being attacked.

Like millions of others at airports throughout our nation, Sandra and Charles went home to watch the terrifying history take place right in front of their eyes through the marvel of television.

Even now, I have to pause as I relive the devastation caused by the Jihadists piloting those two planes, the one leaving Philadelphia filled with citizens who would never see their loved ones again, and the fourth one that crashed into the Pentagon that infamous day known now at 9/11. It has forever changed the way we live our lives. Fear of another such attack lurks in the back of our minds.

I decided to remain with my original surgeon. After the second operation, I started the rehabilitation of my muscles and tendons once again, but this time I did it at home. Although I was told not to expect perfect results, because it was very difficult for most patients my age to fully recover from such complicated trauma, I remained hopeful. The doctor was right. This time, it was more difficult to regain my former agility and my left hand remained limb and numb. There is no denying that my emotions ran the gamut from high to low and back again on a daily basis.

Today, I can attest to the power of prayer and faith. I not only have full use of the hand, fingers and arm, but my handshake is stronger than it ever was. I feared I would never play the piano again, but I enjoy easy and fluid maneuvering of my fingers up and down the keyboard.

Yes, we *can* survive trials and tribulations and come out stronger, without resorting to the addiction that continues to appeal to our weaker selves.

Prayer and trusting in God to provide Divine assistance saw me through yet another of life's traumas. And I didn't resume my sugar yearnings through any of these trials.

21

IN THE TELEVISION movie *Into the Storm*, Winston Churchill and Franklin Delano Roosevelt were sharing their thoughts during turbulent times of WWII. President Roosevelt said, "Faith is power!" Prime Minister Churchill said, "When men are under stress, they will turn to faith."

We can only imagine the endless pressures placed upon these two men and their inner anguish over every lost life and battle with no end in sight. Both understood the necessity for a projection of calm and encouragement to the people of their nations. They dealt with the strain of their offices with eloquence and dependable authority. Both had the support of their citizens, regardless of their station in life.

My father, who had grown to manhood in London, held great admiration for Churchill and quoted him enough times when I was a girl to stimulate my interest in seeing Into the Storm. Now, I will never forget Churchill's resounding pronouncement, "...this is the lesson: never give in, never give in, never, never, never, never—in nothing, great or small, large or petty—never give in except to convictions of honor and good sense."

Churchill was speaking to his compatriots both at home and at battle-fronts on foreign shores. London was being bombed by the Nazis and thousands of the British were killed or wounded, thousands more suffered from food rationing, loss of significant income, and unremitting worry over how they could survive one more day. How is it possible to not be deeply affected by Churchill's words that reminded them of the inner strength, optimism and perseverance that comes from their faith in a Higher Power?

Never give in. As a Science of Mind practitioner, I have worked with many over the past decades who needed this reminder during their own moments of faltering faith, moments that required hard decisions. Some faced life and death situations not unlike those who still experience the traumas of war. Some were in the throes of a life-threatening illness, loss of job, failure of a marriage, or financial ruin. Some dealt with rejection, loneliness, or the inability to end their own addiction to a substance that could temporarily soothe the agony that crippled their will to live joyously.

Never give in. Never give up. Not for any reason.

I have already recounted a few of my personal trials and a few of the distractions that worked continuously on my willpower to put me off course; but, on contemplation now, I know none of them compare to those of the millions who suffer paralysis or the amputation of limbs or who have daily travails that originate from a lifetime of poverty, starvation, persecution, oppression or torture. When their mental anguish seems far worse than the physical crisis, too many of these tortured souls resort to the abusive use of drugs, alcohol or overeating, purposeful starvation, cutting, or even suicide. I *can* compare the overpowering need to deaden the mental pain even for an hour.

Sugar-filled carbohydrates. That was my substance abuse. At the time of every personal distress—each of which seemed serious and insurmountable to me—I gorged and piled on the pounds. Just as the millions of Americans and British needed a reminder from their leaders of the critical importance of a deep and abiding faith during the war years, I learned how to seek Divine wisdom to conquer the reason for my mental anguish. I couldn't do it on my own. I needed help. Only when I experienced the profound effect prayer and faith had on my future, and subsequently on the futures of those closest to me, did I find my way out of the pity pit. Pity is a strong word and many readers are likely to protest.

Think about it. If we hate the way we look or the way we're treated by family members or people at work, or if we don't have a job or hate the one we have, if we think of ourselves as a failure or useless or a burden or inadequate in any way, we worsen what we consider a 'problem' by finding some way to feel better. We use and then misuse a substance because it alters our mood or behavior long enough to push the reason for misery out of our consciousness for an hour, a day or a night. Then we start over again when that 'reason' reappears.

Although I personally abused my body through an out of control sugar addiction, I have known others who abused alcohol, narcotics, prescription (licit) drugs, or illegal drugs. My self-inflected and wounding addiction made my best choices during difficult times next to impossible. Over time and through my studies, I learned that the process of healing of the body, spirit and addictive habit is directly related to our mindset.

I never tire from reading the stories of people who are living examples of courage, inner strength, faith and the power of positive thinking.

Stephen Hawking, a renowned theoretical cosmology physicist, spent thirty years as a professor of mathematics at Cambridge while suffering with ALS—also known as Lou Gehrig's disease. Most patients die within five years after being diagnosed with this daunting disease. Hawking spent years speaking to the public about black holes and quantum gravity from a wheelchair, operating his trademark computer system with his cheek when he was paralyzed from the neck down.

Christopher Reeve, known worldwide as Superman in three films about this superhero, was also an equestrian who participated in show jumping competitions. An accident, when he flew over the head of his horse at a three-bar obstacle, left him a quadriplegic bound to a wheelchair and a portable ventilator. Reeve lived for nine years after his accident and became the face of courage for those in his condition. He set up a foundation for spinal cord research. "We live in a time when the words 'impossible' and 'unsolvable' are no longer part of the scientific community's vocabulary," he said. Reeve also wrote in his 1998 memoir *Still Me*. "I believe that it's what you do after a disaster that can give it meaning."

Charles Krauthammer is another example of some who had the same fortitude and sense of purpose. While in Harvard's medical school, he and a friend played a game of tennis and went to the gym for a swim before the next class. When he dove into the swimming pool, he crashed his head on the cement bottom and severed his spinal cord, becoming an instant quadriplegic.

He was determined to get his medical degree. He did just that and then completed additional years of residency training to become board certified by the American Board of Psychiatry and Neurology. His published research caught the attention of Washington and he worked with the Carter Administration while also writing essays for several national journals and the Washington Post. His writing earned him a long list of awards, including a Pulitzer Prize. Even those with polar-opposite viewpoints consider him brilliant and the most powerful force and voice in American conservatism. Until he wrote his book *Things That Matter: Three Decades of Passions, Pastimes and Politics (c. May, 2015)*, and Fox News produced a one-hour special on his life, the majority of Americans who have watched him on PBS and Fox News productions had no idea he was sitting in a wheelchair.

Antony Weller, novelist, became a gradual paraplegic through multiple sclerosis (MS). Before the disease changed his life, he was a jazz and classical guitarist, and had published several books of fiction and nonfiction. Now he had to write through dictation. About his physical disability, he states that Mark Twain, Henry James and even John Milton (after he became blind) used dictation. He said, "Complaining changes nothing, and doesn't make you feel better—so you learn not to complain."

Then there is Jean-Dominique Bauby, AKA Jean-Do, who was the editor of the French magazine *Elle*. After suffering a massive stroke in his forties, he found himself locked in what he called a 'cage' called 'locked-in syndrome' that kept him imprisoned through total body paralysis, unable to communicate with those his loved. He escaped through his magnificent imagination and was able to not only converse with them, but to write a memoir. *The Diving Bell and the Butterfly* became an award-winning movie. How did he accomplish this fete? By working out a system of dictation using the alphabet and the blinking of his left eyelid. He was able to use his memories and mind's eye to feel alive again and escape his entrapment through the words that needed to be spoken, especially to his children. His indomitable fortitude was a magnificent tribute to the human spirit. Bauby died a few days after publication of the book.

My nephew Brian is another one of my heroes. Due to damage of his motor system, he is unable to look after himself and requires around the clock care. His caretakers bathe, feed and dress him. But Brian, who is bilingual, is blessed with a phenomenal memory and intelligence and has one of the most loving hearts I know.

I have never forgotten the time he received a pair of pajamas. He said, "I'm so lucky." I choke up even as I write this, because it is so humbling. Brian has never felt sorry for himself. Although I have relatives who have never flown to Michigan, Brian has made the trip twice despite the challenges it brought.

My sister spent much of her pregnancy in bed, but Brian was born three months prematurely, weighing in at only two pounds. Prior to the latter part of 1960, there were no intensive care units in any U.S. hospital for premature babies. In fact, there were laws and prohibitions against them, no specialized training, and no precedents for lifesaving techniques. There were only rules and regulations against mixing divisions of babies out of a very real fear of a particular staph infection, which was common at the time. Rampant, in fact, and prone to spread from ward to ward.

And there were no ultrasound machines. The fetus was an unseen, indiscernible, unknowable being whose maturity and weight were only guessed at through palpitation, measurement of the uterus growth, and judgment of heart health through the doctor's stethoscope. Premature babies often have breathing problems, because their lungs aren't fully developed. Because ventilators weren't available for preemies in that day, Brian stopped breathing several times, which resulted in motor damage. He had to remain in the hospital for months.

My sister and brother-in-law changed their customary lifestyle to adapt to their son's needs. For many years, they welcomed people from all walks of life who donated an hour or so of their time to help "pattern" Brian. These wonderful people were dubbed Brian's Angels. They were trained to move his body in a rhythmic pattern that mimicked crawling. Once a year, Sandra would give a party for Brian's Angels, which often gave them their first opportunity to meet each other.

In April, of 2016, Brian celebrated his forty-first birthday. He continues to teach me about unconditional love, perseverance, the beauty of humility and of heartfelt thankfulness for life as we know it.

I have shared these examples of these six real people who overcame their adversity and used whatever talent and facility they had to live productively. Each has inspired me to become a better person, to avoid destructive crutches to bolster my self-confidence and lessen my fear of criticism, and to believe wholeheartedly in the possibilities offered through faith. Both Roosevelt and Churchill would have been proud of these men.

Specifically, I have learned through the examples of such brave souls to focus on *only* today. To be mindful of every decision that will affect the rest of the day, those with whom I interact, and how today's decisions will affect tomorrow.

Twenty-four hours. Nowhere on this planet does anyone get days that are longer than that. No one gets an extra five or ten minutes. Just 1,440 minutes. And each of these minutes is a gift. How we choose to spend them is up to us.

Years ago, I wondered how many hours I'd have if I were to live to be a hundred years old. At that time it was over 500,000 hours. Fascinated with this figure, I reduced it to minutes and then seconds. Looking back, I have greater appreciation for the often used idiom 'how time flies.' According to The American Heritage® Idioms Dictionary, people have been using the phrase since 1800 when it was first recorded. I wasn't the only one to marvel at how the hours of each day, week, month and year can take wing when we focus on something other than the mental whispers that tempt and taunt us to take a mind-number at the first sign of unpleasantness.

How did I want to spend the abundant number of hours, if I should live to be a hundred years old? At the time, I chose to laugh often, to forget past slights, rebuffs and offenses, to forgive my own failings and those of others, and to be worry free. I chose to live in the present, to enjoy and savor simple moments, and to avoid stress.

I experienced plenty of bumpy roads, detours and flat tires on my journey through the years while trying to follow my audacious declaration. In time, I learned to take roads with fewer potholes, to change my flat tires, and to get back on my journey.

As a practitioner of the Science of Mind, I not only pray for demonstrations for myself, but for my clients, friends and family members. What is a demonstration? A demonstration is like making a blueprint to describe something we expressly want or need. In a house blueprint, we try to be as specific as possible; we should do the same when designing our prayer demonstration, with the full intention of receiving it. However, we don't outline *how* it will come about or *when* it will be revealed, because that's what God does. Our job is to ask God for the demonstration, to believe it will be provided, and to wait patiently for the it and in whatever form. If the answer isn't exactly what we had in mind, we must keep our faith and believe the adjusted answer is for a purpose beyond our understanding at the time.

The following personal demonstrations represent a few that resulted in the deepening of my faith and my continued study of the Science of Mind tenets that changed my life. Some of my personal demonstrations have taken a long time, while others have manifested in a matter of minutes. It always amazes and delights me whenever the demonstrations occur and each becomes a momentous event. Our words have a vibratory energy.

For instance, on a visit with family members in Portland, Maine, one year, I left the house early in the morning for a walk. In order to benefit from the exercise, I kept time to the music provided by a tape in the recorder I held in my hand. Suddenly, the tape recorder came apart at the joints. *I need a rubber band to hold this thing together*, I thought. Only a few steps further, I spotted one right in front of me on the trail. I swooped it up, wrapped it around my tape recorder and continued on my hike, as though it were the most natural occurrence. Someone must have dropped a handful of them, because I noticed a great number within the next several feet.

As improbable as this sounds, this demonstration happened in exactly this way. Yes, it was just a rubber band, but I have learned to take nothing for granted. God hears us, even when we don't speak the words directly through prayer.

Another time, while on errands in my car, the driver-side door rattled and distracted me from focusing on the road. When the rattle became as annoying as it was distracting, I drove into the parking lot of a grocery store, found a parking space, and opened the door and stepped out. There on the pavement right beneath my feet was a half-inch-thick piece of black foam rubber. I picked it up, repositioned myself in the driver's seat, and placed the foam where I thought the source of the noise occurred, quickly pulling the door shut to keep it in place. It worked.

A number of years ago, Ian and I had to sell our wonderful 'perfect' home in Birmingham, due to business changes that resulted in a lessening of monthly income. We would have to lease a home, until our financial situation changed for the better.

As unexpected challenges are wont to do, this one came at a tough time that added to the stress. Our daughters were in their senior year at Groves High School and wanted to remain in the Birmingham school district to graduate with their friends the following spring. After that, they would have college expenses, and that was even more important. And expensive.

I rolled up my sleeves and started to scale down, selling some of our furniture at a giant garage sale. Needless to say, our life was turned topsy-turvy. Sleepless nights followed, one after the other. We searched our entire area, but nothing available was suitable. Ian is not a hand wringer. After sober consideration, he liked to make a decision and follow through on it. This situation was different. He felt powerless. If he put up a 'for sale' sign in front of our home before we found a house to lease, we could find ourselves in even deeper trouble. We'd have to add storage and motel bills to our tight budget.

Three weeks before the first day of school, I pulled out a piece of typing paper and wrote out the blueprint for a suitable rental home: a place near water, air conditioning, Birmingham school district, three bedrooms, vacant or ready for vacancy within three weeks. Oh, and it must allow two indoor dogs.

I took this blueprint to God in prayer and asked for a demonstration. Soon. Then I did what I knew best. "Treat and move my feet."

Wasting no time, I left the house and drove directly to the shoreline. On the way through downtown Birmingham, I noticed a "Share Rental" sign. I parked and went into the real estate office. After registering, I shared the specifics about our home requirements with the agent. She gave me three addresses of home rentals in the school district.

Excited, I called Ian. He was reluctant to spend another evening traipsing about town on our own. "We don't really have a choice, honey. Avoidance accomplishes nothing." Right after supper, we headed for the first house on the list. It was beautiful and ideal for us. Unfortunately, the current occupants couldn't vacate in time. The other two homes were unsuitable.

The very next morning, I was on the phone with the agency with my report. "Do you have anything else?"

"Actually, another house was listed soon after you left here yesterday. It appears to have all your requirements."

I wasted no time and called the homeowner immediately. She was gracious enough to say, "Come over this morning."

The second I caught my first glimpse of the brick Tudor home near Walnut Lake, I fell in love with it. The girls were with me and rushed ahead to ring the doorbell. The homeowner told us her husband was going to work for a senator in Washington, D.C., and they would be there for at least a year. Another good sign. Then she asked, "Would it be possible to keep the furniture in the house, rather than putting it in storage? We have to leave fairly soon, and I simply won't have time to deal with that."

Surely I hadn't heard her correctly. A semi-furnished home? Another answer to prayer. I wouldn't have to replace a single piece I had sold at our mammoth garage sale, including bedroom furniture. "That would be fine," I said, trying not to look or sound too eager.

"And one other thing," she said, looking apologetic. "I'm a piano teacher and I'll have to leave my two pianos in the house. I know they take up space, but—"

"I would love that," I said. "I play a little myself and would take great care of your pianos." Talk about abundance; there would be three pianos in the house. I didn't want to get my hopes up. We needed to see the rest of the house. As we toured, she asked a few questions and I chatted about Ian and me, how we had met, and about my early piano training (I skipped the parts about why I quit or how I got hooked on chocolates to soothe my fragile feelings when Daddy wasn't pleased with my progress). Ian and I returned that evening to give him the opportunity to approve and to accept and sign the rental contract.

Our move took place in late August of 1985. Over that year of rental, we spent many hours in the stunning backyard that bordered the waterfront or just peering out the window at the lake from our kitchen table. The vistas changed with the weather and each season—the gorgeous foliage of deciduous trees that turned from green to shades of red and gold and then brown, before they dropped to reveal the recognizable silhouettes of each unique species through the winter months; and then the burgeoning of lush greens that announced spring and summer months with the added vibrant colors of blooming bushes and perennials.

As I watched the dogs chase each other from one end of the yard to the other, I wondered how we would ever be able to leave. The girls were happy and enjoyed bringing their friends home. We entertained with pleasure and pride. Fortunately, Ian's business prospered during this year, once again giving us the opportunity to purchase a home once August arrived.

As the weeks passed, I found myself repairing and fixing minor things with a little spackle here and a little paint there. I didn't want the owners to return to a laundry list of problems. Ian kept reminding me, "Carol, this isn't our house." His reminders kept my 'I Wish' and 'If Only' musing in check.

All too soon, we felt the urge to search for an available home in the area, reluctant to move far from our neighbors, who had become friends. Then a house came on the market just five blocks away. It was the right price and would 'work' for our family, but it fell short of rousing our enthusiasm. Especially mine. I felt trapped, because for some reason it didn't feel right. *Home is where the heart is,* I reminded myself.

After a second visit, we put a down payment on the home. That afternoon, I received a call from the owner of our dearly loved rental house. He said, "I don't want to put you and Ian on the spot, Carol, but I wanted you to be the first to know. I've been offered a new position, and my taking it will require our moving to Philadelphia. After much discussion and a couple visits there, we decided we'd like to build a home and live there, perhaps permanently. You've mentioned often, in the letters that accompany your lease checks, how much your entire family enjoys our house there in Bloomfield Hills. We wondered if you'd be interested in buying it?"

"*Buy* it?" I wanted to explode with joy. "Yes, yes, we would definitely want to buy it. Let me contact Ian. He'll get back with you by tomorrow morning to discuss the particulars."

It was an effortless transaction and the rest is history; as of this writing, we have lived in our wonderful dream home for thirty years. Our daughters have finished college, matured, married, given birth to our grandchildren and celebrated many holidays, dinners and birthdays in it. It is the family home. With each passing year, the trees on the property have grown taller and more majestic. We never tire of drinking in the beauty of our special surroundings. I share this story, because nothing is too large or too small for God to demonstrate his love for us.

This demonstration is particularly special to Ian and me. We received the news, via a Chinese fortune cookie message—ironically, in an Italian restaurant—that our life was about to change. I cracked it open and both Ian and I read its message at the same time.

Our eyes widened. "Grandparents! You're . . . ?"

Lisa and Tim nodded with joy written all over their faces.

Next to hearing of your own pregnancy and sharing the news with your parents, the arousal of the same delight is beyond words when spoken by your own child. "Oh, my dears, a little angel will bring you endless days of love, joy, and smiles. My heart is bursting with excitement!"

I peered into Ian's eyes. "Remember how it felt when you held your daughter for the first time? *Grandparents.* Where have the years gone?"

It was difficult to keep our voices down in the restaurant and even more difficult to finish eating when there was so much to talk about. "Take it slow, Lisa. Savor every moment of this new journey. Before you know it, your little one won't be so little anymore. You are embarking on one of life's greatest adventures. One you will never forget."

The weeks passed and Lisa seemed to grow lovelier. Since she was a twin and her father-in-law was a triplet, our excitement grew with each increase in the size of her abdomen. Her obstetrician wanted an ultrasound to check on the growth of the baby or babies. It was hard to wait for the phone call that would assure me all was well. I tried hard not to dwell on any of the problems I had experienced.

At about eight o'clock that evening, Lisa and Tim arrived. It didn't take any of my psychic intuition to see that something was amiss. This time, Ian and I could read the concern on their faces.

"We have a dilemma," Lisa said. She sat close to Tim and held his hand. "We're having a little girl, but we were told she may have a heart problem."

"The doctor couldn't be certain," Tim added. "There's an unexplainable shadow around the baby's heart. For now, we have to forward know this is a high-risk pregnancy."

Although I heard the words and the worry in their voices, I felt a calmness wash over me. Maybe I was only being a mother whose sense of duty included bringing comfort and support to a hurt child, but what I felt went deeper than that. "She will be fine, Lisa," I said. "The shadow is her inner light. She is a child of God, and he will watch over her."

Over the next several weeks, I prayed and asked God for a demonstration we could all accept and take in hand with great love. I could empathize with Lisa and Tim and knew well how difficult and frightening this experience was for both of them. After numerous tests and consultations, they chose to continue the pregnancy and deliver their daughter in December.

At first, Lisa refused to buy baby clothes and diapers, but her friends and sister urged her to make a few purchases in preparation for those first couple weeks after arrival. "It will be good for you," they proclaimed. "Stay busy. It will help the days pass quickly and bring untold pleasure. You're having a Christmas baby!"

Finally, with restraint, Lisa listened and shopped, but tears welled in her eyes with each purchase. I remember in particular one little red coat with white trim on the collar. It brought her enough pleasure to infuse more interest in setting up a nursery. We hung a mirror on one wall and she painted baby animals around the outside edge.

Beautiful Taylor, our first grandee, was born on December 11, 1997. She was absolutely perfect. No heart problem. The shadow that persistently showed on the ultrasound remained a mystery, but I am convinced it was Taylor's inner light.

Since this joyful event, we have since been blessed with two more equally beautiful grandees, Carson and Hayden. As I write of this life experience, which brought with it weeks of trauma and trepidation, I am thankful and awed by how special and magnificent this demonstration was for everyone in the extended Hunter family.

In treatment work with clients, I continually reminded them to expect a change for the better, but to remember that sometimes the reverse may occur. I reminded myself and Lisa of that, too. God is in charge. We must never give up praying, but include in our petitions a plea for courage and the willingness to accept whatever is given to us as a special gift. Just as my sister and nephew Brian have been living examples of grace and love to us and the hundreds of people who have come to know them through the years, we may also be used by God to inspire others.

Demonstrations sometimes require a deeper knowledge and understanding of a Loving God who does not punish.

In my treatment work with clients, or when praying for a personal demonstration or one for a family member, I found it effective to use specific names, addresses, and even a ZIP Code.

A few years ago, I went to God with particular prayers for my husband and his business. I had always prayed for prosperity and success in all of his ventures. Sometimes he was tested. On this particular occasion, he was busy but felt the projects weren't manifesting as rapidly as he would prefer. Ian had never really understood the Science of Mind process, but he had certainly experienced and seen the results of prayer and treatment work. "I need more work projects," he said. "You know more clients. Do whatever it is you do."

Time passed and he grew skeptical. One day I stopped by the office, while out on a couple errands, and my eyes fell on the brass nameplates in the lobby. R. Ian Hunter. *Not Ian Hunter*. That very day, I changed the name in my prayers to the one on the nameplate and kept the address and suite number the same. Lo and behold, his workload increased.

Similarly, when treating for a hospital patient prior to surgery, I have asked for the patient's room number, the location of the bed if the room is shared, and even the surgeon's name.

Not every blessing that has enriched my personal life came about after prayers of desperation when I struggled with a major crisis, like my compulsive sugar addiction, or when I was afraid, worried, frustrated, confused or dealing with health problems. During such transient times, my need for the Power of God's help drove me to my knees to seek a specific demonstration of understanding and strength of belief.

I have continually been given daily blessings that arrived without a single expressed need. I am still receiving such blessings. We all have. The welcoming voice of a loved one. The laughter of a granddaughter. A wave from a neighbor as I drive past her house. The warmth of the sun. A night sky resplendent with stars. I have never been able to enumerate just one day's worth.

Several times, a blessing comes 'out of the blue.' One evening in July of 2000, I received a call from my sister Sandra. "I'm extending an invitation you can't refuse, Carol. We're going to Morocco. It won't cost you a dime except for your personal shopping."

"Good heavens, Sandra, what are you talking about? Morocco?"

"Yes, Morocco. It's that little country, about the size of California, in the northeast coastline of Africa. Part of it borders the Mediterranean Sea and the other half, on the other side of a mountain, is the Sahara Desert. It's a quick ten-day excursion, Carol, inclusive of all accommodations, roundtrip airfare, most meals and a tour guide. It's a perfect jaunt without our spouses."

"You know I can't turn down an offer like that! I've always wanted to ride a camel and visit Casablanca."

"You can forget any romantic notions you have about Casablanca being like the movie, Carol. It's the largest port city in Morocco and probably the most important financial center in Africa. Besides, if I remember our family history correctly, the movie wasn't even filmed there. It was a Hollywood set production."

"If the city is a financial center, it must have great places to shop and eat. I love couscous and lamb and most spices. I think Moroccan cuisine is prepared with a lot of spices, like ginger, saffron, cumin and cinnamon. And they'll have seafood. I can't wait to tell Ian."

We met up with two other friends in New York, where we also faced our first challenge. Our supposed reliable and trusted guide, Henry, left his passport at home in Los Angeles. Since we really had no other choice and our sense of adventure kicked in, Sandra and I boarded the Royal Morocco plane without him.

The flight was uneventful except that the overhead lights were never turned out. Despite this frustration, many seated around us were either sleeping or nodding off. We quietly chatted most of the flight and were rewarded with a stunning sunrise as we approached our destination.

Happily, we were met by a Moroccan guide, Lotve, who drove a Mercedes van. Ten years old and slightly worn and weary, but it was still reasonably comfortable. Lotve took us around Casablanca, then Rabat, which is the political and royal center of Morocco; evidently each royal city has a prominent color and in Rabat it is white. Then he drove us to Fez, just an hour east of there. Still without Henry.

The first thing I noticed about Fez was the plethora of royal blue tiles. Glorious patterned tiles. Finally, after years of art classes and painting, I understood why this rich color was called Fez blue.

Since no one in our group could speak of understand Arabic, we feared we wouldn't be able to enjoy any city if left to explore on our own. We were also apprehensive about securing rooms at the right hotels. Henry had our itinerary. Did we have accommodations at the Hilton or a refurbished mansion?

For some reason I didn't question at the time, I was able to provide Lotve with names and descriptions, effective enough to impress him with enough information to pave the way for us wherever we went. In addition to the most notable tourist attractions, we visited carpet factories, jewelry and clothing stores, and family-owned gift shops. By now, I realized I was experiencing an unexpected but not inexperienced ESP. Several proprietors wanted to gift me with tokens of their esteem.

Since our group was small, we traveled everywhere together and enjoyed each meal as we exclaimed over the local cuisine. Of course I had to play my 'you taste and tell me about the flavors' game. Indubitably. The more common dessert was fresh fruit and that suited me just fine.

It was in Fez that Sandra and I sat on the floor in robes with white towels wrapped around our wet heads while being hennaed and tattooed on our hands and arms.

The next day we went into the Medea where I was approached by a refined gentleman who offered me 500 camels if I would stay with him in Morocco. That was one offer I had to refuse. Not that it wasn't tempting. I have used this unique proposal to remind Ian of what I was willing to give up to remain with him!

Henry, our Los Angeles tour guide, arrived two days later. He was quite happy and still tipsy from drinking on the plane trip. For the rest of the tour, he had to be satisfied with green mint tea, the beverage of choice in Morocco. Muslims do not use alcohol. At least not while in public and in their homeland.

The most fascinating experience for me occurred at the pottery factory. While a few of us remained in the van, the others headed for the restroom facilities. The van door was open and I could see a group of travelers trudging up the dirt hill directly in front of us. The leader was a white-robed man using a cane for assistance. When he reached the van, he stopped and started to remove a small green Moroccan flag with its lone red star attached by elastic to the cane.

I immediately assumed he was going to offer to sell me the flag. Instead, he handed me the hand-carved orange cane with its silver top. In broken English, he said, "For you." Before I could even open my mouth, he went on his way with the group. The episode had taken mere seconds. The first thing I said was, "Does anyone want the cane?"

A woman named Mary, who had joined our group said, "Sure, I'll take it."

Later, when we were back in our room, Sandra said, "Carol, he really meant for you to have the cane."

I shrugged. "Well, there's nothing I can do about it now. I already gave it to Mary and I'm not going to ask her to give it back to me."

Early the next morning, we heard a knock at our door. There stood Mary with the cane. "Carol, I can't keep this. The man gave it to you for a reason."

From that moment on, I kept the cane with me. We traveled together over the Atlas Mountains, into Marrakesh, and back to Casablanca. Out flight was delayed in Casablanca due to a bomb threat, and when we arrived at JFK airport, I learned I would likely miss my connection back to Detroit. Breathless with anxiety, I rushed up to the Northwest Airline counter to ask what I should do. When the attendant saw the hand-carved orange cane with silver top in my hand, she said, "Wait here. I'll get a wheelchair for you. Don't worry. We'll get you on the flight." And they did. To this day, the cane sits in the foyer umbrella stand. I rarely pass by it without experiencing a flashback of the giver of such delight. The cane has truly become a treasure.

I could go on and on about the fabulous demonstrations that manifest daily, perhaps some not as dramatic as others, but each one valuable and significant. I am an ordinary woman who experienced extraordinary results from finally recognizing my willpower was inferior to that of others. I needed to share the truths of my story with those who have witnessed by struggles and listened to my complaints during the first three-plus decades of my life. I wanted to inspire those with any addiction that takes away the full enjoyment of a life that centers around God, family and friends.

You must take full accountability for your choices. Today's addictions go far beyond alcohol, prescription and illegal drugs, and sex. They include fast food, sugar-infused food, spousal and child abuse, lying, excessive use of social media, especially texting, and spending beyond our means. But work can be addictive, too, and you're not the one who suffers most. World renowned Rick Warren, founder and pastor of Saddleback Church in Southern

California, authored *The Purpose Driven Life*, which has been read by over 100 million people in 137 languages. He recently wrote:

Your work and your worth are two different things. Many of you grew up being told you're worthless, and you're out in the workplace trying to prove everyone wrong. In the back of your mind, you're telling yourself, "I'm going to show them. I'm going to prove them wrong." You work harder and harder, but no matter how hard you work, it's never enough. Just about the time you start to relax, you hear a haunting voice telling you, "Keep pedaling. Somebody's catching up!" You need to get rid of the voice. It's feeding you a lie.

As a pastor, I've been by many bedsides as people died. I've seen many people take their last breath, sometimes at a hospital, sometimes in a home, and sometimes at the scene of an accident. Among all of the people I've watched die in my life, I've never heard anyone say with their dying breath, "I wish I'd spent more time at the office."

Not one.

(Daily Hope, "Your Work and Your Worth Are Two Different Things," Nov.29, 2015, © 2015 by Rick Warren)

Many of you will wonder if I ever filled out another Miracle Card. Truthfully, I have never again felt the need to do so. My three wishes were fulfilled, and in the process I have learned that God hears my prayers even when they come directly from my heart.

One thing more. Remember that white envelope I stepped on the weekend Ian and I first met in San Diego? I loved the Walpole quotation so much I had it engraved on a glass prism and gifted it to Ian much later in our relationship. It was a perfect response to what I felt we both had just experienced. A truly Divine Accident.

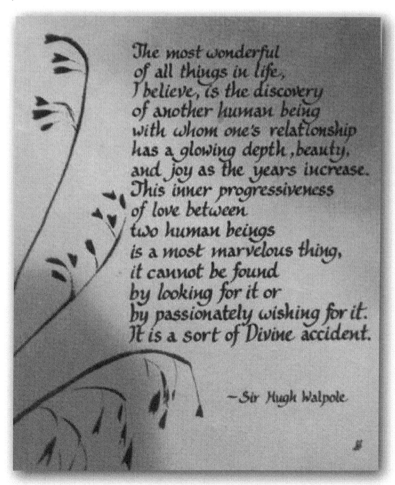

The most wonderful
of all things in life,
I believe, is the discovery
of another human being
with whom one's relationship
has a glowing depth, beauty,
and joy as the years increase.
This inner progressiveness
of love between
two human beings
is a most marvelous thing,
it cannot be found
by looking for it or
by passionately wishing for it.
It is a sort of Divine accident.

—Sir Hugh Walpole

Addendum

MY LESSONS FOR Healing

- Have an attitude of gratitude.
- Focus on what you have rather than what you don't have.
- Set small goals every day and do them. Accomplish one small task, regardless of how small.
- Let nothing stand in the way of achieving your desires.
- Being polite doesn't cost a penny and the rewards are plentiful.
- You don't have to always be right and win the argument.
- Be willing to listen and not interrupt.
- Do not judge by appearances. They can often camouflage the truth.
- One wise thought can result in a new direction.
- Children are like Myna birds; they mimic words.
- Accept people as basically good.
- Be persistent, steady, tolerant and loving.
- Learn to release the useless and keep the treasures.
- Nothing by chance.
- There is not a single painful moment that you cannot release and find momentary comfort.
- Demonstrate by becoming selfless, serene, fearless and confident.
- Learn from your mistakes.
- Speak respectfully. Even animals respond to sounds and tones of voices.
- Cherish all forms of life.

There is nothing special about the words I use or the way I pray. What I do know is that I have an unshakeable faith and remain calm while I seek answers. I don't attempt to compel, manipulate or pressure God to do anything my way or at my convenience. I find that just being my real self, uncomplicated, sincere and forthright is the best and most rewarding way to demonstrate. My children and clients often want a more compelling reaction to their needs and wants. Yes, I do hear them and see their pain and discomfort, but as a Practitioner, I know that the answer will demonstrate to the level of my belief. I have learned to remain composed and steadfast. Here's another personal example of how these traits can work to bring about a positive manifestation of our faith.

Shortly after our daughter Jenny and her dog took up temporary residence with us, while she searched for the perfect condo to buy. Very early one Sunday morning, our beloved Tiptoe started to bark. Jenny called out from her room, "I'll take him out."

About ten minutes later, our bedroom door swung open and Tiptoe leaped onto the bed reeking of a nasty odor. We knew exactly what it was. Jenny poked her head through the doorway. "Sorry. Tiptoe got skunked. Unfortunately, the skunk got into the house. I don't know where it is."

What! *A skunk in the house?*

Ian rolled out of bed, grabbed the flashlight in a bedside table drawer and headed out of the room. Very calmly, I said, "I have to shower first. I'll join you in about five minutes." I noticed that Tiptoe was not only skunked, he was spooked. We couldn't count on him to assist with the search.

When I arrived downstairs, Ian was investigating every nook and cranny in the family room, but from a distance. His eyes followed the beam from the flashlight as it flitted from corner to corner. Jenny had a doggie gate that shut off whatever room we wanted to barricade from entry by any of our dogs. I headed for the fireplace, thinking I'd turn it on for additional light. I stopped in my tracks when I heard a movement in it.

"It's in the fireplace hearth," I announced. "I'll call Critter Control." What I got was advice from them, not on-site help. "They said we should open the nearest door and put on an outside light. They wished us good luck."

Ian inched his way across the room to a door not far from the fireplace and opened it, flicking the switch on the wall that flooded the back yard. Hopefully, familiar sounds and smells of the outdoors would entice the skunk to use this door as an escape route.

Jenny held the doggie gate in front of her to form a barricade on one side of the fireplace. I noticed Ian's wooden Go-Blue sign and snatched it up as my weapon of choice. Now was a great time to give it the old college try!

Remember my narrative of being so freaked out over the water beetles in my art studio that I had to leave it? My more serene self was able to confront a very real skunk with boldness. I softly talked to our unwelcome guest. "Come on, baby, come to Mama. Let's go back outside." I sweet-talked it over and over again. "Come on, honey. You don't want to stay where you're not wanted." Slowly, the skunk crept out of the fireplace. It was so close to me, I could see the cobwebs on its eyelashes.

Without missing a beat, I continued my quiet chatter, only this time, I addressed my two assistants. "Here's my plan, dear family. When our little friend is completely within sight, we should carefully steer it towards the door. Ian, stand on the other side of the doorway so it doesn't dart further into the room."

Although the skunk's tail side was pointed in my direction, I didn't fear being sprayed. Skunks spray when they feel threatened. "That's right, baby, head for the light. Head for freedom." I used the Go-Blue sign to gently push the confused animal toward the doorway. Ian, my beloved husband, remained as far away as possible while giving Jenny and me instructions on what to do next. Amazingly, with the aid of a doggie gate and a college sign, that skunk scurried outside and disappeared beyond the circle of light in the yard.

We bathed Tiptoe every day for more than a week with tomato juice and white vinegar. He slept with us on our bed. As long as we caught a whiff of skunk on his fur, we continued with the bathing.

Jenny decided it was time to write a blueprint for a prayer demonstration of her own. It was specific and seemed unattainable. But no blueprint for a home is too difficult for God. With prayer and faith and patience, Jenny found her condo home after reviewing and turning down at least thirty-five others. She was patient and waited until she received the Demonstration of her exact blueprint.

You Are What You Speak

There is untold power in the words we use. There is a vibration that is sent forth. I pay attention to the words I use in daily dialogue, stating the positive even when I'm speaking to myself. *I can do that. I have boundless energy. I won't give up without trying several approaches.* Negativity is mentally draining. *I can't do that. I'm too fatigued. It won't work, so why try?*

One day, the word WORRY flashed through my mind. *I'm so worried. Don't worry. You're such a worrywart.* I am trained in the use of words in our prayers and the effect they have on our conviction that only God has the power to provide the right answers. We can't cope with or fully comprehend why we or our loved ones have to suffer. Ever. We forget that we're human and not divine. Worrying involved such wasted energy.

Wait a minute.

I stopped what I was doing and breathed a silent thank you. God had given me these thoughts for a reason. It took only a couple minutes to convert WORRY into Waste Of Resources Regarding Yourself. I never hear or use the word *worry* again without its new definition coming to mind. I have shared it with every client.

I continued to receive word examples and started to them down. They became an effective tool in my teaching as I instructed clients in how to become or remain calm and heal their lives. A strong faith doesn't happen overnight; it has taken me years to appreciate the effectiveness of positivity. God never teaches negativity. Our life changes for the better when we turn our thoughts away from *hate, rudeness, bitterness, revenge, conceit, anxiousness, dishonesty,* and a host of other negative traits.

Strive instead for *love, courage, forgiveness, patience, perseverance, tolerance, respect, generosity, selflessness.* And remember that time is irrelevant. Learning how to begin and grow my faith has not been a burdensome undertaking.

Rather, I have gained a sense of inner peace and calm regardless of the circumstances. Some have been traumatic, but the result of purposeful prayer was always astounding.

The following words and their transformations have proven useful on many occasions.

- AGE: Attitude Generates Energy
- AGEING: Attitude Generates Energy In New Growth
- AMEN: Accepting Myself Eliminating Negativity
- CANCER Cells Aggressively Navigate Causing Extreme Results
- DEATH: Divinely Entering Alter To Heaven
- DIET: Directing Intelligent Eating Traits
- EVIL: Empowerment Viciously Infecting Life
- FAITH: Form Attaches Itself to Heaven
- FAT: Feeling Appetite Temperature
- FAT: Food Affirming Tragedy
- FEAR: False Energy Attacks Respiration
- FAILURE: Fear Always Inhibits Learning
                   Uncontested Redemptive Energy
- GOD: Guardian of Destiny
- GREED: Gluttony Robs Everyone Else's Deeds
- GUILT: Growing Unrest Internally Living Turmoil
- HATE: Holding Anger Toward Experience
- HERO: Heartfelt Efforts Reacting Outstandingly
- HOPE: Holding Optimistic Positive Energy
- HUG: Heavens Universal Greeting
- JOY: Jubilancy Occupying Yourself
- KISS: Kindness In Sweet Sensations
- LOVE: Light Of Vibrant Energy
- MIND: Mentally Ingesting New Data
- MIRACLE: Mind Is Receiving At Cosmic-Level Energy
- MOTHER: Masterpiece Of The Highest Everlasting Responsibility

- MORALS: Monitoring Our Responses About Lifestyle
- PEACE: Perfectly Establish A Calm Environment
- PRAYER: Purposely Receiving Answers You Earnestly Request
- PUSH: Provoke Unconscious Senses Harder
- REJOICE: Regenerating Energy Joins Our Inner Consciousness Effortlessly
- SAD: Staying Around Darkness
- SIN: Self Immoral Need
- TRUST: Taking Risks, Understanding Secure Tether
- TRUTH: Trusted Rules Understood Through Honesty
- WORD: Written Or Recited Desire
- WORRY: Waste Of Resources Regarding Yourself
- BUM: Broken Unsupported Mortal

For more than thirty years, I have followed the guidelines set by the Church of Science of Mind. I attended hours of classes, teaching seminars and, ultimately, achieved licensure. What does this mean? Science of Mind is best defined in the first textbook I read on the subject. "It is a study of Life and the Nature, of Laws of thought; the conception that we live in a spiritual Universe; that God is in, through, around, and for us." (*Science of Mind Textbook,* Dodd, Mead and Company, N.Y., c1938)

Since graduating from Founder's Church in Hollywood, California, in 1978, I have taught hundreds of classes and written treatments for innumerable clients. Treatments are prayers consciously spoken with explicit words to achieve specific results.

After the move to Michigan, I located a Science of Mind Church in Battle Creek and became a member. It meant a four-hour round trip, but I never felt these hours were a burden. Sadly, when the minister passed away a number of years ago, the church closed. Then I became a participating practitioner of The Church of the Golden Triangle, based in Eustis, Florida. The members there conducted a conference-call with me every month, and we shared our thoughts. In the process, we shored up our beliefs and discussed the most effective and meaningful ways to assist our clients. This church, too, has now closed with the death of the beloved pastor.

I continue to meet with or have phone conversations with clients throughout the world, demonstrating my faithful commitment and obligation to teach, counsel, and pray for all those who seek to feel better about themselves. Although it was personally satisfying to be awarded Emeritus Status by the Science of Mind Church for my thirty years of service, I have received my greatest joy from the moments I was able to work through the superstitions, fears and doubts of those who needed my help and then witnessed the results of their changed lives. My psychic ability continues to amaze me as well as others. There are no strangers!

At present I do not wear glasses, or have to take daily medication. I hear perfectly. I stay active and do my best to remain healthy. I walk about 30 miles a week and have my teeth thanks to implants. My life changed from one of despair to delight, from poverty to prosperity, from loneliness to lovingness. I owe it to faithfully practicing the principles of the Science of Mind. In my life's journey, I have learned that the energy in the universe is pure, non-judgmental and exquisitely effective. —Carol Sorkin Hunter

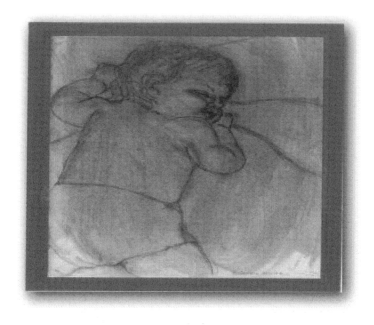

About the Author

ARTIST CAROL SORKIN Hunter's work not only spans artistic genres, it also crisscrosses the globe. Ms. Hunter was born on Long Island, New York, but grew up in California. She studied at the Art Center in Los Angeles and then traveled extensively throughout Europe, specifically to Rome where she spent an extended period of time. Over the past thirty years, Ms. Hunter has put together an extensive portfolio of work, using a wide variety of media to highlight her talent for art.

Ms. Hunter has been married to R. Ian Hunter, a Michigan attorney, since 1979. They currently live in Bloomfield Hills and are parents of twin daughters: Lisa, an art therapist, and Jennifer, a psychologist. In addition to her artistry, Ms. Hunter is a Science of Mind Practitioner who lectures for the Science of Mind Church, composes music, and travels.

Made in the USA
Columbia, SC
31 January 2019